lisaqknecht@gmail.com

PRAISE FOR *BULLY NATION*

"A canny and sobering look at bullying behavior and how it permeates our nation's major institutions. When children do it, we abhor it. When our leaders do it, we usually applaud it. The authors remind us."

Oliver Stone

"This thoughtful study expertly dissects the 'bullying scourge' that poisons lives and society, exposing its roots in the institutional structure of a 'militaristic capitalist culture' that it reflects and nurtures, while also revealing the encouraging reactions that may offer cures for the malady and the factors that engender it."

Noam Chomsky

"*Bully Nation* is the most comprehensive analysis of bullying yet published. It is a brilliant book that refuses to define bullying as merely a psychological concept. Instead, it addresses in great detail the interplay of bullying as having its roots in a range of historical, economic, political, and social conditions. In this instance, bullying functions as a metaphor to connect the private to the public, specific acts of violence to larger forms of systemic violence. Rather than treat bullying as part of a rite of passage confined to the often difficult process of growing up, Derber and Magrass treat it as a systemic force that produces values, social relations, structures, and collective identities steeped in violence and aggression. This is a powerful and compelling book that addresses one of the most important social problems of our time. It should be read by all educators, parents, and anyone else interested in a world free of aggression and violence. *Bully Nation* deserves widespread attention."

Henry Giroux, author of *Zombie Politics and Culture in the Age of Casino Capitalism*

"Clear and compelling. Its case for shifting our focus from individual schoolyard bullies to power imbalances in American society is badly needed in current discussions of bullying. A brilliant example of the sociological imagination at work."

Daniel Geary, author of *Beyond Civil Rights: The Moynihan Report and Its Legacy*

"A welcome departure from the popular habit of reducing distasteful behavior to family pathologies or genetic dispositions, *Bully Nation* is an important example of how intelligent social science can help heal the world. If bullying is rooted in history and structured by institutions, then citizen action can do something about it."

John Ehrenberg, author of *Civil Society: The Critical History of an Idea*

"*Bully Nation* is absolutely terrific—an important, powerful, and timely book that should be read by academic and public audiences alike. The authors have done a remarkable job of taking the topical social problem of bullying, which has received a great deal of attention over the past decade, and extrapolating it to economic, political, corporate, and militaristic bullying. We come to understand that bullying isn't just for the schoolyard, it's a sociopathology woven throughout our culture and guiding much of the way that the political economy is run. Their illuminating analysis illustrates how corporations and governments bully not only citizens—the 99 percent—but also the planet, and with reckless abandon. The consequences are potentially dire—for our culture, for the middle class, for the nation's and world's poor, and for the survival of the planet. Without question, this is a book that will have wide appeal to academics, students, and public audiences. I imagine using this book in my own courses and am already anticipating with great excitement the important discussion that will be opened with my students as they grapple with the bully nation, and with the most important issues facing their generation."

Jonathan White, coauthor of *Sociologists in Action: Sociology, Social Change, and Social Justice*

"Derber and Magrass force us to rethink our concept of bullying. Moving beyond the relatively limited focus on the psychological paradigm and interactions among children, they instead situate the process in a broader institutional context and relationships among adults. Their creative and expert treatment of bullying brings in the economy, the military, dominant political organizations, and indeed global inequalities as well. Their analysis of 'structural bullying' fulfills C. Wright Mills's call for a sociological imagination that links personal problems to our social world. Their contribution offers new ideas, not only on the concept and sources of the behavior, but also on the direction where more humane and effective solutions will be found."

Paul Joseph, professor of sociology at Tufts University, past president of the Peace Studies Association, and editor of *The SAGE Encyclopedia of War: Social Science Perspectives*

Bully Nation

Bully Nation

How the American Establishment
Creates a Bullying Society

Charles Derber and Yale R. Magrass

University Press of Kansas

Published by the
University Press of
Kansas (Lawrence,
Kansas 66045), which
was organized by
the Kansas Board
of Regents and is
operated and funded
by Emporia State
University, Fort Hays
State University,
Kansas State
University, Pittsburg
State University, the
University of Kansas,
and Wichita State
University

© 2016 by the University Press of Kansas

Library of Congress Cataloging-in-Publication Data

Names: Derber, Charles, author. | Magrass, Yale R., author.

Title: Bully nation : how the American establishment creates a
    bullying society / Charles Derber, Yale Magrass.

Description: Lawrence : University Press of Kansas, 2016. |
    Includes index.

Identifiers: LCCN 2015049989| ISBN 9780700622603 (hardback) |
    ISBN 9780700622641 (ebook)

Subjects: LCSH: Bullying—United States. | Aggressiveness—
    United States. | Violence—United States. | BISAC: SOCIAL
    SCIENCE / Violence in Society. | HISTORY / United States /
    20th Century. | HISTORY / United States / 21st Century.

Classification: LCC BF637.B85 .D47 2016 |
    DDC 302.34/30973—dc23

LC record available at http://lccn.loc.gov/2015049989.

British Library Cataloguing-in-Publication Data is available.

Printed in the United States of America

10 9 8 7 6 5 4 3 2 1

The paper used in this publication is recycled and contains
30 percent postconsumer waste. It is acid free and meets the
minimum requirements of the American National Standard for
Permanence of Paper for Printed Library Materials Z39.48-1992.

Contents

Acknowledgments

We first want to thank our editor, Michael Briggs, who proposed that we write this book. Mike not only inspired the volume but also provided intellectual and social support all through the process. We are deeply grateful.

We would like to thank as well the colleagues, reviewers, and friends who read all or part of the manuscript and offered constructive suggestions. These include Jonathan White, Henry Giroux, Paul Joseph, Javier Trevino, David Karp, and John Williamson.

I, Charles Derber, want to thank Elena Kolesnikova for her heroic patience and support throughout the many hours I devoted to working on the book.

I, Yale Magrass, must thank Ana Matos for providing substantial research material and helping edit several chapters. She often called my attention to issues that I had overlooked or misstated, which proved most helpful.

We want to gratefully acknowledge the support of Randall Wallace and the Wallace Action Fund in making this book possible. Randall helped inspire this work and played a major role in helping us disseminate the book and shape the public conversation on bullying.

CHAPTER ONE

Rethinking Bullying
From the Individual to the Institution

A PERSONAL STORY FROM YALE MAGRASS

It is the 1960s, and I am sitting on a wall during outdoor gym at the middle school I attend. Completely lacking in athletic skills and knowing no one will want me on their team, I do not join the games. At times in the past when I did decide to play, each team would fight about which side would be stuck with me. On this day, somebody grabs my tie. (Students were required to wear ties in public school back then.) He pulls it really tight as he puts his other hand under my collar and places an ant down my back. The air passages are cut off. I soon find myself getting dizzy, and my head bops back and forth. Someone else asks me, "What are you doing?" For a moment, I regain awareness and answer, "Nothing." I get up and begin to walk across the field, but I soon collapse to the ground. Everyone who sees it starts laughing.

The next day, I am in the schoolyard. Someone says, "Knock, knock." Naively assuming this is a joke, I respond, "Who's there?" Wrapping a woman's stocking around my neck and squeezing it tighter and tighter, the boy replies, "The Boston strangler." I again fall to the ground. He lets go as I rise to my knees, waiting to regain full consciousness. Once again, everyone who sees it bursts out laughing.

Fast-forward to the high school cafeteria. Someone says my name. Kids next to him start shouting, "YALE, YALE." The people on the next bench join in: "YALE, YALE." Soon, all the students in the entire cafeteria are shouting my name in unison. This happens repeatedly over several days.

Another time, four boys surround me, each grabbing an arm or a leg. They carry me to an open window on a higher floor of the school, where they wave me around, counting one, two, three, and then hold me out the window. On the bus home from school on a different afternoon, a boy grabs my books from under my arm and tosses them to someone else who throws them to a third guy who then tosses them to another student. I run back and forth, unsuccessfully trying to get my books back.

The next day as I get on the bus, the driver warns me, "If you act up again, I'll throw you off."

Bullying has been around since time immemorial, yet only recently has it gotten serious attention. A decade or two ago, it was commonly dismissed or minimized, often being seen as cute, as a joke, or as something to "get over." The victim needed to toughen up. If he couldn't take it and fight back, then he deserved to be a target of ridicule and harassment. Being a bully could actually be a source of pride, marking the individual as someone triumphant and powerful who was likely to be popular and admired, often by the victims themselves.

Only now is it being recognized that chronic bullying can lead to a traumatic childhood, whose scars may be carried well into adulthood. More and more parents worry that their kids will be bullied at school or online, or perhaps they will witness bullying in the schoolyard. Some parents think their kids might have to become bullies themselves just to survive or to be part of the in-crowd. Other parents encourage their children to bully in order to get ahead or fit in. Yet others tell the kids bullying is a terrible thing to do, possibly thinking about the horrific mass killings in schools—from Columbine to Virginia Tech to Newtown—that have been described in popular books such as *Rampage*[1] and *The Bully Society*[2] as the tip of the iceberg of a longstanding bullying problem.

The current conversation about bullying depicts it as a personal, psychological trouble to be solved by counseling or therapy for both the victim and the bullier.[3] The victim needs better communication or adaptation skills. He may need to tell the bully how he feels, as if the bully does not know he is causing harm or does not intend to do just that. There is little discussion about larger social or cultural forces that may actually encourage bullying or about how bullying may indeed serve certain institutional interests. But as the renowned twentieth-century sociologist C. Wright Mills points out in *The Sociological Imagination*,[4] personal troubles are often public issues. A purely psychological approach to bullying is deeply distorting. We need a larger picture showing how key institutions in society—the economy, military, culture, family, schools—all help create and perpetrate the bullying milieu. We need a paradigm shift, with the current microfocus on individual psychology tucked into a new and larger conversation about America's corporate and militarized society.

The psychological paradigm masks the institutional bullying that encourages and reinforces individual bullying. Bullying is carried out by societies and is a characteristic of cultures, economies, and the military. Militarized capitalism is one way of describing the structure of American society. It's a system that gives rise to both institutional and personal bullying.

The idea that bullying has societal roots and reflects the dominant values and interests of powerful institutions may have some intuitive plausibility. After all, we speak of politicians such as Donald Trump or Chris Christie as bullies, of the National Football League (NFL) as encouraging bullying on the field to make big money, of large and powerful nations bullying smaller ones, of companies such as Walmart bullying their workers, and of agricultural corporate giants such as Tyson or Smithfield Farms even bullying animals and the environment. But these are seldom the focus in scholarly or popular books and articles about bullying. A few researchers, such as the sociologist Jessie Klein in her book *The Bully Society*,[5] have begun to talk about widening the frame, honing in on gender relations, but we will show that psychologists and psychiatrists have captured bullying as a subject for analysis. They concentrate on personal bullying in schools and treat it as a psychological and individual problem, seldom considering how it reflects structural problems embedded in our society. Even Klein, despite having a chapter on the "bullying economy," focuses overwhelmingly on kids and violence in schools.

In this book, we take a different path. We shall show how bully nations operate on the world stage, even as they bully their own citizens and, in the age of climate change, the environment itself. Our spotlight is on the United States, the most powerful bully nation in the world today—yet hardly the only one. Bully nations have operated throughout history, but we want to explain why bullying has such a significant part in American life, how it developed, and what can be done about it.

Since we need a paradigm shift, we will first look more carefully at the current psychological paradigm and show why it is deeply flawed. We will then turn to an alternative approach.

THE MICROPARADIGM: SHRINKING THE BULLY

Whom do you think of when you hear the word bully? Maybe a big guy in the schoolyard or cafeteria, like the tough jock with a buzz cut who tries to rough up Michael J. Fox's short, small-framed character in the film *Back to the Future*?[6] Or maybe a mean girl in a clique of popular girls who goes around attacking others as "fatties" or "sluts" or "geeks"?

And whom do you think of as the victim? Perhaps a gay boy who is taunted for being "girlie"? A girl who is chubby or looks "funny"? Or maybe a skinny boy who is uncoordinated and weak looking or "geeky," one who would never be captain of the football team?

These are certainly the images that are presented in most books, media articles, and movies on the topic, including comedies (among them *The Diary of a Wimpy Kid*)[7] that treat bullying as something to laugh at. Carrie Goldman wrote a widely read book entitled *Bullied* that described the not-so-funny experiences of her daughter, Katie, a girl who had been taunted and teased mercilessly because of her looks and so-called geeky interests.[8] Katie came home in tears after a first-grade classmate named Jake called her "Piggy." Jake got other boys in the class to call her by that name, and the constant teasing and taunting grew worse. Breaking down in sobs one day, Katie told her mother that she did not want to go back to school. She couldn't take it anymore.

Goldman wrote a blog about her daughter's experiences, and it went viral. Thousands of other parents wrote in to sympathize and tell stories about their own kids who were bullied in school and online. Some of the children's supposed crimes were looking funny, wearing the wrong clothes, being "nerdy," being gay or a minority, or having a disability. The bullied kids included the boy who was not tough enough to make the football team and the girl not pretty enough to be a cheerleader.

By "bullying," Goldman refers to the use of power by tough kids to repeatedly taunt, threaten, intimidate, humiliate, or hit her daughter. She says that all the kids whose parents wrote her—the parents of gays, geeks, nerds, and others who typically get bullied—are subject to this kind of traumatizing abuse. This is consistent with the psychological paradigm's general definition of bullying as a repeated emotional, verbal, or physical battering by a more powerful or tougher child of a weaker one. We will return to the definition of bullying soon.

Goldman's story shows that the popular images about fatties, geeks, gays, nerds, sissies, "uglies," or "weirdos" are not just stereotypes. They refer to hundreds of thousands of real kids who are players, usually victims, in the bullying drama. But they also reveal only a small slice of the world of bullying, and they highlight the serious limitations of the current way of thinking about bullying.

The psychological paradigm is centered on schoolyard bullies and traumatized kids. Its first premise, which most people take for granted, is that bullying is a matter of individual behavior. The bullier is a person, and the bullied are also individuals.

Moreover, within the psychological paradigm, the bullies and the bullied are all a particular type of person: they are children or young people. Their bullying is usually seen as a nearly inevitable part of growing up, especially as students in grammar schools, high schools, or colleges and universities.

The focus on young people is a second and critically important dimension of the current bullying paradigm. The bullying world is populated by kids. Adults, especially parents and counselors and teachers, are affected, but they are not central players in the direct bullying drama. They are rarely highlighted as the bulliers or the bullied.

As we will show shortly, both of these assumptions—that bullying is mainly behavior by individuals and that it specifically involves kids—are wrong. They take the spotlight off the world of adults, which is itself a vast arena of bullying and has a pivotal role in creating the bullying world of children.

If we conceive of bullying as personal behavior among children, we immediately move to a third unstated premise of the microparadigm: that the problem lies largely in individuals and their psychology. The scholarship on bullying is laden with analyses of personality, mental health, and psychological challenges related to being part of a group that is targeted by aggression.[9] It also highlights child psychology rather than the psychology and behavior of adults, as if people might be expected to grow out of their roles in the bullying drama. In fact, the opposite may well be true, for reasons about adult society that we will explore throughout the book. And in any case, the emphasis on children is a convenient way to hide an inconvenient truth: that bullying in the schoolyard mirrors the larger adult social world that kids see every day. Within the psychological paradigm, there is little space for an institutional and political analysis that would uncover these grim realities of the adult social world and its leading institutions, except for some discussion of the way schools are operating and how they might intervene to reduce the problem.

Cutting to the chase, the psychological paradigm frames the conversation about bullying as a therapeutic discourse. In this way of thinking, adults—especially parents, trained counselors, and psychiatrists—learn to see bullying as a phenomenon having to do with the psyche, the psychology of cliques, and the biology of the brain itself. The ruling conversation falls within the claimed professional expertise of psychologists and psychiatrists. Consequently, bullying analysis centers on categories of psychological disorder, and treatment relies heavily on psychiatrists and counselors, with teachers and parents as secondary supporters.

This is yet another reason why we need to move beyond the ruling paradigm. Psychiatry claims scientific expertise, but there is a growing challenge to the scientific validity of the profession itself, as well as its diagnoses and drugs.[10] Psychiatry has succeeded in creating a medicalized world for children, with millions of youngsters on drugs or in therapy. But whether this is a solution to bullying—or good for children—is problematic at best, and such treatment can often do more harm than good. One obvious harm is that it moves attention away from the real causes of bullying, as we will discuss. A common social and political assumption in the psychological paradigm is that bullying is mainly caused by misunderstanding, by a lack of communication. If geeks, nerds, funny-looking kids, gays, or children from minority backgrounds were only brought together with jocks, popular children, and mean girls, they would learn to appreciate each other and bullying would cease. But what if there are underlying societal conflicts leading some individuals or groups to have an interest in tormenting others and reinforcing differences in power? Woody Allen offers an alternative perspective on what could happen when children of different or conflicting backgrounds are brought together: "I won two weeks at interfaith camp where I was sadistically beaten by boys of all races and creeds."[11]

The psychiatric paradigm blinds us to the role of the larger society. And this point is central to our argument that bullying, though it may reflect or cause psychological disturbances, grows out of the wider society's mainstream institutions and cultural values. Clearly, individual bullying has psychological dimensions and can cause deep and lasting emotional scars. We in no way wish to minimize the trauma associated with almost all forms of bullying. Indeed, we know firsthand that the psychological curse of being bullied, which can damage a person for life, is often understated. But the current psychological paradigm is a deeply inadequate way of thinking because it does not offer the socioeconomic and political analysis necessary to understand—or even recognize—the massive amount of bullying that arises from and is fueled by the core values of the most powerful institutions of our society.

Our talk about social institutions such as corporations and the military will sound odd to many readers who pick up a book about bullying. Though some of us do, as noted earlier, casually refer to politicians or corporations as bullies, almost all of us have learned to think of bullying as such a personal issue that we forget the institutional or societal context surrounding it. Say the word *bully* and you think of a tough boy or mean girl in school. We have unconsciously absorbed the idea that bullying has little to do with our economic, political, or military organizations. In fact, we had to do reality checks of our own as we developed our analysis. And we are certain that many readers will think that we have missed the point, that we are diverting attention from the kids and schools that need help, and that we probably have our own axes to grind.

But remember that we do *not* dismiss the importance of the bullying of children by children that is the main topic of the current conversation. Part of what we are saying is that if we really care about kids bullying each other, we need to widen our angle of vision and consider issues that are now outside the bullying conversation, taking us on new journeys into the heart of our corporate and militarized society.

In our society, a "structural bullying" is built into the DNA of leading institutions, such as huge corporations and the military. It is a different and larger scale of bullying, but as we will show, it has many of the same basic features of the school-aged bully's abuse of power—and it is a core cause of the schoolyard jungle.

Yet the large-scale institutions helping to shape the adult and child worlds of bullying are not subjects of study for psychiatrists. Psychiatrists are not trained to analyze societal institutions and the economic organization of society. They usually try to help their patients "adjust," seldom considering whether this a society to which anyone *should* adjust.[12] Society is usually treated as an unseen, automatic given or an inherent good. In their training, psychiatrists learn that societal forces are distractions from inner psychological dynamics and biological brain disorders. This professional training—emphasizing psychodynamics, mental illness, and the like—blinds them to the role played by the huge corporations and militaries that bully millions of adults here and abroad, as well as individual adults in workplaces and families in the home. These same institutions drive much of the bullying of kids on kids, while also perpetrating corporate, military, and other violence against animals and the environment.

Psychiatrists who dominate the academic discourse about bullying are involved not just in crimes of omission but also in crimes of commission, for they direct our attention away from larger social forces, denying that they play a major role. Because the psychological paradigm is dominant, our argument that bullying is rooted in society's major institutions may seem surprising and confusing to some of you. But if you stay with us, you will begin to see how thoroughly the real problem has been mystified and shrouded.

Part of the trouble is that we live in a culture that "psychologizes" almost all social problems. We think of behavior and behavioral problems as being driven by individual rather than institutional or structural causes. This is true of everything from poverty to inequality to individual aggression and violence. And psychological reductionism is nowhere truer nor more misleading than in regard to bullying. It has led to a shrunken understanding—in fact, a nearly complete blindness—about the causes of bullying and about what bullying is, who or what the targets are, and who does it.

For all these reasons, understanding bullying requires a shift in virtually all our current assumptions and ways of thinking about bullying itself. C. Wright Mills highlighted the psychological reductionism of American thinking that separated personal problems from social and public issues.[13] His idea of the sociological imagination was intended to remedy this intellectual warping. And for much the same reason, we argue the need to expand the discussion about bullying from the psychological paradigm to the paradigmatic thinking, following from Mills, that we call the sociological imagination.

THE MACROPARADIGM: THE SOCIOLOGICAL IMAGINATION, INSTITUTIONAL BULLYING, AND DEFINITIONS THAT HELP US RETHINK AND REFINE THE BULLYING CONCEPT

The essence of the sociological imagination is to link private problems with public issues, the central theme of Mills's *Sociological Imagination*.[14] In it, as well as in an earlier book entitled *Character and Social Structure*,[15] he argues that we Americans are taught to believe that our personal problems are separate from our public institutions in the economy, political system, and international relations. The personal and public worlds are planets apart.

But Mills contends that personal problems are rooted in societal values; power hierarchies; and the values and interests of economic, political, and military systems. He believes that, contrary to American common sense, it is impossible to separate private troubles and public (and political) issues and that to attempt to do so would lead to nothing but myths and illusions, a form of cultivated ignorance.

In fact, Mills asserts that there is nothing accidental about this artificial segregation of personal problems and public power. His other great book is *The Power Elite*,[16] published in 1957. In it, he argues that though America may look like a democracy, it is actually dominated by a trifecta of economic, political, and military elites. Each group sits on top of established and intertwined hierarchies of power, and together they control much of what happens in America and the rest of the world.

This includes control of the mind and of public discourse.[17] The sociological imagination suggests that the psychological way of framing the bullying conversation serves the power and profit interests of dominant institutions; further, the elites work hard to ensure that any conversation about bullying does not become a critical analysis of our corporate, militarized society. That would become a threat to the system that they control, leading ordinary people concerned about the bullying that causes their kids pain and suffering to begin raising questions about the existing social order and power structure.

From the perspective of the sociological imagination, then, the psychological paradigm about bullying is predictable and merely part of a larger way in which American intellectual life is conducted. Societal problems are psychologized; social systems are viewed as simply aggregates of individuals; and both personal and social behaviors are seen to be caused by personal, psychological needs rather than by the institutional priorities of the ruling elites.[18]

The sociological imagination is a broad, critical approach that challenges the way almost all public discourse is conducted in America. In this book, we want to demonstrate how this approach applies to the conversation about bullying. It gives us an entirely different angle of vision, moving the narrow focus on the psychological needs of disturbed children tormenting each other in the school cafeteria or fighting in the schoolyard to the way in which our society is institutionally structured. It shows how our militarized corporate system drives the same kind of bullying in the adult world as in the child world. The corporation and the military are, in key ways, programmed to act like the schoolyard bully, and they actually end up doing much of the programming of the schoolyard bullier. They are responsible for the bullying of millions of adults and children, as well as animals and other species now facing extinction.

At the heart of the sociological imagination—and bullying itself—is the study of power. Power is one of the core realities of all societies, and it creates multiple overlapping economic, social, and political hierarchies. Where each of us is perched on these hierarchies largely determines our power and our prospects for success and status. It also shapes who bullies and who gets bullied and tells us much of what we need to know about bullying that has been rendered invisible. Bullying is, in fact, all about power and the way it is exercised—from the halls of the Pentagon, Congress, and corporate suites to the playing fields of the schools.

But before moving to the bullying issue, let us briefly look at the broader perspective of the sociological imagination paradigm vis-à-vis power and American society. This perspective gives the context for understanding how and why our paradigm turns America's thinking about bullying in a new direction and why it sees bullying as an expression of the core values and power systems of our society.

America, according to Mills, is largely controlled by elites at the top of the economic, political, and military structures.[19] These elites, though very powerful, are not free actors themselves. They must work largely in the service of the institutions they govern, including big global corporations, governments at all levels, and the military. If they don't maximize profits or extend the nation's military influence or sustain public faith in militarized capitalism, they will be thrown out. So, the sociological imagination considers not only powerful people but also the huge institutions seeking power and profit.[20]

The sociological imagination goes one step further, arguing that the leading institutions are bound together in a more or less coherent system. In the United States, Mills has described a system that we call militarized capitalism.[21] The idea that America is a capitalist system marked by unprecedented military power is not particularly controversial; analysts of all political views tend to agree with this assessment. But the sociological imagination does provoke argument by the way in which it analyzes and critiques the values, structure, and role of power within this system.

The conventional wisdom asserts the United States is a democracy that is ultimately accountable to the people. Everyone has one vote, and the society is organized around the founding documents, such as Thomas Jefferson's Declaration of Independence, that emphasize the equality and rights of all citizens. Many social scientists and economists view these ideals as a reasonable approximation of American realities and aspirations. The system is not perfect, but it is "exceptionalist," tilting, over the long run, toward more democracy and equality than any nation in history.[22]

The sociological imagination bluntly challenges this exceptionalist thinking. It argues that although the United States is, like other Western societies, organized around formal democratic procedures such as voting, it is governed by power elites—and the institutions they control—with enormous wealth and influence. Thus, what distinguishes the United States is *not* its degree of democracy or equality, which research shows is increasingly falling below that in many European nations; in fact, most Americans are losing power and wealth to their own national elites faster than is the case for their counterparts in most of Europe. In a book whose message has reverberated around the world, economist Thomas Piketty presents data documenting this startling rise in inequality.[23] He contends that this has led to a castelike stratification of power in which you inherit your place in a deeply divided American society for life and thereby inherit a serious vulnerability to economic and political bullying throughout adulthood—an assessment that is reinforced by many other important studies of growing inequality in the United States.[24] We shall return to Piketty's argument about inequality later. But we should note here that despite his analysis and the evidence produced by many others about the cancer of extreme inequality in this country, most Americans do not see that their own society has become more stratified by power and wealth than that of other developed nations. Nor do they realize this is jeopardizing their own well-being and leading to a political culture of increased repression and violence, with frightening implications for the bullying scourge that we will turn to shortly.

The sociological imagination hones in on the broad tendencies that are for the most part invisible to much of the American population because of the grip of exceptionalist ideology.[25] The sociological imagination sees social problems of all forms as linked to the concentration and abuse of power in the wider society. Power inequality, especially when extreme, creates a society of haves and have-nots. It disenfranchises large sectors of the population in the middle and bottom of major hierarchies, and then it bullies them into submission.

Of course, abuse, like bullying itself, is a subjective concept that exists to a large degree in the eye of the beholder. The victim may feel he is subject to the bully and his abuse of power, whereas the bully, who may deny the label, may feel entirely entitled and believe he is behaving in a perfectly moral manner. One's position in the power hierarchy will heavily shape such perceptions.

The sociological imagination sees bullying as a structural problem. By structural, we mean power inequalities that are built into the DNA of the corporation, the military, and the broader state. Such structural inequalities are fundamental factors not just in the corrosion of democracy but also in repression or violent subjugation in all spheres of life, with bullying being one major illustration.

The emphasis on social and political power structures makes clear our difference with the psychological paradigm, for we essentially invert it or turn it on its head. Whereas the psychological paradigm argues that individuals, with troubled psyches, create social problems and their own personal difficulties, the sociological imagination argues that the society itself—in the American case, militarized capitalism, an organized system of power inequality—gives rise to both the social problems of the dispossessed and the psychological disturbances that follow from the loss of power.

But before turning directly to the sociological paradigm on bullying, let us look at two or three perspectives it shares with the psychological paradigm. Both paradigms see power—and specifically inequality of power—as a defining concern. Nearly every definition of bullying by microinvestigators that we have found (you can see them in online dictionaries) begins by saying that bullying involves aggressive, hurtful behavior arising in relations of unequal power. Here is a typical definition of bullying, found in the standard literature:

> In order to be considered bullying, the behavior must be aggressive and include:
>
> - An Imbalance of Power: Kids who bully use their power—such as physical strength, access to embarrassing information, or popularity—to control or harm others. Power imbalances can change over time and in different situations, even if they involve the same people.
> - Repetition: Bullying behaviors happen more than once or have the potential to happen more than once.
> - Bullying includes actions such as making threats, spreading rumors, attacking someone physically or verbally, and excluding someone from a group on purpose.[26]

Here is another commonly used definition in the standard microparadigm, again highlighting bullying as a form of aggressive and harmful behavior made possible by an inequality of power:

> Bullying is the use of force, threat, or *coercion* to *abuse, intimidate,* or aggressively impose domination over others. The behavior is often repeated and habitual. One essential prerequisite is the perception, by the bully or

by others, of an imbalance of social or physical *power*. Behaviors used to assert such domination can include verbal *harassment* or *threat*, physical *assault* or coercion, and such acts may be directed repeatedly toward particular targets.[27]

We think that these definitions, which focus on the way that power inequalities enable repetitive hostile and hurtful behavior, are apt and useful for our macrostructural paradigm. Our own definition of bullying behavior within our new paradigm is in line with the orthodox concepts defined in the current academic microliterature:

> Bullying is behavior (1) reflecting an imbalance of power, and (2) involving threats, harassment, intimidation, or attacks—often repetitive—that are designed to secure domination or control and create fear, harm, or submission. The bully seeks to establish a sense of inferiority in the target and reinforce the sense of superiority of the bully, legitimating the power hierarchy on which the bully and the bullied are both perched.

Both paradigms agree that inequalities of power are key to domination and abuse of power. The two paradigms embrace the same basic idea that power inequality is a principal precondition and cause of bullying. The difference between them, though, which we expand on throughout the book, is that the psychological paradigm concentrates on inequalities of personal power, power in cliques and small groups, and the psychological forces that lead individual people, mainly kids, to seek power and abuse it,[28] whereas the sociological paradigm looks at the larger inequalities of power in the society that lead to institutional power abuse. It shows that children actually seek and abuse power in a way that mirrors and mimics larger institutionalized power relations, threats, and violence in the adult economy and society.

The second and closely related parallel between the two paradigms is that they both recognize the victims of bullying tend to be people at the bottom of power hierarchies.[29] These include gender hierarchies but also, especially in the sociological paradigm, race and class hierarchies and lifestyle caste hierarchies such as gay and straight or jock and nerd. The only strong "societal" aspect of the psychological paradigm is its focus on gender hierarchies and values, a concession to the societal emphasis that is pivotal in the sociological imagination.[30] And the psychological paradigm cannot help but observe that the bullied kids tend to be the kids on the bottom rungs of other social power hierarchies, including those involving physical strength, physical beauty, and sexual orientation, as well as the rich over the poor, the abled over the disabled, and the jocks over the nerds.[31] However, with the exception of gender, these factors do not lead psychologists to do serious analysis of the crucial role played by societal power structures in bullying, especially those endemic to a corporate and militarized system.

The third parallel is that both paradigms recognize that certain cultural values contribute to bullying, among them toughness, competitiveness, dominance, aggression, and violence. All these values are associated with holding and abusing power, as typified by President Teddy Roosevelt, who gloried in blood, guts, and violence and rejoiced as he rushed into what he called the "splendid little war" pitting the United States against Spain in Cuba and later in the Philippines.[32] But in the psychological paradigm, these values are interpreted as personal norms and are considered to be psychological symptoms reflecting personality disorders, sometimes tied to masculine values in a traditionally male-dominated society. In the sociological imagination, we talk not just of values but also of a bullying culture, constructed by elites and leading institutions. The bullying culture is seen as related to gender but rooted as well in other crucial institutional systems of militarized capitalism.

A fourth parallel involves serious complexities in the definition of bullying itself. Although the macrostructural paradigm extends our definition of just who bullies are, it shares with the psychological paradigm some commonalities in the complex and tricky questions associated with the definition of bullying. In both paradigms, bullying is defined around unequal power and dominating or controlling behavior, and in both paradigms, the definitions can easily get muddied. In both, bullying is a broad concept and overlaps extensively with violence and competition, particularly in societies with significant power inequalities. It might seem so broad as to encompass all "bad behavior" or even almost all social behavior, especially in very hierarchical societies. In both paradigms, then, it is important to clarify what is and is not bullying behavior.

The issue of motivation helps distinguish bullying from nonbullying, but this has to be carefully qualified. The motive to control, coerce, harm, or dominate the target and create a sense of inferiority in the bullied person is central to the concept of bullying that most Americans hold, and it helps define what bullying is. If the controlling people or institutions say their motive is cooperative or intended to help others, therefore, this might suggest bullying is not involved. But that depends on another factor: does the controlling behavior have the free and true consent of the target?

The issue of consent is crucial in assessing motive and identifying bullying. Almost all bullies justify their own aggression as being for the good of the other. When George W. Bush and Dick Cheney invaded and occupied Iraq, they claimed to be helping that country become free and democratic. We would argue, as many critics do, that oil and US power were the real motives, but even if Bush and Cheney believed their own rhetoric, the war would have been bullying because the occupation did not have the consent of the Iraqi people. Motive matters—but so does consent, as the bullying in Iraq illustrates. The same is true of violence perpetrated by bullies in the schoolyard who attack other kids without their consent.

But when a person in power—whether a teacher, a manager, or a military officer—demands that a person lower in the hierarchy do something, is it automatically bullying? We have three answers to this question. One is that it depends, again, on motive. If a manager issues an order to a worker but is doing so not to humiliate her but simply because he is following the rules of the company—and the orders of the managers above him—then this is not full-blown bullying, but it has an element of it. The manager may be feeling bullied to bully those below him, even if he doesn't want to do so. This could apply, as well, to a teacher who demands something from his student. Both the manager and the teacher may be bullying in the sense of repeatedly ordering those below them on the pecking order, but they are not doing it to humiliate them or make them feel inferior. They are acting as agents of a bullying institution, even if they are not completely comfortable with the bullying role assigned to them. In this case, the use of power to coerce suggests a strong bullying element, but it may not be full-fledged bullying because the motive is not to humiliate or create a sense of inferiority.

All this suggests that bullying is not necessarily an all-or-nothing proposition. In power hierarchies, those on top may exercise power with different motives. There is always an element of bullying when a power hierarchy is involved, but it is only partial bullying if the person on or near the top feels compelled to exercise power but is not doing so to humiliate or foster a sense of permanent inferiority in the target. Again, we emphasize that bullying is not simply a psychological personality trait. In a bullying society, some "nice" people may bully when they themselves are bullied into carrying out the mandate of a bullying institution. Bullying is best understood as conduct falling along a spectrum, whereby the behavior may be full-scale bullying, have strong bullying dimensions, have fewer bullying dimensions, or have no bullying dimensions at all. This spectrum can be linked to the difference between "potential" or "latent" and "actual" or "actuated" bullying that we refer to repeatedly in this book. The closer to the full-scale side of the spectrum, the more likely it is that the behavior is actuated rather than potential, with use of the word *potential* being another way of saying that the conduct has bullying elements but is not full-scale bullying. However, the steeper the institutional hierarchy is and the more its culture involves establishing feelings of superiority and inferiority, the more likely it will be that the person on top and all those situated on the hierarchy will find themselves enmeshed in full-scale bullying relations.

A third important consideration is that behavior can sometimes be seen as institutional bullying even if doesn't qualify as personal bullying by the individual who carries it out. Consider the presumably nice corporate manager who does not want to bully but feels compelled to outsource or reduce wages as part of his institutional responsibility. His threat to outsource may be full-scale institutional bullying, since it is a way that the institution is seeking to bully its workers into submission and create the sense of inferiority that the corporation requires. But because the manager does not personally want to humiliate the worker, his behavior may be institutional bullying but not full-scale personal bullying. He may feel guilt or remorse. The subtlety here is that he is acting in a dual capacity: he is a bully as an agent of the institution, but at the same time, he is not a personal bully if he has not adopted that institution's bullying culture and if he is acting against his own personal values and motives.

This leads to another knotty set of definitional issues involving the relation between bullying and violence. There is a great deal of overlap, but much bullying is not violent, and some violence is not bullying.

Often, the bullying in both paradigms is not physically violent; making verbal threats and issuing insults are examples. In fact, the preponderance of bullying in everyday life does not involve physical violence, as we will illustrate vividly in our chapter on bullying in the family. When bullying is nonviolent, it is frequently more effective, for it is disguised and harder to discern. The fact that most bullying is not expressed in violent acts is a key reason why bullying should not be defined simply as violence. For the same reason, we need to distinguish bullying from crime, since most bullying, whether by individuals or by institutions such as the corporation and the state, is legal. In fact, powerful bullying institutions usually write the laws and are in a position to define what crime is.

In both paradigms, there are also forms of violence that are not bullying. For example, self-defense that requires immediate violence to protect one's own life is not necessarily bullying. This, again, must be qualified because bullies typically justify their violence in the name of self-defense, whether they are individuals—such as the self-appointed Florida community watch team leader George Zimmerman, when he killed Trayvon Martin, and the Ferguson, Missouri, cop Darren Wilson, when he killed Michael Brown—or whether they are American leaders who fight offensive wars in Vietnam or Iraq under the banner of self-defense. Claims of self-defense do not mean bullying has not occurred, for bullies almost always use such claims. But there are situations where a thief or murderer can be stopped only with immediate and violent self-defense, and in rare situations of this type, the violence may not be bullying. By contrast, revenge killing, which is also carried out in the name of self-defense but at a later time, typically *would* be a form of bullying. Some acts of violence are single, desperate moves made by people who feel they are bully victims, in order to assert themselves. This kind of act can literally be a one-shot attempt to feel the power of the bully. Examples include school shooters, who perceive themselves as tormented social rejects, or suicide bombers, who sacrifice themselves to offset their people's or their cause's lack of power.

Another important definitional question involves the relation between bullying and competition. In both paradigms, bullying is often a way to win competitions, whether over status, money, or power. But not all competitive behavior is bullying, even though most bullying involves competition in some form of hierarchy to establish power and dominance.

What kind of competitive behavior is *not* bullying? That depends on whether or not the competition is a zero-sum game and also on whether people have cooperated to establish the rules and entered the game voluntarily. In a zero-sum competition (which typifies most capitalist competition, as we will discuss in chapter 2), one competitor's gain is another's loss: to win, you must "conquer" and ultimately destroy your rival. But if I am working as a student or a writer to do the best job of writing that I can, my success may not necessarily harm or destroy other students or writers. In a classroom situation where grading is done on a curve, however, the student competition may become a form of bullying, since my winning typically will mean that other students lose out; if the grading is not on a curve, my good mark does not mean that others will get a bad grade, and thus, bullying is less likely.

Even if there is a zero-sum competition, it is not always a bullying game. If you go out to play a game of pickup basketball, there will be winners and losers. But if all players agree to the rules and all choose freely to play, the game will not necessarily involve bullying. The issues of consent and consensus, again, prove to be crucial in establishing bullying. If all players truly consent to the game, then the competition may not lead to bullying—although, as before, we need to be careful in our assessment here, for not all consent is consensual. Sometimes, people are bullied into agreeing to terms they are not entitled to challenge. They may fear a social stigma, such as being labeled weak or cowardly. A famous example is when Aaron Burr, known to be an expert marksman, challenged Alexander Hamilton, who barely knew how to fire a gun, to a duel. Hamilton accepted, even though he knew that if they fought, he could be killed.

As we will explore in chapter 2, most capitalist market competition involves bullying, and many conventional economists describe participation in the market as a free choice. But since most workers and consumers did not establish the rules—and the same is true of many small business competitors—what appears to be cooperation and consent is something quite different, a form of market involvement dictated by survival. Here, competing to win often becomes indistinguishable from bullying.

HOW THE SOCIETAL PARADIGM IS DIFFERENT

The sociological imagination paradigm is not meant to minimize or distract from the psychological impacts of bullying on kids or adults, which can't be overstated. But it shows that the roots of those impacts lie in the competitive and violent adult world of militarized capitalism. Let us look at the main new and distinctive points arising out of the macroparadigm we are offering.

First, bullying is not a personal aberration or form of deviance. It is programmed into major institutions, endemic to our entire society, and it is useful (if not always necessary) for surviving and prospering in militarized capitalism. If you want to move up the ladder, you are going to have to bully, and you must ultimately embrace without too much questioning the big corporate institutions that bully large segments of the population into submission. The individual bully is a product of the bully nation.

Second, bullying is a core feature of power and arises out of social systems organized around steep power hierarchies. The greater the inequalities of power in a society, among nations, or even across species, the more likely it is that both institutional and personal bullying will become commonplace. Bullying is about the more powerful bending the less powerful to their will and ensuring that things stay that way. In that sense, the militarized imperial state models bullying for the corporate manager, the military commander, and the schoolyard bully. It all follows a Machiavellian script: social life and international affairs are all about power, and bullying is simply one way in which inequalities of power are created and abused. If politics or political economy is about the study of power, then the sociological imagination tells us that to understand bullying, we need to move away from psychologists and toward political analysts and sociologically and environmentally oriented political economists.

Third, although power and power inequalities are the structural roots of bullying, setting the conditions for bullying to occur, they are *not* absolutely determining. The relation is *contingent,* as we will discuss more fully in the next section—dependent on cultural and political factors that vary across societies and personal relations.

This is not an academic point. One of the more surprising elements of our argument is that a strong antibullying movement is developing in parts of US society. Even as power and wealth inequalities grow larger, we are seeing a revulsion in significant sectors of society against personal bullying, especially among children. This is a largely unnoticed aspect of the "culture wars," and we will examine it in chapter 9. Our point here is that this shows contingency is real. There is no simplistic formula that automatically translates all social inequality—or every form of corporate society—into bullying. And society can become even more unequal and yet, paradoxically, see the growth of new values as well as groups whose stated mission is to end bullying, especially in schools.

Nonetheless, this does not mean that bullying behavior is now less common in the larger society or among kids in school. A powerful bullying culture still exists in the nation, and the bullying problem has deep historical roots in American society—from the annihilation of Native Americans to the slavery that defined the Deep South before the Civil War. It continued after the war in the rise of the corporate robber barons, who bullied an immigrant population of powerless workers.[33] Today, it persists because bullying values and power inequalities remain deeply embedded in the nation. Despite our emphasis on contingency, it is difficult to imagine a society of deep power and wealth inequalities in which the rich do not bully the poor and humans do not abuse the environment. Likewise, it is hard to see historically militaristic societies that do not bully weaker nations or large sectors of their own populations. As long as there are serious power inequalities, elites will almost certainly bully subordinate groups into submission, and stronger higher-status people, both adults and children, will bully weaker lower-status people whom they meet every day.

We have already introduced other framing arguments about bullying as seen from the perspective of the sociological imagination. For clarity, we will briefly recap them here:

1. Bullying is as much about the adult world as about the world of children. The current focus on kids is an orchestrated distraction from the role played by adults and adult institutions in creating bullying. It leads to a warped discussion that makes bullying appear to be something specific to child psychology and behavioral disorders that tend to fade as people mature—something that, once outgrown, leaves few permanent impacts. The sociological imagination challenges this view, asserting that bullying is created by the adult world and the institutions that structure adult behavior. The focus on kids and child psychology masks the reality that bullying reflects the institutional and cultural values and power hierarchies of our society. We therefore need a new conversation, centering on adults and how adult bullying has resulted in the bullying scourge among kids.

2. Institutions as well as people bully. In the United States, corporations, the military, the police, sports leagues, the family, and other organizations all commit institutionalized bullying; accordingly, the bullying will take place somewhat independently of the psychology or personality of any particular institutional leader, since it is embedded in the DNA and legal structure of the institution. This happens on a large scale. In the sociological imagination, institutionalized bullying is the leading cause of personal bullying. When the conversation about bullying is largely about individuals who bully (and their psychology), it essentially enables more bullying because it distracts attention from the true sources of the problem.

3. The national focus on personal and child bullying is shaped to a large degree by the elites who control the institutions that are themselves the biggest bullies of all, such as the corporations and the military. This reflects simple self-interest, since it diverts attention from institutional bullying and its horrific, rippling effects on the social lives and pervasive bullying among both adults and children. Such twisted control of the discourse gains popular acceptance because it allows

parents and teachers to believe that they can protect and support their children through their own psychological interventions, rather than by having to challenge the biggest and most powerful institutions in history, which, like air, are everywhere around us but actually unseen.

4. Institutional bulliers are closely tied to the bullying system that we call a bully nation. In the United States, a system of intertwined corporations, governments, and military institutions constitutes militarized capitalism. The system itself carries out "systemic bullying," to create profits and sustain its own power. This gives rise to the bullying endemic to both the US version of capitalism and the culture and practices of the US military, used against other nations and America's own domestic population by militarized police forces. It also creates other repressive institutions of control, including schools, sports organizations, and the family.

5. The military, sports, schools, and the family are all "bridging" or "transmission" institutions. They help create and channel a bullying culture from institutions to individuals. They are, in a sense, the kitchen that churns out food for the bullies. They dish out the bullying values and conduct that nourish militarized capitalism, making them palatable and part of the daily routine of millions of Americans.

6. The targets of bullying include not only adults and children but also animals and possibly other nonhuman species. We call this environmental bullying, and in the age of climate change, it may prove to be the most dangerous variant of all. In militarized capitalism, corporate capitalism teaches us to treat animals and other species as resources to be used to produce profit and satisfy our own material needs. Corporations seek to dominate all of nature for profit. Environmental bullying—with humans as the hegemonic species and animals and natural resources as prime targets—could ultimately result in consequences that end the human experiment as we know it.

UNEQUAL POWER AND CONTINGENCY: WHEN DOES POWER INEQUALITY CREATE BULLYING?

Socioeconomic systems based on unequal power are the root cause or enabler of all kinds of bullying, both institutional and personal. But does this mean that any power inequality in any institution, economic system, or social relation leads inevitably to bullying?

This is such a critical issue that we want to address it in more detail. If any system of unequal power always created bullying—and continuously so—all social life would be bullying all the time in all relations, since inequality is omnipresent in most societies. Now, the idea of omnipresent bullying is not absurd (just watch sitcoms such as *Everyone Loves Raymond,* where bullying in family interactions happens almost constantly). We believe that bullying takes place in all social, economic, and political systems and has done so in all historical eras; further, it always has strong roots in unequal power relations. In this sense, all social relations are vulnerable to bullying, and the social sciences are disciplines involving the study of bullying as a core issue.

Nonetheless, as highlighted earlier, we also believe in the idea of contingency. The notion of contingency is that there is no iron law dictating that unequal power in all cases leads to bullying. Potential or latent bullying, always present in relations of unequal power, leads to actual bullying only under certain conditions, mainly when the degree of inequality, political norms, social mores, and psychological dispositions encourages it. We do not argue that there is an iron law guaranteeing that power inequality will always lead to active bullying. But we see differences in power and inequality as enabling bullying—making it possible and probable but not guaranteeing that it will move from latent or potential bullying to active bullying.

So what are the contingencies that most strongly affect the likelihood that potential bullying will turn into actual bullying? Here are some of the most significant:

1. *The Power Gap:* We propose that the greater the power inequality, whether personal or institutional, the higher the likelihood of abuse and bullying. As power inequalities increase, so too do the chances for frequent and harmful bullying. In relations of systems marked by very high power inequality, the more powerful have more certainty they can get away with bullying, achieve their goals, and not harm themselves by bullying.

2. *Political Norms:* Capitalist societies, for example, may legally or politically encourage, tolerate, or even require, by law or custom, bullying behavior—behavior that we shall argue tends to be more prevalent in the United States than in many other capitalist societies. In northern Europe, by contrast, there are legal and political norms that discourage bullying (explaining the low bullying rate in Sweden, which

some investigations have shown has the lowest rate in all countries studied).[34] The political culture is shaped historically and will reflect national values that vary by country and from one capitalist nation to another. Of course, policies will not always work as planned, and antibullying state or school rhetoric will not always translate into a reduction in bullying behavior.

3. *Culture and Social Mores:* Every society has cultural norms that value or discourage different uses of power, including bullying. These differences may reflect family structure, religion, the culture of schools and sports, military values, ideas about domination, and other historical forces and views. Social approval or social mores about bullying behavior may be very different in societies with the same levels of structural power inequality. The potential for aggression and bullying may be part of human biology, but the key factor is whether the culture nurtures this potential or discourages it. Militaristic and competitive societies encourage bullying, whereas other societies discourage it: our concern is to identity the cultural forces that are crucial in making the difference.

4. *Psychological Patterns:* Dispositions toward aggression and domination may vary by society, and they may be quite different in societies with the same levels of structural inequality. Again, family patterns, school cultures, and biological temperaments may also vary by society, creating different rates of "bullying personalities." Again, however, we propose that the greater the systemic inequalities of power, the more likely it is that we will find a higher percentage of such personalities. Nevertheless, in all cultures, biological, psychological, and other factors, combined with power inequalities, create latent bullying; differences pertain mainly to the frequency and extent of harm created by active bullying behavior, whether by institutions or individuals.

Why are these contingencies so important? The sociological imagination points to major institutions, such as corporations and the military, as causes and enablers of bullying. And as we will discuss shortly, it also points to whole systems, such as capitalism itself, as the roots of bullying. This immediately leads to the question of whether capitalism in all nations and all forms is a bullying system. In answering such a charged question, we argue that contingencies always play a large role. In capitalism, as in all socioeconomic systems, bullying will occur. But what forms of capitalism are most likely to create high and harmful levels of bullying? And how will those levels compare to bullying in noncapitalist societies? The same questions can be asked about institutions such as corporations, the military, sports, or the family. Bullying will always take place—because there is always unequal power—but a crucial issue will be what forms of businesses or sports or families are most likely to create the high and harmful levels of bullying? These are the kinds of issues we will sort through in the rest of the book, and that effort will require understanding both the socioeconomic systems themselves and the cultural, social, and psychological contingencies translating potential into actual bullying.

MILITARIZED CAPITALISM

The sociological imagination ultimately turns our attention to society. Every society has a particular economic order, political structure, and culture that become part of what we mean by a "system." In America, the system is militarized capitalism, and it extends its dominion throughout the United States, across the globe, and into the planetary environment. It is a system primed to create pervasive bullying that affects adults, children, and all species.[35]

Militarized capitalism is most fully developed in the United States, which is one of the reasons why we focus on our own society. By looking both at America's history and at its current function, we see how a bully nation can flourish, gaining enormous power and wealth as well as moral legitimacy.

But are we looking at a nation or a system as the cause of bullying? In our view, they are intertwined. Militarized capitalism is the commanding structural reality of the United States today, and thus, we cannot disentangle the United States from its own system.

Militarized capitalism is hardly the only system that can produce a bully nation. Although we highlight America as a bully nation—and concentrate on militarized capitalism—we must not ignore the diversity and savagery of many other bully nations around the world, most of which are not systems of militarized capitalism (even though they may have strong military and financial power centers). These include other giant nations such as Russia and China and most Arab countries, among them Iraq, Iran, Saudi Arabia, Egypt, and Syria. They also include terrorist groups such as the Islamic State of Iraq and Syria (ISIS) and Al Qaeda, which may or may not identify as states; both state and nonstate terrorism are horrific forms of bullying, whether carried out by brutal groups such as ISIS, which we discuss later in the book, or by states that terrorize their own populations. Whether a state, a group, or a person, the bully always terrorizes, and terrorism is always bullying.

Militarized capitalism is just one system of unequal power that can create a bully nation, but since America is the most powerful country in the world and promotes its system as a model for the world, it deserves our attention. Yet as we see when we discuss the military and militarism, we cannot think of bullying at a purely national level, for bullying operates as a foundation of the American global order.[36]

As will be shown in chapter 2, nonmilitarized capitalism is very much a bullying system in its own right. The fundamental power inequalities between owners and workers foster the structural conditions that give rise to institutionalized bullying. Both capitalism and militarism can, on their own, create bullying societies. But as in America, where we have a deeply militarized capitalist system, the effects are amplified: the scope and harshness of institutionalized bullying become overwhelmingly powerful.

If we were looking at societies such as Germany or Sweden today, which both have forms of nonmilitarized capitalism, we would still analyze bullying as a product of capitalist forces, even though European capitalism differs significantly from the American variant; for example, it is far less militarized, and because it is a "social welfare" model, its bullying social effects are less intense.

In the United States, it is simply impossible to disentangle capitalism and militarism, leading to our analytical focus on militarized capitalism. Yet this does not mean we ignore the purely capitalist structural roots of bullying. In chapter 2, we will begin with a close examination of how a capitalist system produces a bullying society, an analysis that does not center on militarism and could be applied to other capitalist societies that are not militaristic. Later, in chapters 4, 5, and 6, we will turn to militarism and its own contributions to a bullying American society. These are partially autonomous but, in the United States, deeply intertwined with capitalism.

We believe that capitalism and militarism are the two fundamental institutional systems of political economy that give rise to a bullying society. We consider them to be parts of a unified structure in the United States. However, we need to make clear that if we extend our macroparadigm of bullying societies to other nations, the conceptual unit of analysis might be capitalism itself (in nonmilitarized capitalist societies) or militarism itself (in militarized noncapitalist societies).

The basic elements of a bully nation are a bully economy, a bully political/military order, and a bully culture. In the United States, these are the defining foundations of militarized capitalism. Note that these are the three interrelated power hierarchies identified by Mills in *The Power Elite* and *The Sociological Imagination*.[37] These hierarchies are fundamental to every bully nation, but they take different forms in different countries: what unites them across all nations is the way they divide a society into controlling elites and relatively powerless masses; in each, the powerful are small groups seeking to sustain control over the rest of the population and the natural environment.

A bully economy is one with significant wealth and power inequality, where the economy is structured to maximize profit or wealth for the rich and force submission by the rest, while at the same time subordinating animals and all of nature to the will of the wealthy. Inequality is endemic to the bully economic system; if you eliminate the inequality, the economy cannot long endure, as we will address in chapter 2.[38] Corporate capitalism is the American version of the bully economy. It is founded on the basic division between a small ownership class and everyone else; all of the latter are dependent on those owning productive property or the "means of production." This can also be described as the difference between those who own capital and those who don't.[39] If you eliminate this division, you no longer have capitalism as a system; it is the system's defining quality, and it ensures a great inequality of power in which the rich bully the rest into submission. This was the basic insight raised in recent times by the Occupy movement, which targeted Wall Street as the headquarters of the capital ownership class and dubbed the chief executive officers (CEOs) there as "the 1%." In the process, the movement clearly signaled that wealth concentration and power inequality were burgeoning to unbearable proportions.[40] *The Wolf of Wall Street*,[41] a popular film in 2013, dramatized the growing inequality and the bullying elements of our capitalist economy, as did Oliver Stone's classic film *Wall Street*,[42] which became famous for its motto of the bully economy, "Greed is good," as voiced by Michael Douglas's character, Gordon Gekko. Gekko symbolized the new financial tycoons who were running the economy, innovative mainly in their strategies to bully the world and the domestic workforce to ensure their own massive wealth.

In the real world, the bullying is not fully seen because of the ideology and morality promoted by the wealthy and by the economists who wittingly or unwittingly serve their interests. By arguing that the rich are worthy "makers" who have earned their money through hard work and talent while also creating jobs for the "takers," they turn bullying into a moral meritocracy that builds prosperity and rewards virtue.[43] It is hard to see a virtuous elite as a bully.

A bully politics is one based on a political ruling elite controlling both global and domestic populations, ultimately through military threats or even invasions. Such bullying may be promoted as a high moral cause and pursued under the guise of maintaining democracy, civil order, and virtue.[44] The United States is by far the most dramatic example of such a militarized political order, both externally and internally. Its military has appointed itself as the world's police, committed to using force to secure American and corporate power. Both the Bush and Obama doctrines, which argue that the United States has the right and the duty to attack countries where it feels threatened or sees a breakdown of "civilized order," are classic statements of the principles of a bully military and politics, as historically exemplified by, among others, the British, French, and Spanish Empires.[45] The United States has built its own form of empire, and it has routinely resorted to force to ensure "friendly" client states and bully them into submission.[46] The bullying is again carried out in the name of high moral principles, whether that is pursuing "manifest destiny"; saving democracy; or fighting communism, fascism, or terrorism.

Militarization in the United States has also redefined the relation of the police and the state to the American population, demonstrating how militarism can also be a source of bullying at home. Today, America has the largest population of jailed persons in the world. The 2014 case of Michael Brown, an unarmed black teenager who was shot to death while running away from a Ferguson, Missouri, policeman, illustrates the terrifying form of bullying that confronts many in the most powerless segments of the population. If you are black, brown, or white and poor, just walking on the street or sidewalk in many neighborhoods is to risk being bullied by police, and even many in the middle classes have had their own less frequent experiences of being bullied by cops during traffic incidents or political protests.[47] Meanwhile, immigrant populations, especially those crossing the border, are subject to intense levels of increasingly militarized bullying. As the police become loaded down with surplus military gear from the Department of Homeland Security, militaristic bullying is becoming more and more a part of daily life in thousands of US cities and towns, as we will show in chapter 6 when we discuss militarism at home as well as abroad.

A bullying culture is the third pillar of the bully nation. As noted previously, this culture's central values and norms of conduct are competition;

self-interest and self-defense; material acquisition; power seeking; toughness; dominance; security; the right to guns; and violence. Many nations incorporate *some* of these values, but every one of them has had a key historical place in American culture; they were enshrined during slavery and the frontier days, followed by the Industrial Revolution and the application of these values after the Civil War to promote military expansion and maximize corporate profits. The moral justification for these values initially grew out of the social Darwinism of the nineteenth-century's Gilded Age, leading to today's "greed is good" culture and the view that the virtuous rich have the moral obligation to force the "moochers," as Ayn Rand named them,[48] into submission and a "disciplined" life.[49]

Bully culture in the United States is associated with religious ideologies, such as Puritanism, that are related to repressing external and internal evil or hedonism; economic ideologies inherent in market competition and expansion; and military ideologies involving the spread of American values and defending both domestic and foreign populations against external threats. Again, the bullying elements are redefined in public discourse as moral virtues sanctioned by God or nature to ensure the flowering of civilization and prosperity in a world of evil. The bullying culture moralizes violence but hides its bullying dimensions in the language of controlling evil and the unworthy.[50]

A bully culture can coexist with other "countercultures" in a bully nation. In the United States, we have had "culture wars" almost since the beginning, where different groups or regions assert different value systems. Since the 1960s at least, culture wars have pitted the bully culture against another culture that emphasizes values of compassion, equality, nonviolence, simple living associated with a rejection of consumerism and materialism, peace, and harmony with nature. This counterculture, though hardly free of its own violence and bullying, has helped nourish a strong "antibullying" sensibility in parts of the population, as will be discussed in chapter 9. It has roots in major changes in the economy, demography, and education. And it proves that none of the features of bully nations are uncontested or necessarily permanent: there is always the possibility of change.

All three of the key elements in America's militarized capitalism—bully economics, politics, and culture—combine to produce the most invisible but perhaps ultimately most consequential bullying of all: the bullying of other species and nature itself. Corporate capitalism treats animals and other species, indeed nature itself, as property owned by corporations or individuals who can use all of it for their own profit.[51] This is a more extreme form of inequality than the kind dividing capitalists and workers; it more closely resembles a slavery system in which the workers were owned. So too are animals and natural resources "owned," and thus, they have virtually no rights and no voice at all. This extreme inequality of power creates a structural bullying relation between people (particularly the wealthy) on one side and animals and nature on the other. The situation is most obvious in industrialized agriculture, where huge corporations own and control vast numbers of animals that they raise and slaughter for profit. The same violent treatment is perpetrated by other corporations that use other species or natural resources as nothing but "inputs"—with no rights or voice—in production and profit making.[52]

Thousands of nonhuman species are going extinct as we extend militarized capitalism to all parts of the planet and all of its resources. We have fought our wars mainly for oil and other resources necessary to fuel the capitalist engine, and in the process, we have subjected all species and natural resources to control for profit. The environmental movement may, ironically, become one of the leading forces of cultural change and help create an antibullying sensibility.

We shall argue that anyone concerned with the bullying scourge needs to understand and seek to change key aspects of our culture and society. This is a tall order, and it is easy to fall back on personal strategies for saving oneself or one's kids, a problem facing all movements for social change. But societies are historically complex and are never entirely homogenous in their economic, political, and cultural legacies, a point made especially clear in the very recent rise of an antibullying culture in the United States. The country has been surprisingly receptive to social movements historically, as identified by Howard Zinn in his classic *People's History of the United States*.[53] That historical legacy is of vital importance for anyone who is alarmed by our bully nation and seeking a new way forward that can nurture the antibullying forces already rising into a broader movement for social change—a movement that can expose the horrors of bullying and move us as a society beyond it.

CHAPTER TWO

Capital Bullying

Capitalism, Power, and Economic Bullying

WORKERS IN A PICKLE

On October 1, 2014, the National Labor Relations Board ruled that a Burger King franchise in Ferndale, Michigan, near Detroit, had bullied a part-time worker, Claudette Wilson, by sending her home two hours early for not positioning pickles correctly on her burgers. As Judge Arthur J. Anchan put it, the company illegally sent Wilson home for failing to "put pickles on her sandwiches in perfect squares."[1]

Such absurd but intimidating and humiliating bullying of a very low-paid worker was retaliation aimed at intimidating Wilson from continuing her efforts to organize low-wage Burger King workers. A few days earlier, she had stopped at the store to ask workers coming off their shifts to fill out a questionnaire about their wages. A manager had written her up for violating the store's "loitering and solicitation" policy, something that Judge Anchan also said was "protected activity" and thus illegal. Wilson said she had not done the pickles quite perfectly because of her anger about the earlier unfair treatment.[2]

The story gets bigger because Wilson was one of several workers, including Romell Frazier, who were members of a group called D15, part of the Fast Food Forward Network trying to unionize Michigan Burger Kings. Wilson's "pickle problem" was really part of a larger and more serious pickle faced by the workers. The Michigan Burger King franchisee was systematically going after workers who were part of D15 and threatening them with sanctions, including firing.[3]

Frazier, for example, had talked up a union and had spoken about striking to his fellow workers. A manager told him that "if he was talking about striking again, he'd soon be picking up his paycheck," a clear threat intended to bully any workers who were engaged in organizing others. The company claimed that it had the right to prohibit workers from talking about unionizing on the job, but such activity is actually "protected, concerted activity" under the law. It's against the law to punish any workers for discussing unionizing or other forms of organizing. And as Judge Anchan underscored in his decision, the workplace is the "particularly appropriate place" for such talk and distribution of material because it's "the one place where employees clearly share common interests"; further, he said, "this is particularly true in the instant case where some of the workers are lower paid individuals who commute to work via bus."[4]

The pickle gets even bigger because the incident took place during a nationwide organizing campaign for fast-food workers. D15 and the Fast Food Organizing Network were partly funded by the nation's largest union, the Service Employees International Union (SEIU). The union was a leading supporter of the grassroots organizing spreading like a prairie fire among workers not only at Burger King but also at McDonald's, Kentucky Fried Chicken, and other fast-food chains. As the workers organized for unions and a higher minimum wage, the big companies were striking back. The threats and retaliation aimed at workers such as Wilson and Frazier might be called "capital bullying"—a type of bullying that is built into the DNA of corporate capitalism and that occurs at workplaces everyday, much like the pervasive bullying happening daily in schoolyards.

CAPITAL BULLYING: CAPITALISM, COMPETITION, AND WINNERS VERSUS LOSERS—HOW THE RICH BULLY THE POOR

Though the bullying of vulnerable kids in schools gets a lot of attention, the bullying of vulnerable workers usually is ignored. If the mass media mention it at all, they typically parrot the corporate view that the agitating workers are troublemakers who deserve punishment. The failure of scholars in the "bullying field" to see even illegal (not to mention legal) corporate threats, intimidation, and retaliation as bullying is another profound failure of the psychological paradigm that views bullying only as a "kid thing" in schools. Such scholars are blind to the adult and institutionalized bullying that is endemic to our economic system.

We refer to the bullying against workers such as Wilson and Frazier, whether pertaining to something as small as Wilson's pickle bullying or as big as being fired en masse, as *capital bullying*, meaning bullying inherent to Western and especially American capitalism. We must move from the micro-psychological to the macrosocietal paradigm to discuss capitalism as a bully-ing system. Only a macroanalysis can analyze capital bullying and help create structural changes to reduce it, a deeply destructive type of bullying carried out mainly by corporations. The bullying problem at Burger King and all the big fast-food firms is not a result of the personal psychological problems of the managers; rather, it is something that is systemically dictated and enacted no matter what the psychology of management.

In chapter 1, we explained that any economic or social system based on power inequality creates potential or latent bullying that often translates into active bullying, by institutions and individuals. So this is not a problem ex-clusive to capitalism; bullying was brutally manifest in systems claiming to be socialist or communist, such as the Soviet Union, and it is also obviously a major problem in China today. But capitalism is the dominant system cur-rently and has its own, less recognized, institutionalized bullying propensi-ties. They are not discussed in the academic bullying literature, but they are directly or indirectly responsible for much of the bullying we see in Ameri-can schoolyards and among both kids and adults.

In this chapter, we look mainly at institutional bullying by corporations in capitalism. We need to remind the reader of the definitional points we made in chapter 1. In many cases, corporate institutional bullying should not be viewed as personal bullying because the managers involved, though they are threatening and harming workers, are being required to act as agents of the company. As individuals, they may not deliberately be seeking to humiliate or harm their workers. Such "decent" or "nice" managers may cut wages or fire workers, but in doing so, they are carrying out institutional imperatives and orders rather than fulfilling personal motives to dominate, intimidate, and humiliate. In what follows, we primarily concentrate on institutional bullying by corporations, but keep in mind these two points: (1) such insti-tutional bullying may or may not involve personal bullying by the managers themselves, some of whom are being bullied to bully by their superiors, and (2) even top managers may be bullied by the larger market system, which is structured, as we show, to force corporations to become institutional bullies, even if the CEO is not personally a bully.

The greatest early critic of capitalism, Karl Marx, firmly believed that unequal power is inherent in capitalist systems—and that this creates power hierarchies and market structures that require institutional bullying.

Capitalism puts ownership of capital into the hands of one small group—the "capitalist class," often dubbed "the 1%" today. Most of the rest of the population is part of a huge underpaid working class or a growing poverty-stricken and jobless group, with no or very little capital or power. Marx argued that this unequal class power is the essential capitalist ingredient for profit, enabling capitalists—and specifically their corporations—to bully workers into accepting the wages and working conditions dictated by the owners. Put another way, workers have to accept their inferior position, a hallmark of bullying on which the entire system depends.[5]

Thomas Piketty, in his blockbuster best seller *Capital in the Twenty-First Century,* has spread public awareness of capitalism as an inequality machine.[6] In his book, Piketty presents data about the distribution of capital ownership in more than twenty countries over the last three centuries. He finds that capitalism, with only one exception in the last 300 years, has created wide, sustained, and often extreme inequalities of both income and wealth. Piketty argues that this does not reflect markets gone wrong; rather, it is the way capitalist markets are designed to work.[7]

Piketty is very explicit about this: "Specifically, it is important to note that [inequality] has nothing to do with any market imperfection. Quite the contrary: the more perfect the capital market (in the economist's sense), the more likely" that inequality will be created and grow.[8] There are no self-correcting market mechanisms to limit inequality, he argues, but only political interventions that are difficult to achieve. "It is possible," he says, "to imagine public institutions and policies that would counter the effects of this implacable logic: for instance, a progressive global tax on capital. . . . It is unfortunately likely that actual responses to the problem—including various nationalist responses—will in practice be far more modest and less effective."[9]

Put simply, inequality in wealth and power is baked into capitalist systems, and it is fundamental to structural and institutional bullying. But why does this inequality lead capitalists to bully workers and the poor—and also other groups, such as consumers, and even other capitalists? The answer has less to do with the psychology of executives than with the structure of the capitalist marketplace.

Capitalism is a ruthlessly competitive system in which all capitalists—whether corporations or individual entrepreneurs—have no choice but to compete furiously. Karl Marx argued that capitalists who do not compete with the ferocity of sharks, going for the kill, will be destroyed by rivals who are committed to the economic battlefield and to winning at all costs. This is an economic version of militarism, and it also mirrors the ethic of the schoolyard bully—dominate or die.

This systemic competition incentivizes even so-called nice or "socially responsible" capitalists to bully workers, consumers, and fellow capitalists. (As noted earlier, such executives are carrying out institutional bullying but are not engaged in personal bullying, for reasons discussed in chapter 1.) Corporations that do not bully workers—by paying low wages, breaking unions, and constantly harassing those who seek to challenge the power of the companies—will typically be at a competitive disadvantage compared to those that do; this is because the bullying leads to high corporate profits, as in McDonald's and other fast-food giants, and thus attracts more capital from the financial markets. Investors follow the money, just as sharks follow blood in the water. Corporations that do not bleed their workers by cutting wages and benefits—and intimidating those who challenge their degradation—will tend to see reduced profits and lose out to their competitors in the capital markets. A failure to bully workers into accepting low wages and the loss of other benefits also reduces profits, since increases in wages and benefits are drains on profit. This is a structural reality faced by all capitalists, whatever their personality, and it demonstrates the need to move from a psychological paradigm to one focusing on structural imperatives.

The same logic leads capitalists to compete intensely even with giant rivals in the 1%. The system will not be kind to competitors who are unwilling to threaten, undermine, and destroy their rivals; they are vulnerable to being put out of business. This results in bullying within the capitalist class; it is, we show, both similar to and different from the cross-class bullying of workers that is class warfare. In both cases, the strong must defeat competitive rivals, and they can win only by devouring the weak.

Structural competition in the marketplace encourages other types of capitalist bullying, including bullying of the unemployed, of consumers, and of politicians. As we will discuss later, these bullying relations, too, are structurally dictated by the marketplace. As on the bully schoolyard, nice guys finish last.

Before moving forward, we must illustrate the generic way in which competition in most capitalist societies leads to the rich (the winners) bullying the poor (the losers). This is particularly true in the United States, where the competition is harsh and the ideology of winners and losers conveyed in a particularly bullying discourse. At least since the nineteenth century, American capitalists have seen the competitive process as a form of social

Darwinism, in which the strong overcome the weak and the best triumph.[10] Thus, the rich deserve all their wealth and blessings, whereas the poor deserve their low station and misery. Since the market is seen as a Darwinian selection process, it is only natural and good that the rich—those who have proved their worth—assume control over the society as a whole, including all the specific groups that we discuss in this chapter. The system will not function unless the poor learn that they deserve their fate; workers must be bullied until they embrace this Darwinian view that they are inferior and deserve their fate.

This view emerged in early American Puritanism, where competitive success was seen as a sign of God's grace. The winners proved themselves a higher order of being, entitled to deference and special power and status. Competitive failure in the markets was, to the Puritans, a sign of being damned, in this life and the next. The degree of loss was a measure of the degree of worthlessness; it justified the winners treating the losers as drags on the social order who had to be controlled and kept in their place.[11] Workers who didn't accept their inferiority as losers would be bullied until they did so. This sense of inferiority is a "hidden injury of class, the enduring trauma of capital bullying."[12]

This ancient Puritan view has survived in various forms to the present day, with the wealthy winners seeing their success as a sign of virtue—and seeing the poor as losers whose nature is inferior and parasitic. In the 2012 presidential election, Republican candidate Mitt Romney made his famous comment about makers and takers, expressing perfectly his view that the poor were parasites leeching off the wealth created by capitalists like himself. He claimed that 47 percent of Americans were takers, thus condemning much of the population to the status of dependent moochers on the body politic. The implication was not hard to fathom: people in Romney's class would have to take charge of society and take control of the takers, through political and sometimes coercive means, in order to maintain a prosperous and virtuous social order.[13] They had to bully the takers to embrace the view that the makers deserved to be in power and legitimately claimed their wealth.

This is, of course, a bullying view of society, in which the winners of capitalist competition must assume control over the losers to preserve social well-being. To offer help to the losers—through welfare or other social benefits—is to divert resources to the undeserving and encourage their dependency and parasitism. Politically, this leads to austerity policies that are designed to be punitive to the poor and maintain the "natural" and "fair" unequal order that the competitive selective process has established. All people deserve their positions in the hierarchy, and those who question this primal assumption must be bullied into accepting their inferiority. Austerity has become the contemporary policy most clearly symbolizing capitalist bullying, in which the worthy rich threaten and withhold benefits from the unworthy masses, who in turn recognize their own inferiority.[14]

This bullying perspective was articulated lucidly by the writer Ayn Rand, who turned it into a broad philosophy about the morality of capitalism. Rand divided the population into the strong and the weak, the worthy and the unworthy, the productive or "creative" and the moochers.[15] The virtue of capitalism was that the free, competitive market provided a sure way of distinguishing these two orders of people, and it ensured that the worthy would triumph over the unworthy, the makers over the takers. To intervene and seek to reverse that order by helping the losers was immoral and would lead to social decline. Society thrived only when it allowed—indeed forced—the strong to dominate the weak in the Darwinian world, structured and managed through the market.

Rand is useful because she so clearly described the bullying philosophy and practices that govern US capitalism and its basic social Darwinism. The idea that the strong must dominate the weak is central to the schoolyard bully. The bully is strong and a winner and therefore entitled to control the weak, who are seen as sissies, cowards, and losers. The weak must accept the definition of themselves as inferior. The bullies in school essentially enforce their own austerity on the out-crowd—the loser kids deserve the humiliation, injury, and ostracism administered by the winner kids in the in-crowd.

In the rest of this chapter, we will consider how capitalist market competition is a macrostructural version of bullying in the schoolyard, playing out in the bullying way corporations treat others. We will look in some detail at the bullying of workers, which is central to the operation of capitalism, the profit drive, and the system's competitive warfare. We will also devote sections to capitalist corporations bullying capitalist rivals, as well as bullying consumers and politicians—all part of the DNA of the capitalist marketplace.

BULLYING FOR PROFIT: ROBBER BARONS SHOW
HOW TO BULLY WORKERS AND MAKE A MINT

In 1892, one of the most famous American strikes took place at a Carnegie steel plant in Homestead, Pennsylvania, near Pittsburgh. Andrew Carnegie had been known as one of the less ruthless tycoons of the era, but when the union, the Amalgamated Association of Iron and Steel Workers, organized a strike at the Homestead plant to increase wages, Carnegie decided to break their will and destroy the union for good. Before things were over, workers were threatened and attacked, and some were even killed; proud workers who asserted their right to earn a living wage and enjoy basic American rights were ruthlessly bullied into submission and defeat. The Homestead tragedy is an iconic symbol of capitalist bullying, whereby, in the name of property rights, profits, and prosperity, employers threaten and harm workers who seek a degree of workplace power and decent wages.[16]

As early as 1889, the union had effectively taken over the plant and established work rules to limit management's absolute power to control every detail of the work. A series of negotiations ensued, and Carnegie, who had nominally accepted unions, decided enough was enough. He instructed his man on the scene, Henry Clay Frick, to lock out the workers. Frick sealed the plant, built a high barbed wire fence, installed cannons capable of spraying boiling liquid, and turned the site into an armed camp.

On July 20, 1892, the Strike Committee resisted the intense bullying pressure that Carnegie and Frick imposed, issuing this defiant proclamation:

It is against public policy and subversive of the fundamental principles of American liberty that a whole community of workers should be denied employment or suffer any other social detriment on account of membership in a church, a political party or a trade union; that it is our duty as American citizens to resist by every legal and ordinary means the unconstitutional, anarchic and revolutionary policy of the Carnegie Company, which seems to evince a contempt [for] public and private interests and a disdain [for] the public conscience (commemorated on a plaque at the pumphouse of the plant).[17]

Such open resistance by the bullied was unacceptable. Frick responded by calling in the Pinkerton guards, an armed private security service that would attack the striking workers while helping bring in new, nonunion employees. Fighting broke out when workers refused to leave, and several of them were shot dead. As the fighting continued over the next few days, the union tried to defuse the situation, but Carnegie and Frick were not ready to concede anything. They turned to Pennsylvania's governor, Robert E. Pattison, a politician who had been elected as part of the Carnegie political machine and was in no mood to tolerate workers confronting his corporate patron. The governor immediately ordered 4,000 soldiers to surround the plant—and within a day, the strikers were dispersed. Some of them were bayoneted to death by state militiamen.

The strike ended, and the plant reopened with nonunion workers. The union collapsed. The consequences were disastrous for workers across America. In the next several years, Carnegie and his fellow robber barons destroyed unions at steel and other plants across the country. By 1900, there was no unionized steel plant left in Pennsylvania, and the labor movement was effectively destroyed.[18]

Homestead is a symbol of the capital bullying that has kept workers weak and intimidated up to the present day. Carnegie called himself a pacifist and had been seen, as noted earlier, as the most compassionate of the robber barons. He had given hundreds of millions of dollars (billions in today's money) to build public schools and libraries, and he so opposed the expansion of the American militaristic empire that he offered to pay $20 million to "free" the Philippines. But the crisis at Homestead proved that wages and profits require a bullying system that keeps workers disorganized and submissive, with military force being used when necessary.[19] This is true whatever the personality of the managers, with Carnegie exemplifying a "benign" capitalist pulled by the imperatives of market competition into bullying. The regime change of the New Deal led to a peak of about 36 percent of US workers being organized in unions, yet the Reagan revolution decades later resurrected the work Carnegie and the other robber barons began; as of 2014, some 94 percent of private sector workers had no union.

The minimum wage workers at Burger King and other fast-food companies, as well as at huge businesses such as Walmart, are struggling to create a new labor movement to help prevent the return of Gilded Age conditions. They are beginning to see that without the countervailing power of unions, corporate bullying—keeping wages low and workers submissive—will never end and that American workers will be like the bullied weak kids in the schoolyard. As we will see later, corporate employment in capitalist societies creates latent or active bullying against all employees, including unionized ones. To work in America is to inevitably experience substantial structural bullying, and those on the lower end of the totem pole suffer the most and yet somehow must learn to view it as a fair situation—much like the kids who are far down on the totem pole of power and "coolness" in school.

EXIT POWER AND BULLYING: GLOBALIZATION AS A BULLY REGIME

On April 24, 2013, an eight-story factory building called Rana Plaza in Bangladesh, housing 3,500 sweatshop workers, collapsed. The workers were mostly young women, sewing clothes for big companies such as Benneton, Primark, Joe Fresh, and other well-known brands. A total of 1,129 workers died, and 2,500 others lost hands, feet, and arms or suffered head traumas. It was the worst garment labor tragedy ever and the deadliest industrial accident in history.[20]

The tragedy could have been prevented. Just the day before, workers reported seeing huge cracks appearing on the floors and walls of the building. They knew they were in danger, but management refused to let them leave the workplace. Managers threatened them that if they didn't come to work the next day, they would be docked a month's pay.[21]

The workers labored, on average, thirteen to fourteen hours a day and earned wages between 14 and 26 cents an hour. Despite the miserable pay and their fear that the building was unsafe, the workers succumbed to their managers' threats and returned to work. They did so knowing that doors and windows would be locked and that they would be prevented from escaping if disaster struck. Ultimately, this corporate bullying resulted in mass death.

But why did the bullying work? Bangladesh is one of the poorest countries in the world, offering workers some of the lowest wages. But as meager as the wages are, millions of Bangladeshis have no way of surviving without their sweatshop jobs. The big companies, fully aware of the workers' desperate condition, know they have the power to get them to do whatever is necessary to keep their jobs. Since they have plenty of workers to pick from—there are 3.5 million garment workers in Bangladesh and many more waiting—the companies are in the catbird seat. They have the power to threaten the workers with any demand they choose, and the workers have no strong union or allies in the government to protect them.

It is a classic capitalist bullying situation, where the supply of global workers greatly outstrips the demand for them. In such a situation, the bargaining power shifts overwhelmingly to the companies, fostering enormous potential bullying that global market competition structurally translates into vast institutional bullying.

But in the age of globalization, the corporate power to bully is even further enhanced because of global companies' "exit power." Bangladesh is hardly the only country where global apparel firms can get work done for pennies an hour. They can go, for instance, to Vietnam or El Salvador or China. When workers in any country resist management demands, the companies can simply threaten to leave. A credible exit threat is a powerful tool for bullying, and it is a key to capitalist bullying in a global economy.[22]

Exit power is one of the fundamental forms of social power.[23] Consider a marriage in which one spouse has the financial or emotional power to leave the marriage and the other does not. It doesn't take a PhD in psychology or sociology to realize that the spouse with exit power has more influence in the relationship than his or her partner. And it is obvious that exit power creates latent bullying, which can easily be turned into active bullying when a spouse who can leave actually threatens to do so unless the other agrees to his or her demands. The partner whose survival—psychological or financial—is at stake if the other leaves will likely submit to the bullying spouse.

Globalization is an organized system of exit power for global companies. Corporations have created the architecture of a global system, in tandem with their allies in large and wealthy states, precisely because it gives them the freedom and often the necessity to leave or threaten to leave if they are to survive global competition. This system enables and often requires bullying on a mass scale, as Derber has discussed elsewhere:

> Corporate globalization is a game of global musical chairs—a master strategy for maximizing profits by pitting national workforces against one another. Corporations able to hire cheap labor around the world can threaten to leave a community unless workers submit to lower pay or local governments agree to various incentives to keep companies from pulling up stakes. Such intimidation, a vicious form of corporate bullying, has long been one of business's trump cards, played 75 years ago by Massachusetts and New Hampshire textile mill owners, for example, who relocated from New England to the South after northern workers unionized. But musical chairs became a game plan for unparalleled wilding when the theatre shifts from the nation state to the world—and the mill owners can relocate to South Korea or Mexico.[24]

Or, of course, they can move their operation to China, ground zero of the global workforce. China is the prize jewel for corporate bullies, since global companies can produce a dizzying variety of goods and services there at rock-bottom, starvation wages. Whether their work involves manufacturing jobs (producing computer keyboards, shoes, caps, solar panels, automobiles, toys, or almost any other good imaginable) or high-tech and service jobs, corporations can credibly threaten to go to China. Of course, they can also credibly threaten to outsource jobs to Mexico, Vietnam, South Africa, Indonesia, Guatemala, and especially India, which will soon compete with China as the corporate bullier's dream.

Globalization sets up a situation in which the big US corporation bullies both domestic workers and those in poor countries such as China. In the 1980s, the Big Three US auto companies—General Motors (GM), Ford, and Chrysler—repeatedly went back to officials of the major labor union, the United Automobile Workers (UAW), and demanded that they tear up contracts and accept major cuts in wages and benefits. If they refused, the companies would shut the plants down and move to Mexico, China, or other low-cost producers. The autoworkers capitulated to this bullying, accepting lower wages and cuts in pensions, health insurance, and other benefits, because their jobs were at stake. But eventually, the Big Three moved much of their production abroad anyway, cutting more than 60 percent of US-based auto jobs with little concern for the impact on the employees or their communities. They transformed prosperous metropolises such as Detroit into impoverished, Third World shells. Like the schoolyard bully, the corporate bully forces the weaker "kids"—workers in this case—to submit and then beats them up or finishes them off even when they give him what he demands.

Meanwhile, as in the case of the Bangladeshi worker, those getting the jobs in places such as China are bullied as well. Charles Kernaghan, the most authoritative chronicler of sweatshop conditions in the world, has described the conditions of workers in the Metai factory in southern China, who produce keyboards and other computer parts for giants such as Microsoft, IBM, Dell, and Hewlett-Packard:

- "Workers sit on hard wooden stools as 500 computer keyboards an hour move down the assembly line, 12 hours a day, seven days a week, with just two days off a month. The workers have 1.1 seconds to snap on each key, an operation repeated 3,250 times an hour, 35,750 a day, 250,250 a week and over one million times a month."
- "Workers are paid 1/50th of a cent for each operation they complete."
- "Workers cannot talk, listen to music or even lift their heads to look around."
- "All overtime is mandatory and workers are at the factory up to 87 hours a week, while earning a take-home wage of just 41 cents an hour."[25]

It's hard to say whether the US worker who lost her job or the Chinese worker who got it is the greater bullying victim. What is clear is that both are subject to bullying that is inhumane and potentially life-threatening treatment. For the corporate bullier, it is the best of all worlds, since the bullying works against both the domestic and the foreign worker, and the exit threat can be used repeatedly against workers in any country. Governments could intervene to lessen the bullying, partly by modifying the terms of international trade treaties, but governments are themselves subject to corporate bullying—through the withholding of campaign funds, lobbying, and the like—and typically draw up treaties that increase exit power and lead to ever-more corporate bullying.

ADJUNCTIVITIS: ADJUNCT PROFESSORS, CONTINGENT LABOR, AND STRUCTURAL BULLYING—WHEN LATENT BULLYING IS ACTUATED BULLYING

Colman McCarthy, an adjunct professor who has written eloquently on his own plight, writes that "we are the stoop laborers of higher education: adjunct professors."[26] What does that mean? McCarthy gives us a hint: "Benefits, retirement packages, health insurance? Hardly. Job security? Silly question. An office? Good luck. A mailbox? Maybe. Free parking? Pray. Extra money for mentoring and counseling students? Dream on. Chances for advancement? Get serious. Teaching assistants? Don't ask."[27]

And then there is the pay. According to the American Association of University Professors (AAUP), the median adjunct salary is $2,700 for a three-credit semester course. Colman puts this in vivid context: "Hordes of adjuncts slog like migrant workers from campus to campus. Teaching four fall and four spring courses at $2,700 each generates an annual salary of $21,600, below the national poverty line for a family of four. . . . This fall and spring I expect to teach 13 peace studies courses. My university pay totals $28,300."[28] Teaching thirteen classes an academic year is a mighty heavy load—and often, the adjunct will teach at multiple universities, increasing the number of classes even further! This pace would be almost unimaginable to professors on a tenure track, for they normally teach only two or three courses a semester.

Yet the tenured professor is no longer the norm. The AAUP reports that 75 percent of professors in higher education are now off the tenure track, and more than a million professors are adjuncts who have virtually no chance of getting into a tenured job. Most of them will be working beneath the poverty level, and all of them will be, by definition, insecure, since adjuncts have no promise of a job beyond the current semester.[29]

The adjunct position is worth examining for two reasons:

1. It creates a form of structural bullying in which latent and full-scale bullying converge. Every adjunct is bullied simply by the structure of the job.
2. Adjuncts not only comprise the great majority of the professoriate but also reflect the structural position of millions of workers in other parts of the economy, increasingly defining what work in the United States is all about.

Consider the first point. The adjunct is in a particular position of being structurally bullied: the position itself creates bullying simply by its own intrinsic dependency and vulnerability. Its core attribute—an absolute lack of job security—translates into uncertainty and anxiety about whether one will have a job or any pay at all when the semester ends. To be an adjunct is to be in a position of such vulnerability that it is virtually certain the person will (1) be in a state of anxiety about the job, and (2) do whatever is asked because of the lack of power. To challenge any dictate or order from the department head or dean is exceedingly risky. And to do anything unorthodox in one's teaching, to speak about controversial topics, to deviate from the prescribed teaching lessons—even if one's superior is not barking orders or telling one what to do—remains threatening. One toes the line because the consequences are so severe if one does not.

The adjunct position creates a bullied professor even when he or she is in a benign department or university. Latent bullying becomes full-scale bullying, and nice department chiefs must institutionally bully even if they personally are not bullies. They are being bullied to bully, required to act as agents of the university against their own values—and thus are engaged in what we described in chapter 1 as institutional but not personal bullying.

All adjuncts are bullied simply by the terms of the job, for latent bullying is built into a structural relationship that has little to do with the psychology of the person in power. The tenured professor who asserts the latent bullying upon the adjunct may herself be bullied by the university to impose rules she does not believe in. She may sympathize with the adjunct professor and be grateful she herself is not in that position. The tenured professor usually has no control over the university budget or university policy, and she may be forced to impose a salary and a schedule she considers exploitative.

The adjunct relationship itself creates bullying for four reasons:

- The power inequality between the adjunct and the administration is so extreme.
- The power inequality always creates insecurity, poor wages and working conditions, and other indignities or humiliation.
- The adjunct position always creates perpetual threat, no matter what the administration actually does, because the risk of losing one's employment is part of the terms of the position.
- The adjunct position inevitably creates fear and intimidation, leaving the adjunct always fearing that no matter what he does, the job may disappear the next semester for reasons outside his control.

Put differently, the latent bullying inherent in almost all power relations, including employment relations, is also full-scale bullying in the adjunct position. The adjunct position vividly illustrates why we need a structural and institutional paradigm of bullying. The bullying does not require any intervention or overt threat by the superior; it is written into the job and the institution.

Perhaps that is why people talk about the disease of "adjunctivitis." The replacement of the tenured position with the adjunct position embeds structural bullying deep into the heart of higher education and teaching.

Adjunctivitis, however, is not restricted to the university, where 75 percent of professors are subjected to it. It is increasingly the norm in all US jobs. Full-time, secure employment has succumbed to contingent, temporary, and involuntary part-time labor. Today, the fastest-growing sector of jobs and workers is composed of contingents, temps, and part-timers, representing about 35 percent of all workers today. One 2013 report noted that "temporary staffing jobs accounted for 91 percent of total nonfarm job growth from June 2009 through June 2011, according to the U.S. Bureau of Labor Statistics data cited by ASA."[30] By 2020, all kinds of contingent workers, including freelancers, are expected to make up 40 percent of all US employees.[31]

Contingent workers all suffer variants of the adjunctivitis disease endured by adjunct professors, for they are subject to structural inequalities of power, insecure and often low-paying work, and threats of job termination no matter what their performance; in turn, they experience fear, anxiety, and isolation. Derber did a series of interviews with contingent and temporary workers and found high levels of anxiety, isolation, and depression among almost all of them. Many reported being "invisible" to other full-time employees.

One temp worker found it so distressing to be "not part of the group" that he would take his lunch and eat it alone in the parking garage. This feeling of being "outside the in-group" is a classic sign of the bullied student as well.[32]

Another contingent worker, who worked as a clerical temp in a campus police department, told Derber that when she came in each morning and walked to her desk, nobody looked up and said hello, which made her nauseous (although the very fact of having a desk can feel like a privilege to the contingent worker). Yet another worker reported that he was not assigned a desk and had to work on an improvised chair or table, sometimes even sitting on a windowsill, which left him feeling humiliated and marked him as not part of the group. It was common for those in the sample to tell Derber that they were not introduced to full-time workers and that nobody knew their names or noticed if they were present at work or if they had been terminated.[33]

The millions of contingent and temporary workers outside the university are, in some respects, more structurally bullied than adjunct professors are. In contrast to the adjunct professor, they are often not doing work that they love. Moreover, their job security extends as far as the end of the day, not to the end of the semester; one temp told Derber her work was like a "one-night stand." But like other contingent workers, the adjunct professors are usually also invisible to tenure track professors; they are aware that the tenured professors do not know their faces or names, and they are not allowed to participate or vote in department decisions. Some contingents call this the disease of "tenurism."[34]

All workers or employees in the United States are in positions that create latent bullying because the country has an "employment-at-will" legal structure, a feature of most contemporary capitalist economies (though not all, as will be discussed). This means that their supervisors or bosses can fire them for any reason they choose. Except for tenured professors and some civil servants, virtually everyone works in a power hierarchy within the corporation, with a supervisor who has authority over them and can threaten to fire them. One does not have to be a contingent worker in an employment-at-will capitalist economy to face the possibility of being terminated for lack of merit as judged by one's supervisor or to have one's job outsourced or to be replaced by a robot. And since the new US norm is high unemployment, fueled by globalization, corporate control of the labor market, and the crushing of unions as well as technological changes, the threat of losing one's job is a serious concern for all US workers and is baked into virtually all work in modern America.

The difference between the full-time and the contingent worker is thus largely a matter of degree. Because of employment-at-will, all workers face structural bullying, for to be employed is to be automatically vulnerable to the threat of dismissal. Most union contracts do not eliminate this threat even for full-time, unionized workers; in any case, as noted earlier, 94 percent of private sector US workers have no union, and public sector unions are under relentless attack. Further, even tenured professors and civil servants face latent bullying because university and government contracts have clauses allowing the administration or top executives to decide if a tenured employee has breached an ethical contract or a performance standard that would permit termination of the employee.

But tenured professors or civil servants have a unique position in the United States, one in which latent bullying is not necessarily actuated bullying. For these employees, job security and autonomy are strong enough that the threat of being fired does not hang over their heads, and there is substantial (though far from total) freedom to do one's job—and to voice one's views—without being terminated. In this case, one might speak of a genuine distinction between latent and full-scale structural bullying. It takes an unusual intervention by those on top to actually make the threat of dismissal vividly real—something that creates the insecurity experienced by most other workers. That is why one of the authors' colleagues reported that during the approximately ten years she worked in various universities as an assistant professor on tenure track but without tenure, her first thought every day before getting out of bed was about tenure. Even after getting tenure, however, professors are constrained in a subtle way, for their fear of doing something controversial often leads to self-censorship and prompts them to stay within the bounds of "respectable discourse."

For most full-time workers without tenure, the distinction between latent and full-scale structural bullying is even blurrier. For those who have high-level skills or are toward the top of the power hierarchy, the structural bullying may be more latent than full blown. But for the great majority of untenured full-time workers, the threat of losing one's job is strong, especially without union or state protection of the kind that many workers in European capitalist societies enjoy. (They also enjoy the protection of legal employment doctrines that are not based on employment-at-will, as in the United States.) The full-time American worker is always under threat, and the threat grows for workers who are lower on the totem pole in the business or corporation. Increasingly, the full-time worker thus occupies a structural position in which latent and actuated structural bullying converge.

Consequently, adjunctivitis is becoming the condition of nearly all workers, whether they are full-time or contingent employees. To be employed in capitalist America is to experience structural or institutionalized bullying as an important part of one's life. The adult worker therefore may be even more subject to bullying than many kids in school, and that is saying quite a lot! This situation clearly illustrates that the adult world is rife with bullying and that corporate power and capitalist economies make the problem a visceral and agonizing experience for workers, much as schoolyard bullying is for their kids.

CAPITALISTS BULLYING CAPITALISTS: BULLYING OF THE 1% BY THE 1%

As noted in chapter 1, capitalists don't just bully workers. They also bully each other, driven by the merciless competitive structure of the marketplace. This bullying was evident more than a century ago in the Gilded Age, when the robber barons cooperated with each other but also viewed one another as sharks and reacted accordingly, as seen in this account about Andrew Carnegie:

> Carnegie, playing the game, double-crossed his competitors with as much regularity and glee as they double-crossed him. . . . Carnegie . . . never liked to cooperate with his enemies. When he entered his first rail pool, he was allotted a small part of the market by the other members. Carnegie leaped up, announced that he wanted an amount equal to the largest quota, moved his finger around the table from magnate to magnate telling each one his own business and costs and threatening to undercut them all. It was a typical Carnegie display and it worked.[35]

Carnegie was seen as a so-called nice capitalist, but he knew he had to play the shark. This incident reveals the contradictory relations of the 1% vis-à-vis one another. On the one hand, they cooperate and often collude, forming cartels, trade organizations, and collective lobbies to advance their collective interests. But they are playing a double game, also seeking to weaken and ultimately destroy each other. John D. Rockefeller, Sr., built an even larger fortune than Carnegie by demanding a rebate from railroads that carried his competitor's petroleum. Rockefeller's Standard Oil controlled such a large share of the market that he could bully the railroads into fearing that if they did not give in to him, they risked annihilation.[36]

We see examples of capitalists bullying each other everywhere today. One instance is the high-profile issue of Amazon's conflict with the huge publisher Hachette, regarding the price of e-books. When Hachette resisted the lower prices that diminished its profits, Amazon retaliated by postponing the appearance of new Hachette books, slowing down deliveries, reducing Amazon discounts, and even refusing to display some Hachette books. This was classic corporate bullying, matched by Hachette trying to work with other publishers and its famous authors to degrade and undermine Amazon's reputation as a new high-road mass retailer working for the consumer and authors.[37]

Corporations use multiple bullying strategies to get a competitive advantage, increase market share, and weaken rivals. One very common strategy is suing a rival. Since 2011, hundreds of big companies just in the high-tech smartphone world have sued each other over patent rights, each company seeking to prevent the other from selling a competitive product purportedly stolen from its own design or technical inventions. Apple sued Samsung in 2014 for $2 billion for allegedly copying features on its new phones. HTC has sued Apple. Samsung countersued Apple. Apple and Microsoft started legal action against Google, Huawei, Samsung, LG, ZTE, and others. Oracle sued Google. Microsoft sued Motorola.[38]

Corporations spy on each other, try to recruit their best employees, and seek to undercut each others' reputation and market share through advertising, lawsuits, and cost cutting, often using unfair or illegal trade or sourcing practices. Many use what is explicitly called "brand bullying" strategies. Facebook will sue a company for using "face" or "book"; Blue Shield will sue another insurance company that uses "blue" or "shield."[39] These are all forms of capitalist bullying, carried out by institutions regardless of the personality of their leaders.

Another form of capitalist bullying involves big companies bullying small businesses, often wiping them off the map. One example involves big box stores such as Walmart undercutting mom-and-pop stores by offering extremely low prices, then raising prices again when the moms and pops are wiped out. Another variant occurs when smaller businesses sell products to giant retail outlets and then are bullied over price and other contract issues. A CEO who owns and runs a small medical supply company sells wholesale to CVS and other big chains. He reports how CVS puts his product on its shelves but then begins reneging on all aspects of the original contract, threatening to withdraw the product entirely if he does not agree to revised terms. The bullying by CVS and other retail chains, he says, never stops, and he has no choice but to capitulate; otherwise, his business will be eclipsed by his competitors who accede to the bullying.[40]

But is all capitalist competition bullying? Not necessarily. A corporation can compete simply by developing a better product, with no intention to wipe out rivals. It can also have superior management and marketing. Moreover, the same companies that bully one another often work closely with each other—and sometime merge—to get greater control of the market or more favorable regulations and taxes for the whole industry. Corporations have a love-hate relationship with each other, not unlike many marriages marred by bullying.

Capitalism's strongest defenders proclaim that competition is its operating principle, but competition must, by its very nature, produce losers as well as winners, with the advantage going to the most aggressive bully. As Marx pointed out, capitalist competition is an inherently self-destructive system. The strong wipe out the weak, and there are fewer and fewer survivors. Competitive capitalism mutates into monopoly, with monopolists capable of extreme, enduring bullying of workers, consumers, and potential rivals.[41]

Early in the twentieth century when automobiles were first introduced, there were over 200 car manufacturers. In a relatively short time, there were only 3. Later in the century when personal computers first became common, thousand of young, technically trained "nerds" started writing software in their garages, dorm rooms, or apartments. Today, the market is almost entirely controlled by Microsoft and perhaps Apple. In the 1980s, mom-and-pop software and video stores could be found in almost every neighborhood. Now, they are nearly all extinct. Supposedly to encourage competition, the Reagan regime "deregulated" the airline industry in the 1980s. But rather than producing more competition, deregulation brought greater monopolization. Even giants such as Eastern Airline, Continental, TWA, US Air, and PanAm succumbed. The survivors bullied not only their competitors but their captive passengers as well. They now felt free to exclude meals from the cost of tickets and to charge baggage fees of hundreds of dollars.

Rather than fostering innovation, capitalist bullying, especially in monopoly capitalism, can squelch it, causing great harm to fellow capitalists, customers, and the environment. Auto companies hold patents for engines that would be more efficient and less ecologically destructive than internal combustion engines. However, these alternatives would compete with existing technology, and developing them would require paying to retool plants that were already yielding adequate profits, at least for the time being. The patents were therefore locked in vaults to prevent other people, companies, and countries from using them. Oil companies gave solar and other green energy technologies a similar treatment.[42]

The capitalist marketplace is a ruthless system of economic battle, not unlike competition among militarized nations. The more powerful seek to expand their power and control, sometimes allying with one another and sometimes fighting; the weak fight back with whatever they've got in order to survive. The most powerful typically will win and rule the market. The parallels with the schoolyard are obvious. The powerful kids use whatever means are necessary to establish their dominance. They compete with rivals to become the ruling bullies. Once they've established their positions, they may build strategic alliances with other powerful kids; these are often love-hate relations. The goal is to manage the alliance to ensure their bullying position over their rivals and over all the weak kids. Every school bully will recognize the corporate bullying game—and will be well prepared to use the bullying skills necessary to overcome corporate rivals, partly by more effectively and ruthlessly dominating his or her workers.

CAPITALISTS BULLYING CONSUMERS:
ON BRANDING AND CORPORATE MIND CONTROL

In her classic book *No Logo: Taking Aim at the Brand Bullies*, Canadian journalist and activist Naomi Klein argues that brand bullying is at the heart of capitalism today.[43] We have already mentioned brand bullying, but Klein is not just talking about corporations suing other corporations for patent violations. She is talking about how corporations are now more committed to creating an iconic brand than to making a good product or offering a good service. And she shows that branding—as in branding the soul of the consumer—is necessary for corporations that wish to compete successfully.

Brands are used as a core competitive strategy to lure consumers to view the corporation's product as magical, something they can't live without. The charismatic brand is actively promoted—endorsed by celebrities, advertised as essential to being "cool," shown in popular Hollywood films or sitcoms (for a price)—in order to hook the consumer. Brands are powerful techniques for essentially coercing consumption, making consumers, especially the young, feel that they cannot be popular without buying whatever it is that branding turns into a magical, cannot-live-without product—perhaps a type of smartphone, a brand of dress or handbag or jeans, or a branded video game or other toy product.

Klein is talking about the process that Karl Marx, in the first chapter of his most famous book *Capital,* called the "fetishism of commodities."[44] Marx argued that capitalism cannot survive without a massive demand for corporate goods that people used to make or grow at home rather than buy, whether food, clothes, or entertainment. To create that consumer demand, the corporate product has to be "fetishized," or turned into something miraculous. Whatever you make at home could never be as magical as a fetishized brand you buy: it could never have the mysterious seduction. Fetishizing the product is profound bullying of the consumers, since it invades their minds, transforms their desires, and creates a potent addiction, a kind of coerced consumption of fetishized goods.[45]

Corporations create the magic through endless advertising and strategic marketing, starting with kids at a very young age. Much of this now takes place online—via YouTube videos, video games, and sponsored online ads—but much of it is also "on the ground." Parents take their kids to McDonald's and the kids will get hooked not just on the Golden Arches and the burgers but also on the toys placed in the store by Toys "R" Us. Teenagers see Brad Pitt wearing a certain hat or cologne and race to the store to get it. The bullying may be subtle, but it is a form of power that only Big Brother could approve. It takes over the mind and changes the brain and values and lifestyle of the consumer. Happiness becomes, most of all, a trip to the mall.

Corporations have been frighteningly successful in bullying young consumers. Students who do not buy the essential branded product, whether that's a type of sneakers, a certain telephone, or a particular haircut, are highly vulnerable to bullying by other students. They are shunned and ostracized, mocked and humiliated. Corporate bullying through commodity fetishism has succeeded in creating the conditions for acceptance, success, and self-respect among young people and at the same time creating targets for bullies.[46]

The kids are being bullied through a system the great sociologist Thorstein Veblen called "conspicuous consumption."[47] Veblen described this as a major stratifying and bullying mechanism in the adult world, with wealthier Americans displaying their money, special breeding, and social prestige by acquiring expensive and ostentatious goods, such as a Rolls Royce or a private plane. Conspicuous consumption creates in-groups and out-groups, with members of the in-group denigrating and shunning those in the out-group, a classic bullying dynamic. Corporations are now spreading conspicuous consumption into the schools and the youth population. This institutionalized bullying by corporations—with kids bullying other kids who can't afford conspicuous consumption and thus can't make the in-group—is a major cause of kids bullying each other.

The psychological paradigm highlights kids' bullying, but it doesn't address the crucial role of corporations in setting up the drama and promoting mass institutionalized bullying of both young and adult consumers. Corporations are dream masters, and they mesmerize and coerce the consumer, exercising a form of mind control that is indisputably bullying. Virtually all corporations engage in branding and fetishism, whatever the personality of their executives, because these strategies have become crucial to winning market share and crushing corporate rivals.

Sociologist Stuart Ewen, in his classic work *Captains of Consciousness,* traces the historical process by which capitalists actually created consumers.[48] Ewen points out that before the 1920s in the United States, mass consumption on a national scale did not exist, certainly not the current branded and fetishized form that enables bullying. In the 1920s, corporations turned to public relations experts to develop modern, sophisticated advertising. Catalogs were first put out in the 1880s by companies such as Sears Roebuck, but they did not reach their full impact until after World War I. The catalogs featured goods that people used to make for themselves; now, these people learned that they could only gain self-respect by buying the products from there. The foundations for corporate bullying based on conspicuous consumption were laid in earnest among the masses.

Juliet Schor, in her book *Born to Buy,* asserts that this bullying of the consumer begins at birth.[49] Pregnant mothers are inundated with products as they bring their infants into the world, and every new mother heads home from the hospital with her arms full of magical products for baby. From then on, parents, doctors, and teachers become part of the corporate sales force, essentially imprinting on the most impressionable young minds how life and identity are all about consuming the goods.

We should add that there are many other crucial forms of consumer bullying, including selling a faulty product on credit and then threatening the consumer if he or she doesn't pay the loan. The most egregious recent example is the 2008 housing crisis. The big Wall Street banks and mortgage companies, such as Merrill Lynch and Countrywide, sold houses with sub-prime loans that were designed to go bad. When the mortgagee could no longer pay back the loan, the bank threatened to foreclose. Although the borrower was often deceived—and lured into buying a home without reading the fine print that called for the interest rate to spike up—banks put all kinds of pressure on the victim, with foreclosure being the scariest prospect. Similarly, college students taking out problematic loans from unsavory creditors often find themselves bullied to pay back their debt for years, even if the university they attend can't deliver a credible curriculum or degree and even if they ultimately have to drop out for financial reasons.[50]

In addition to making unnecessary products attractive, corporations have devised other ways to bully the consumer. It could be argued that since the consumer's response is voluntary, whether or not this constitutes bullying is up for debate. However, monopolies can bully their customers to buy their products or services because the corporations deny them alternatives, which amounts to a form of coerced consumption. In addition, very large companies can manipulate the market and transform optional products into necessities. Los Angeles once had one of the finest public transit system in the world, but Standard Oil and General Motors jointly bought it and closed it down. They then pressured the California legislature to build freeways. And soon, life in Los Angeles became almost impossible without a car. Homes, stores, businesses, and even schools and recreation centers were now so far from each other that they could only be reached by automobile.[51]

The variety of ways in which corporations bully consumers is staggering. But the worst among them is the branding of the soul involved in creating the consumption addict in the first place.

CAPITALISTS BULLYING POLITICIANS: THE BEST DEMOCRACY ONE CAN BUY

Money and democracy are a bad mix. Supreme Court Justice Louis Brandeis once famously said, "You can have great concentrated wealth or democracy but not both."[52] This is being proved in the United States today—reflecting, in part, political bullying by corporations. The great wealth of the corporations corrupts democracy and bullies politicians and the state itself.

Marx offered a classic quote in observing that the capitalist state or government "is the executive committee of the bourgeoisie."[53] He did not mean that capitalists directly run the government but rather that capitalist wealth soaks into the political and policy process. In recent times, this has happened through campaign donations and lobbying, and it ends up leading top politicians to serve corporate profits as opposed to the general interest. This occurs when political leaders become captives of corporate money and influence and are bullied to implement the corporate agenda.

By focusing on the market as self-regulating and self-correcting and as the only source of wealth, neoclassical economic theory has masked the enormous role government plays in creating wealth and shaping the market to meet corporate needs. Corporations rely on the state for everything from favorable tax treatment to billions of dollars in subsidies (often called corporate welfare), advantageous trade laws, union-busting efforts, deregulation, and numerous other benefits. Corporations cannot survive without commandeering the state for their own agendas, and to do so, they must coerce and bully politicians, much as they coerce and bully consumers and workers.[54]

How capitalists bully politicians is a fitting subject for a book, but here we will identify just three of the most important ways:

1. *The Koch brothers strategy:* This is shorthand for buying politicians through huge campaign contributions. The Koch brothers, multibillionaire oil tycoons who are among the ten richest people in the United States, have spent astronomical sums on elections, mainly to support oil-friendly conservative candidates for high office. The Koch strategy is to exploit the opportunities of the landmark *Citizens United* and *McCutcheon* Supreme Court decisions, which allow corporations and wealthy individuals to spend unlimited funds on "issue advertising," through entities that do not have to disclose their donors. These shady organizations, with names such as Americans for Prosperity, bankroll the political campaigns of most members of Congress and candidates for the White House itself. *Citizens United* and *McCutcheon* are among the most important Supreme Court decisions ever, overturning decades of campaign finance laws.[55] Both are corporate bullying enablers, allowing corporations to dictate agendas to politicians who depend on them for their jobs.

The Koch strategy is carried out by hundreds of giant corporations seeking to commandeer national, state, and local governments. The capitalists and their corporations can be conservative or liberal, but they use the same bullying strategy. A candidate cannot be elected to Congress or other high office without spending millions on a campaign. And the biggest donors get the greatest access. Thereafter, their money provides the basis for decisive influence through threats that the funding will be withdrawn. If the politician does not follow orders, she will lose the corporate money and face a real threat of seeing her career come to an end.[56]

This applies to both parties. President Barack Obama was elected in 2008 with the help of millions of small donors, but 60 percent of his campaign funding came from Wall Street firms and other big corporations. In fact, these corporations pour in more than two-thirds of all the money campaigns receive. Money assures access and influence. Ultimately, he who pays gets to play, and if the politicians don't play their own role in the game—to carry out the corporate agenda—they won't be successfully playing the political game much longer.

Campaign money from big corporate donors is one of the most insidious forms of political bullying conducted by corporations. It is structural in that no politician can get elected or survive without big corporate campaign donations. Obama wanted public financing or limits on private financing, but he embraced unlimited private donations because it was the only way to win. This bullying is baked into the capitalist political system, and it does not rest on the psychology or the views of individual politicians. All of them have to do it. And this, of course, undermines democracy in an obvious way, as political leaders become beholden to their corporate patrons rather than the general public. Threatening to close the wallet in the next election cycle is the surest way a corporation can bully politicians and commandeer the state.

We should note that bullying also goes the other way. Tom DeLay, a Texas Republican who served as whip of the House in the late 1990s and early 2000s, was indicted for shaking down corporations and rich individuals in his "pay-to-play" strategy.[57] If corporations didn't pay up, they could not play, that is, they could not get access to the politicians who wrote the bills affecting their businesses. So bullying in capitalist politics is a two-way street.

2. *Lobbying:* Lobbying is an extension of campaign finance bullying. Armies of lobbyists camp out permanently on K Street, near the White House. Many of them are paid by corporations to buttonhole legislators and draft laws that comprise a corporate wish list. Legislators listen and often deliver. Why? Because these are the corporations that fund their campaigns and can bully them with threats of cutting off the money, as well as besmirching their reputations. When these corporations turn against you, your influence in Washington is going to sink. The lobbyists are often "revolving door" agents

who have worked back and forth between congressional offices and corporate headquarters; they know how to build the consummate bridge between corporations and Congress or the White House or the governor's office. And they know how to threaten, when necessary, to ensure that corporations get the policy and laws they want.

Back in the robber baron era, lobbyists didn't try to hide what was at stake. Rockefeller would send his men onto the floor of Congress with briefcases full of money, a practice that was frequently satirized by cartoonists in the newspapers of the era. The legislators took the money—and often the laws that Rockefeller had drafted and stuffed in the briefcases along with the money. The quid pro quo was up front, and the shameless bullying helped create the term *robber barons* to describe the corporate tycoons of the era.[58]

Today, lobbyists are a more polished lot. They operate behind the scenes, wear suits, and claim to be "public advocates" or issue advocates, purportedly educating legislators and the public on policy questions. The truth is that, though they work for many different types of organizations, from unions to charities to nongovernmental organizations (NGOs), the most influential and well paid are corporate lobbyists representing giant global firms. These firms officially spent $3.3 billion on lobbying in 2013 (and actually more than $10 billion according to some researchers). One report indicates that "James Thurber, an American University professor who helped the Obama Administration craft its lobbying rules, believes that the industry has 'gone underground' and is actually far larger than just the 12,000 registered federal lobbyists—he says it's more like 100,000 people bringing in north of $10 billion annually."[59]

Not surprisingly, the biggest industries with major stakes in Washington policy hire the most lobbyists and pay the most each year, with the following ranking in 2014:

Pharmaceuticals/health products	$65,420,126
Insurance	$40,008,093
Electric utilities	$38,288,418
Computers/Internet	$35,597,059
Business associations	$35,448,590
Oil and gas	$33,880,219
TV/movies/music	$28,511,338
Securities and investment	$26,670,959
Miscellaneous manufacturing and distributing	$23,650,110
Hospitals and nursing homes	$21,985,808[60]

Of course, $3.3 billion—or perhaps the $10 billion spent by 100,000 lobby-ists—buys a lot of influence, at local, state, federal, and global levels. The lob-byists are strategists, bridgers, and enforcers who make sure that the money does its job. The corporations are the bulliers, but they use suave operators to get their deals done. This is not entirely different from the situation on the schoolyard, where the ruling bully may use some of his powerful friends to handle the dirty jobs so he won't have to soil his own hands.

3. *Exit power:* Earlier, in discussing how corporations bully workers in a glo-balized economy, we introduced the idea of exit power. This is a basic form of power, involving the capacity to credibly threaten to leave a relationship or institutional partnership. Those with the capacity to exit almost always have more power—and the ability to bully partners who feel they cannot survive the loss of the relationship. Anybody in a marriage can easily understand this dynamic: just think of the power of the words "I'm going to divorce you."

Globalization is a system designed for corporate exit power. It allows corporations operating in any one country to threaten to shut down opera-tions there and move to another country. Workers can't easily migrate, but money flows seamlessly across national borders. This asymmetry of mobility between capital and labor produces the superior corporate exit power that enables bullying of the global labor force. Corporations can say to entire na-tions, "I'm going to divorce you."[61]

Exit power lets corporations bully nation-states in exactly the same way they bully workers. Nations depend on the capital, jobs, and infrastruc-ture that foreign companies invest in their economies. When corporations threaten to pull up and leave, they initiate a traumatic bullying process against nations that are dependent on them. Corporations make exorbitant bullying demands if the countries want them to stay, asking for such things as tax holidays whereby firms pay no taxes for ten years, no enforcement of environmental or labor laws in their plants, and special export zones where companies can operate without regulation or public accountability.

If the countries don't comply, the corporations' threats to exit carry great credibility. It isn't always simple to leave, but because there is so much out-sourcing by companies all over the world from one nation to another, there can be no doubt about the credibility of such threats. One need only think of periods when global banks have invested heavily in nations, as in Thailand and other Southeast Asian nations in the 1990s, and then suddenly pulled the plug, leaving these countries with half-built office complexes and devastated economies. This situation created the "Asian flu" of the late 1990s that set back Thailand and neighboring nations for years. Any country, rich or poor, should be afraid about the prospect that its economy can be thrown into a depression overnight through decisions by global companies to disinvest and leave.[62] Often, the people who lose their economic security will blame the state, which can easily forfeit its legitimacy. Politicians can lose elections, or the government may risk being overthrown. When Salvador Allende of Chile nationalized the copper mines, which had been owned by Rockefeller-controlled corporations, the World Bank reduced Chile's credit rating. Allende could not raise the capital he needed to manage the mines and was forced to close them. The displaced workers struck, which provided an opportunity for the Chilean military, with the support of our Central Intelligence Agency (CIA), to overthrow Allende; this resulted in a junta, led by Gen. Augusto Pinochet, ruling Chile for the next sixteen years.[63]

The schoolyard bully uses exit power in a slightly different manner. He can threaten other kids with the withdrawal of attention and membership in the group—that is, total ostracism. He can bully by getting the in-group to exit from any dealings with the kids he is bullying. Such shunning is actually one of the most terrible punishments humans can experience. In ancient China, a severe punishment entailed prohibiting the offender from having any eye contact with others, thereby subjecting the individual to total isolation from genuine contact. Some accounts suggest that it was brutal ostracism that led to rampages by bullied kids such as Eric Harris and Dylan Klebold, the mass killers at Columbine High. Put another way, bullying can have fatal consequences even if it involves no physical violence at all. Sometimes, all it takes is averting one's eyes.

CHAPTER THREE

Environmental Bullying
Bullying Animals and Bludgeoning Nature

Beyond focusing on children, discussions of bullying have largely assumed that bullying is solely about humans. In this chapter, we will argue that this is a mistaken notion. People can bully not only other people but also animals. Moreover, in the age of climate change, it is becoming apparent that we need to discuss how humans can bludgeon nature itself.

This takes our new paradigm into relatively unexplored terrain, at least in the academic literature on bullying. Although some bullying researchers occasionally address military and corporate bullying, none, to our knowledge, has introduced the idea of environmental bullying.

In popular conversation, however, it does not seem strange to talk about bullying animals. Many of us know somebody who bullies or abuses his or her dog or another pet. We have also heard scary stories about how giant agricultural companies, such as Tyson, Smithfield Farms, and Perdue, operate slaughterhouses that mistreat the cattle, chickens, and other animals that end up on our dinner plates. And most people know that corporations and individuals are engaged in other forms of environmental behavior that are grossly polluting air and water, hurting not only millions of people but also many thousands of species of animals and plants. Indeed, two hundred species of animals are going extinct every day. The worst environmental destruction is human-caused climate change, which threatens the survival of civilized human life and the ecological balance sustaining all life species, whether human or not.

One can readily ask whether such environmentally destructive and abusive behavior should be called bullying. As mentioned at the outset, bullying is typically viewed as behavior that only involves humans—not animals, plants, or natural resources. But in ordinary conversation, we also speak of a person who kicks or abuses a dog as bullying, and thus we move beyond human targets to animal ones. We do not, however, generally speak of people bullying plants or air or water, even if they are killing the plants or badly polluting the air and water. Of course, many environmentalists and indigenous cultures think differently, celebrating all of life and nature as precious or sacred.[1]

Here, we distinguish two distinct types of environmental destruction: bullying and bludgeoning. Environmental bullying is carried out by people or organizations that threaten and harm animals. Environmental bludgeoning is carried out by people or organizations that harm or destroy plants and natural resources such as air or water or soil.

Environmental bullying and bludgeoning are closely related, and they share key attributes. First, both involve power inequalities. People who bully animals have more power than their pets or other targets, and the agricultural companies that bully animals have enormously more power than the animals they raise and slaughter. People and corporations that bludgeon plants and natural resources have the same or even a greater power advantage over their targets, at least in the short term.

In both environmental bullying and bludgeoning, superior power is used to create harm or destruction. In both cases, there is a mind-set of domination, whereby the perpetrators believe in their right and even their responsibility to bully animals or bludgeon plants and natural resources in order to satisfy their own needs.

The major difference has to do with the consciousness of the targets and their ability to experience threat and pain. This distinction is crucial to the bullying act; if the animal cannot detect a threat or have consciousness of harm or pain or inferiority, then it is difficult to argue that bullying is taking place.

The great majority of animal species have consciousness and can feel pain and violence—perhaps this is, in fact, true of all animal species. But even though scientists are increasingly finding that plants "think" and have other forms of sensory consciousness, such as smell and hearing, it is not clear that they have the type of consciousness that would allow them to experience either threat or pain, at least not in the same way that humans and animals do.[2] That distinction defines the difference between bullying and bludgeoning: the former is used against targets (animals) with consciousness of threat and pain, whereas the latter is used against targets (plants, air, water, or rocks) that do not, to our knowledge, have that specific type of consciousness.

The distinction here revolves around the consciousness or sentient capacity of the target. Plants and inanimate resources have forms of intelligence and sensory awareness and responsiveness that are remarkable, and as indigenous cultures recognize, this constitutes an evolved consciousness, rooted in forms of DNA shared with humans that has largely been unknown despite the unfolding scientific discoveries.[3] But we do not know whether they have a kind of sentient capacity involving the experience of threat and pain resembling that of people or animals (though many indigenous cultures have believed they do for thousands of years).[4] Since we do not have full clarity about these matters, we reserve the idea of environmental bullying for animals and describe the destruction of plants and natural resources as bludgeoning.

If consciousness or sentient capacity is a defining distinction, we must consider questions about which animals have the level of consciousness that would make them vulnerable to bullying. Primates and other mammals obviously have consciousness and awareness of pain and suffering, as do most other vertebrates such as fish and birds.[5] Whether invertebrates have this specific form of consciousness is clear in the case of octopuses, but for mosquitoes or fleas, we do not know whether they have a type or level of sentient capacity that would make them vulnerable to what we call bullying. So some animals—those with a very primitive consciousness—could be viewed as vulnerable to bludgeoning rather than bullying. Yet it is also plausible, as Peter Singer's work suggests, to argue that all animals have forms of life consciousness that would incline us to view them as vulnerable to bullying.[6]

Some might raise the same issue in regard to very young children: do they have the consciousness or sentient capacity to understand threat and experience pain? If one thinks of the shaken-infant syndrome, it seems relatively obvious that even young infants can be bullied. The same is true of elderly demented people in nursing homes who can be mistreated and bullied. So our perspective suggests that humans of any age should be viewed as potential bullying victims.

Despite the distinction we draw between bludgeoning and bullying, they often occur together and are closely interrelated. Bludgeoning plants or inanimate objects in nature, such as soil and water, can seriously harm people and animals, upsetting the underlying ecological balance on which all people and animals depend. We shall show that bludgeoning of nature is a major way in which powerful people, companies, or armies bully both people and animals, while simultaneously degrading plants and natural resources; this is one of several ways in which we illustrate that bullying and bludgeoning are tightly intertwined—and may, in the end, prove to be indistinguishable from one another.

Environmental bullying and bludgeoning are forms of environmental destruction that are integral to both militarism and capitalism. Militarized capitalist societies, such as the United States, embed environmental bullying and bludgeoning in their DNA; they could not function without either form of environmental destruction.[7] And as just noted, they reinforce each other. In wars, environmental bludgeoning by bombs, destroying individuals' land and homes, is a major way to bully people. In capitalist industrial agriculture, soil erosion and depletion, a form of environmental bludgeoning, often leads to bullying of people, by forcing them off land or giving them little choice but to eat unhealthy products.

Perhaps the most compelling argument today in the discussion of both environmental bullying and bludgeoning is that human-caused climate change—the most existential environmental threat that humans have experienced—is endangering the existence not only of humans but also of thousands of other animal and plant species. Much of the natural world is in peril. And that reflects the enormous power that humans now exercise over nature, as well as the extraordinarily destructive and violent way that power is being used.[8]

Later in this chapter, we will address the question of how human-caused climate change is a form of bludgeoning that leads to bullying in multiple ways. Here, we will offer just three quick observations. First, climate change is tied to actions we humans, the most powerful species in nature, take in order to use power for our own ends, even though this may be suicidal for us and has already killed off thousands of other species. Such actions reflect a practice and mind-set of dominance that we see in the schoolyard bully.

Second, climate change has historically evolved out of Western corporate capitalism, the subject of our last chapter and a focus of our book. Environmental bullying can be seen as an extension of systemic "capital bullying." But we should acknowledge, first, that precapitalist society certainly reeked with environmental devastation. Ancient militaristic empires callously burned fields to bully the people who lived off them, pushing them into starvation.[9] And bullying through biological warfare is nothing new. Medieval knights would catapult dead bodies over castle and city walls in the hope of provoking plagues.[10] It is believed when humans first reached the Americas, they brought about mass extinctions, including among them most of the larger mammals.[11] In some ways, of course, today's environment is cleaner and healthier than in the past. For all the environmental injury caused by the automobile, cars relieved city streets of horse manure, which had caused epidemics of typhoid, diphtheria, cholera, tuberculosis, and other communicable diseases.[12] In fact, these illnesses were the leading causes of death at the time, but today, hardly anyone dies from them, at least not in the rich West.

The capitalist drive for profit accelerated the pace of technological innovation, with the environment treated as an "externality"—that is, as nobody's responsibility and in any case not something for producers or corporations to worry about or be legally required to pay for.[13] Accordingly, capitalism also intensively sped up climate change and other forms of environmental bludgeoning. Although Western and especially US capitalism is far from being the only economic system contributing to climate change, it *is* the most important historical cause, and climate change is baked into America's capitalist model.[14] One might thus argue that intertwined environmental bullying and bludgeoning, especially in an age of climate change, resulted in some of the most significant bullying practices as well as legal codes that are endemic to corporate capitalism. This includes the concept of property and the idea that humans can own nature, whether water or air or trees, and abuse or destroy these resources for profit. More generally, almost all capitalist values—growth, consumerism, short-term profit—contribute to climate change; further, almost all corporate behavior involves bullying of the environment, as we will flesh out in our climate change section. Corporate capitalism is so deeply bound up with climate change that we cannot solve the latter problem without changing the former.[15] If we reject any idea of environmental bullying, we are abandoning a serious analysis of the capitalist system and corporate behavior. We are also neglecting the connection between our economic system and the way we relate to animals and nature, a relationship that is central in all societies.

Similar arguments apply to militarism. Militarized societies conduct wars that are devastating to the environment—due to carbon-intensive military aviation and other military technology, the oil and other natural resources that wars are fought to secure for fossil-fuel industries and nations, and the destruction of animals and plants as well as people that wars cause. Bludgeoning of the environment almost always facilitates bullying of people in war. Think only of the ecocide the United States committed in Vietnam, graphically involving environmental bludgeoning that led to the bullying of hundreds of thousands of Vietnamese. Powerful examples include the US military's use of chemical weapons such as Dow Chemical's napalm and its spraying of environmental poisons and defoliants such as Agent Orange to burn forest and land, especially around guerrilla tunnels. (One American commander declared in Vietnam, "Trees Are Our Enemy."[16]) This environmental bludgeoning helped US soldiers move in and bully Vietnamese soldiers and peasants as part of the war strategy. Moreover, the mind-set of power and dominance endemic to militarism mirrors the mind-set of environmental bullying: I will take what I can conquer. This is also the mantra of the schoolyard bully.

We must make two further observations here. The bullying behavior seen in humans is widely observed among other animal species as well. Scientific literature documents how animals cooperate with each other and nurture one another but also bully members of their own and other animal species. This, of course, does not make bullying a good thing; humans have the capacity to act toward each other and toward animals in ways that do not simply reproduce the less appealing forms of animal behavior. Nonetheless, we must recognize biological realities, as Woody Allen, a famous skeptic about romanticizing nature, whimsically observed in his film *Love and Death*: "To me nature is . . . spiders and bugs, and big fish eating little fish, and plants eating plants, and animals eating. . . . It's like an enormous restaurant."

We have choices about which principles in nature we want to emulate and which we want to avoid. Mahatma Gandhi urged, "Be the change you want to see in the world." We do not accept all that nature bequeaths us, and though we may not be able to eliminate all the bullying found among animal species in nature, we can at least create a society that does not reward it.

Although we focus almost entirely on destructive forms of human environmental bludgeoning and bullying in this chapter, we recognize that many argue there may be morally acceptable forms of such behaviors. For example, certain medical experiments on animals that might help cure terrible human diseases are often seen as justifiable reasons for harming or abusing animals—a notion that has preoccupied ethicists and concerned citizens for many years. Similarly, when people drain a swamp to eliminate mosquitoes that carry malaria in order to protect themselves or when they kill deer carrying deadly Lyme disease, this again can be seen as a form of environmental bludgeoning or bullying that many view as morally acceptable or desirable. We find that humans, schooled as they are in human-centrism, are generally too ready to sacrifice other species for human benefit. In this chapter, however, we will focus on environmental bludgeoning and bullying that we think should clearly be ended—because it is largely motivated by the drive to dominate and profit rather than to protect humans and because it is carried out on a scale threatening the survival of thousands of species of animals and plants. In our opinion, these forms of environmental bludgeoning and bullying are central to militarized capitalism.

In the rest of this chapter, we will look briefly at three types of environmental destruction that involve environmental bullying. The first is people bullying animals for fun or profit. The second is corporate environmental bullying and bludgeoning on and off the farm. The third is systemic environmental bludgeoning that leads to climate change and endangers humans, nonhuman species, and precious resources such as air, water, and earth—in other words, nature itself. Such bludgeoning leads in many ways to more bullying by individuals and organizations of other people and animals.

BULLYING ANIMALS: DO WE TREAT OUR DOGS AS OUR BEST FRIENDS?

Michael Vick, the famous professional football player who was the highest-paid NFL player in 2004 on a ten-year, $130 million contract, helped make animal bullying a national story. In 2001, at age twenty-one, Vick, together with three of his friends, started a dogfighting business called Bad Newz Kennels in Virginia. Vick and his colleagues bought land, hid it from public view behind a fence, and then began buying pit bulls and other dogs that were tested for their fighting abilities and violent tendencies. According to a federal indictment, they "executed approximately 8 dogs that did not perform well in the various testing . . . by various methods, including hanging, drowning and slamming [one] to the ground several times before it died, breaking the dog's back or neck."[17] Other atrocities were applied in order to bully dogs to fight better, and "dogs who lost fights were sometimes executed."[18] One of Vick's friends executed a losing female pit bull "by wetting the dog down with water and electrocuting the animal."[19]

The bullying impact of the treatment they received was painfully obvious in many of the dogs that survived. A team from the American Society for the Prevention of Cruelty to Animals (ASPCA) found that "two had to be put down—one was excessively violent and the other was suffering from an irreparable injury. Then there was a group characterized as 'pancake dogs'— animals so traumatized in their training they flattened themselves on the ground and trembled when humans approached."[20] It was no surprise that the pancake dogs saw people as violent bulliers. Police who went to Bad Newz Kennels found a torture chamber where they observed:

- Approximately fifty-four dogs, mostly pit bulls, some with scars and injuries; most were underfed.
- About half of the dogs were chained to car axles and just out of reach of each other, a typical arrangement for fighting dogs.
- A blood-stained fighting area.
- Animal training and breeding equipment, including a "rape stand," a device in which a female dog who is too aggressive to submit to males for breeding is strapped down with her head in a restraint.
- A "break" or "parting" stick, used to pry open fighting dogs' mouths during fights.[21]

The Vick case clearly demonstrated how dogs and other animals are subjected to bullying both for fun and profit. To enjoy themselves, Vick and his friends would sometimes set the trained pit bulls on other peaceful pet dogs because "they thought it was funny to watch the pit bull dogs belonging to Bad Newz Kennels injure or kill the other dogs."[22] The many fights they staged had big gambling purses of up to $26,000, so this was a profitable business.

Matthew Bershadker, president of the New York ASPCA, has made observations about the Vick case that highlight the bullying aspect of the horror. He writes that dogfighting remains common in all regions and among all classes of people in America, despite being illegal in all fifty states today. He points to the key bullying dimension of dogfighting: "[It] represents the ultimate betrayal of the unique relationship that exists between humans and animals. Manipulating a dog's desire to please its owner to perpetuate a life of chronic and acute physical and psychological pain is the most horrific form of animal abuse."[23] This observation suggests the power inequality involved in the practice, with the owner controlling and threatening or manipulating the dog that is his property—effectively his slave—to get the dog behavior that he wants. The dog is trying "to please its owner," but it cannot avoid being subjected to horrific abuse and violence, no matter what it does. This is something a bullied kid in school would understand.

Studies are actually finding a strong connection between human and animal bullying. People who bully other people, including violent criminals and murderers, often start out as bulliers and abusers of animals. A People for the Ethical Treatment of Animals (PETA) report observes:

Studies have shown that violent and aggressive criminals are more likely to have abused animals as children than criminals who are considered non-aggressive. A survey of psychiatric patients who had repeatedly tortured dogs and cats found that all of them had high levels of aggression toward people as well. According to a New South Wales newspaper, a police study in Australia revealed that "100 percent of sexual homicide offenders examined had a history of animal cruelty." To researchers, a fascination with cruelty to animals is a red flag in the backgrounds of serial killers and rapists. According to the FBI's Ressler, "These are the kids who never learned it's wrong to poke out a puppy's eyes."[24]

The same report notes that much murderous school violence is carried out by kids who have been bullied themselves and have also abused animals and talked about it with fellow students:

> The deadly violence that has shattered schools in recent years has, in most cases, begun with cruelty to animals. High-school killers such as Kip Kinkel in Springfield, Oregon, and Luke Woodham, in Pearl, Mississippi, tortured animals before starting their shooting sprees. Columbine High School students Eric Harris and Dylan Klebold, who shot and killed 12 classmates before turning their guns on themselves, spoke to their classmates about mutilating animals.[25]

Likewise, men who batter their wives or children frequently are animal abusers as well:

> Sixty percent of more than 50 New Jersey families that had received treatment as a result of incidents of child abuse also had animals in the home who had been abused. In three separate studies, more than half of the battered women surveyed reported that their abuser threatened or injured their animal companions. In one of those studies, one in four women said that she stayed with the batterer because she feared leaving the animal behind.[26]

Bullying animals may, in effect, serve as a means of transmitting bully values—a way in which people learn to bully other people and come to see bullying as routine and acceptable. The fact that bulliers of people also tend to be bulliers of animals helps confirm the view that animal bullying is closely tied to human bullying. Ultimately, bullying is bullying, whether the target is human or animal. The behavior is much the same, involving power inequality, threats, and harm often associated with violence, all of which suggests that if we stop animal bullying we may reduce bullying by children or adults.

What distinguishes animal bullying is the degree of the power inequality. Human bullies, whether at school or at work, have power over their victims.

But owners of animals have *unfettered* power; their victims are their property, and pets or other animals are so disenfranchised that their legal position, as in a slave system, creates a kind of deep and permanent structural bullying. The structural power inequality is so great that, as in the case of the adjunct or contingent worker (not to mention a slave), latent bullying is effectively built in, and that routinely translates into actual bullying. One defender of dogfighting told a reporter the dogs were his property and that gave him the right to do whatever he wanted with the animals. Most pet owners would not say that, of course, but they have extraordinary power as owners, much as slaveholders did, since their dogs are their property. Even benign and loving pet owners have latent bullying power because of the structural power vested in them. The schoolyard bully would certainly understand the advocate of dogfighting because he views the schoolyard as his property and embraces his power as a mandate to keep the other kids in line, in whatever way he chooses.

CORPORATE ENVIRONMENTAL BULLYING AND BLUDGEONING: ON AND OFF THE FARM

In the last chapter, we discussed how corporations bully workers, competitors, consumers, and politicians. But they also engage in environmental bullying against animals and environmental bludgeoning against plants. And almost all corporate behavior involves polluting the environment, which can be seen as a form of bludgeoning nature that often harms people or leads them to bully others.

Such behavior is structurally dictated institutional bludgeoning and bullying, for it occurs whether or not the corporate executives are personally interested in preserving the environment. (Recall from chapter 1 that institutional bullying can be carried out by corporate managers who personally are not bullies but act as their firm demands even if that contradicts their own values.) The incessant institutional bludgeoning takes place because of the same competitive structure discussed in chapter 2, which jeopardizes the competitive advantage of corporations spending the necessary money to preserve the environment—something that is expensive and not always possible with many products, from oil to industrial agriculture to aviation. Environmental destruction can be mitigated, but the inner logic of capitalist production—which turns natural resources into private profit and almost everything into a commodity for mass consumption and profit—leads to inevitable environmental degradation.[27]

The corporate mind-set involved is one of conquest and dominance. The corporation views the environment as property to be owned, mastered, and controlled. This mirrors the philosophy of the schoolyard bully, but it is written into the DNA of the corporation and is structurally embedded, whatever the personality of the executive; the culture of the firm and its success in molding the psychology of the managers also make a difference in the degree of bullying.

The bullying elements become clearer when we look at some examples, one of the most horrifying being the bullying endemic in our industrialized agriculture system. Giant factory farms, such as Tyson, Cargill, Swift, Perdue, and Hormel, now produce 99 percent of the animals we eat; they raise animals for slaughter and sale, and the processes they use vividly demonstrate environmental bullying. According to a Pew report, "The present system of producing food animals in the United States is not sustainable and presents an unacceptable level of risk to public health and damage to the environment, as well as unnecessary harm to the animals we raise for food."[28] We shall see that all these practices involve environmental bullying because they threaten and force animals to act and live in ways that cause pain and harm in order to maximize profit.

Another report on the industry, which slaughters billions of animals each year, summarizes the horrors:

Cows, calves, pigs, turkey, ducks, and other animals live in extremely stressful conditions and subject to threats and violence if they resist:

Kept in jam-packed sheds or on filthy feedlots, often with so little space that they can't even turn around or lie down comfortably.
Deprived of exercise so that all their bodies' energy goes toward producing flesh, eggs, or milk for human consumption.
Fed drugs to fatten them faster and keep them alive in conditions that could otherwise kill them.
Genetically altered to grow faster or to produce much more milk or eggs than they naturally would, many animals become crippled under their own weight and die just inches away from water and food.[29]

Once the animals are ready for slaughter, corporations ratchet up the violence, clearly reflecting the bullying institutional dictate that the animals must be dominated and intimidated in whatever way necessary to squeeze out more profit:

> When they have finally grown large enough, animals raised for food are crowded onto trucks and transported over many miles through all weather extremes, typically without food or water, to the slaughterhouse. Those who survive this nightmarish journey will have their throats slit, often while they are still conscious. Many remain conscious when they are plunged into the scalding-hot water of the defeathering or hair-removal tanks or while their bodies are being skinned or hacked apart.[30]

Beyond this terrible bullying of animals, industrial agriculture leads to major environmental bludgeoning of plants and soil, incorporating many of the elements of bullying: this requires a mind-set of domination to extract profit in a way that is coercive, and it inflicts long-term harm. One can think of many such bludgeoning practices, including the use of dangerous fertilizers and pesticides and farming through monocropping. Monocropping involves growing a single crop, such as corn, soybean, or wheat, over and over year after year, instead of rotating crops to replenish the soil. Monocropping can be efficient in the short term and hugely profitable, which is why corporations do it and how they justify it. But the environmental costs over time are considerable, as Rachel Carson first noted in *Silent Spring*, her pioneering critique of industrial agriculture and pesticides.[31] Since her classic work, numerous environmentalists have documented the dangers of monocropping. For instance, it creates easy niches for parasites, making plants or crops more vulnerable to disease and requiring more fossil-fuel fertilizers and pesticides that can leach into the water and nearby soil. It also creates soil depletion, since the rotation of crops replenishes key soil nutrients. And monocropping requires more irrigation and more fertilizers to undo the effects of industrialized agriculture.[32] Organic farmers have turned to radically different ways of growing plants and farming the soil, but the scale of their operations is typically smaller and the profit margins more modest. This explains, in part, why "big ag" uses its bludgeoning technologies.

Interestingly, early critics of capitalism, including Karl Marx and Frederick Engels, wrote extensively about how capitalist agriculture would lead to major environmental damage, including soil erosion. Sociologist and environmentalist John Bellamy Foster has written important books documenting Marx's and Engels's focus on environmental exploitation and degradation.[33] Engels wrote:

And the original appropriation—the monopolization of the earth by a few . . . yields nothing in immorality to the subsequent huckstering of the earth. . . . To make earth an object of huckstering—the earth which is our one and all, the first condition of our existence—was the last step toward making oneself an object of huckstering. . . . It was and is to this very day an immorality surpassed only by the immorality of self-alienation.[34]

The most famous capitalist critics have thus seen clear parallels between the exploitation of humans and the exploitation of the environment. Engels's commentary reveals that he and Marx viewed the relations of capitalists to labor and the environment as intertwined and analytically difficult to distinguish: environmental expropriation gives rise to the conditions of human expropriation, and the environmental "hucksterism" or abuse is just as serious. Marx and Engels treated the domination of both people and the environment as inseparable foundations of the capitalist system. Thus, the language of domination and exploitation we use in discussing capital bullying would apply as well to animals, and it vividly evokes the idea of bludgeoning the environment, crops and soil included. Both are driven systemically by the search for short-term profit and competitive advantage.

But if the corporate bullying and bludgeoning of the environment is perhaps most obvious on the farm, it is just as present outside agricultural sectors. Corporations in every sector develop environmentally harmful products in environmentally destructive ways, making environmental bludgeoning a chronic feature of corporate behavior. And corporate environmental bullying is nearly indistinguishable from the general "capital bullying" against workers, consumers, competitors, and politicians addressed in chapter 2. Whether we are discussing the obvious perpetrators of bludgeoning—the big oil and coal companies or chemical, pharmaceutical, aviation, high-tech, retail, and other corporate sectors—all are constantly expanding production that is depleting finite resources; degrading land, air, and water; and contributing to climate change. All are bludgeoning the environment for profit, and they do so because structural imperatives of survival in the market demand it.[35] In the process, they often increase the tendencies of people to bully other people, as when retailers sell cheaper goods—whether food, drugs, or cars—that are dangerous to their customers' health. Capitalist environmental bludgeoning, as noted earlier, routinely leads to more human bullying, either in other stages of a bullying production process or in the salesmanship of commodities that are harmful to their human users.

In the United States, the market is blind to most environmental impacts, which economists call externalities.[36] These are costs (or benefits) that the market doesn't price into the product, such as many greenhouse emissions. The producer typically does not have to pay the costs of polluting, which often become apparent long after the production process. Corporations damage land by endlessly extracting coal or oil or natural gas, by cutting down forests in logging, by creating and dumping plastics used in production and packaging, by dumping sewage into rivers and lakes (recall when the rivers flowing into the Great Lakes burst into flames from pollution), and by burning fuel in commercial flying. Some forms of production are more damaging than others, but in the United States, powerful companies keep regulation limited and taxes on pollution low, so that almost all corporate production bludgeons and harms the environment—and the cost is not paid by the corporation. Again, this bludgeoning of the natural world often leads to human bullying, as people compete to sell harmful products or turn against nearby communities to find shelter from toxic waste and occupy the most secure land.

Production in all economic systems has harmful environmental impacts, but the problem is greater in some national systems than in others. In the US capitalist model, the corporate activity produces high levels of environmental damage because (1) the corporation doesn't have to pay, (2) the corporation aims for short-term profit and doesn't consider the long-term costs, and (3) the US production process is "extractive" rather than regenerative, that is, it extracts resources and returns waste but does not regenerate the environment to its original condition or to an even healthier state.[37]

Much of this environmental destruction, carried out by virtually all large corporations, is bludgeoning rather than bullying. For corporations "off the farm," this bludgeoning involves many bullying elements; these are all related to power inequality, domination, and destruction. Corporations have property rights over their environment and products, and they enjoy legal and political power to produce, within the law, as they see fit. In US capitalism, the competitive system requires rapid expansion of production at lower cost, without consideration of the environment except when that is specifically mandated by law, to gain market share and profit while destroying competitors. And as in all bullying, corporate power is creating harm, with bullying of rival competitors leading to bludgeoning of the environment.

Capitalist competition and the human bullying it fosters thus can lead to bludgeoning of the environment, just as environmental bludgeoning can increase human bullying. The cheapest corporate production, which neglects environmental externalities, will adversely affect the health and lives of people and animals, thereby bullying them. The drive for immediate profit results in both bludgeoning and bullying, which in turn can reinforce each other and spiral into even more harm to people and the natural environment.

Corporate bludgeoning and bullying both reflect the mentality of schoolyard bullies. Blowing off mountaintops or clear-cutting forests or dumping into the human water supply dangerous pollutants and wastes that are by-products of production reflects a schoolyard bully's mind-set of domination. Like the school bully, the corporation is acting to consolidate a power position and to threaten or harm anybody or anything in its way.

CLIMATE CHANGE: BLUDGEONING NATURE IN EXTREMIS

Today, climate change has to be the ultimate subject for any discussion of environmental destruction. The reality of climate change is itself one of the strongest arguments for entertaining the ideas of environmental bullying and bludgeoning. And it also underscores the view of capitalism as a bullying system, as discussed in the last chapter, with unprecedented consequences— seen as so-called externalities that do not need to be recognized—for human civilization as well as nature itself.

A growing literature connects capitalism with climate change, including Naomi Klein's bestseller *This Changes Everything: Capitalism vs. Climate*; John Bellamy Foster's books, such as *The Ecological Rift* and *Ecology against Capitalism*; and Charles Derber's book *Greed to Green*. Climate change is, along with nuclear war, the greatest threat to human civilization ever known, and understanding its causes is essential if we are to have any chance of limiting the damage.[38]

Capitalist values and structural forces drive destruction of the earth, and they must be changed to mitigate climate disaster as well as reduce all the ways in which environmental and climate bludgeoning lead to greater bullying by people of people. Even the Pentagon has argued that climate change is emerging as one of the central causes not just of environmental destruction but also of wars over scarce land, food, or water that may massively increase militarized bullying among nations and communities.[39]

Our argument is not that capitalism is the sole economic system engaged in environmental bludgeoning or bullying—and causing climate change. As noted previously, all economic systems have harmful environmental effects, and authoritarian self-proclaimed socialist and communist regimes—in the Soviet Union, China, Venezuela, and Bolivia—have engaged in some of the worst environmental practices. But historically, climate change developed as industrial capitalism took root in Europe and America, and the United States today practices the model of capitalism that yields the highest per capita greenhouse gas emissions in the world—by far!

We have already made the case that corporate bullying in the United States, in all economic sectors, is causing massive environmental damage, much of it in the form of greenhouse gas emissions. The Worldwatch Institute has argued that raising animals for consumption through industrial agriculture produces an astonishing 51 percent of all greenhouse emissions and is thus a huge cause of climate change.[40] Any significant mitigation of climate change is going to require major structural changes in our capitalist model of agriculture and in other corporate sectors that will end capital bullying. And ending such bullying will require and foster a different social and moral philosophy, as well as more life-affirming economic institutions and lifestyles—among them a shift away from raising animals for food, for that is arguably the single greatest cause of climate change.

We have already indicated the key aspects of US capitalism that generate climate change: markets blind to environmental costs; competitive forces that advantage companies engaging in low-cost production and ignoring environmental consequences; financial markets dictating short-term profit maximization through unlimited production, an imperative of expanding sales and mass consumerism; and a lifestyle and social philosophy that prioritizes private property and wealth over public goods.

We have explained elsewhere how these features of capitalism cause climate change, so here, we want to focus on why these capitalist values and practices should be understood as bullying in relation to animals and bludgeoning of plants and natural resources. There are three basic considerations at play: the overall philosophy of the capitalist system in the United States, the basic values in that system, and institutional corporate practices that are dictated by the market philosophy and system.

Capitalist philosophy is based on domination. The goal is to control the market and society in order to create conditions for continuing power and profit. All capitalist actors must pursue domination; if they fail to do so, the system will ensure they will be replaced by competitors more intent on achieving such domination.[41]

Climate change is the extension of the philosophy of domination, since it reflects a belief in the unfettered human control of nature itself. Western capitalist philosophy is so structured around ideas of dominance that it is difficult to conceive of any relations—including our relations with the natural world—that are not hierarchical and based on power. (Nature itself generates its own power relations, but humans arguably change the scale and impact by virtue of the extraordinary power they have accumulated.) Some cultures, especially indigenous ones, have developed philosophies based on concepts of harmony with nature or seeing humans as part of an ecological balance of life on the planet composed of thousands of interdependent species, with no one species in control.[42] These cultures do not necessarily end all environmental bullying or bludgeoning; for example, Native American tribes that had philosophies less oriented toward domination still engaged in hunting animals such as buffaloes. (Some might consider that a bullying of animal species, but such hunting is typically done in restrained ways that maintain natural ecological balances.) Hunting in general by people who think of themselves as environmentalists and seek to live in harmony with the land leads to caution about how to characterize different philosophical or ecological orientations. Nonetheless, cultures that do not prioritize domination would be less likely to cause climate change, for such cultures would tend to question whether humans can and should dominate the natural world and whether they have the capacity and right to bludgeon it.[43]

Climate change reflects a mentality of power and control in which nothing is left to the control of others. All means, including violence, are used to get and keep control. We emphasize this aspect because it is at the core of all bullying, exemplified by the schoolyard bully and leading to the bully's small domain of control in the school, just as it leads to human control of all of nature. Domination is the end in itself, and the bully needs no argument to justify gaining and using power over rivals and weaker kids or weaker species; it is the "natural law" of the bully's world.

The broad philosophy of capitalist dominance—leading to the ideal of domination of the environment and the natural world—is embedded in several values that are at the center of the capitalist culture and legitimate both environmental bludgeoning and bullying. The most basic is human-centrism. Humans sit at the top of the hierarchy of species. This presupposes an ecology of power and a natural ordering of the universe in which humans control all other species. This conviction is at the heart of a philosophy of dominance, and it is central to bullying, for bullying is about power in-equality and the abuses of power that arise from hierarchy and dominance. Human-centrism is not exclusive to capitalism, but it is intimately tied to the capitalist system, perhaps more so than any other, because control over nature is so central to the ideas of profit and competitive dominance. Cap-italism has often been conceived as social Darwinism, according to which capitalist theorists argue that just as evolution leads to the survival of the fittest, so too do all social and natural relations reflect the survival and rule of the fittest—those most equipped by nature or God to rule, including ruling over the environment.[44]

This general philosophy of social Darwinism and rule by the fittest is rooted in at least three more specific but core capitalist values. One is the concept of private property, which roots all value in the market and private enterprise. Capitalism extends the idea of property into the environment and natural world, arguing that, in the pure form, nature is subject to private ownership and sale on the market. This would include land, air, and water, as well as all nonhuman species. If these elements can be privatized and subject to ownership, then the human proprietors have legal claims to power over nature, and they may subject it to their own ends, through both bludgeoning and bullying.[45]

This notion of the legitimacy—or necessity—of subjecting nature to ownership with rights to bludgeon and bully is at the foundation of climate change. Without this idea, nature would be conceived as part of a natural "commons," which would not be subject to the rules of human dominance, ownership, or profit. Because bullying and bludgeoning arise within capi-talism under the legal frame of private ownership or property, with own-ers having power over their property, owners can dominate animals and all of nature (consistent with societal norms) within the private property paradigm.[46]

According to the property concept that is central to capitalism, value and wealth are possible only within a privately owned system. In other economic models, private property is limited, and proposing an environmental com-mons that is not privately controlled becomes a way of thinking about creat-ing value and protecting nature. But in a private property system, where value can only arise from the market and private owners, the commons makes no sense: it is not privately owned and thus cannot have or create value. That is why "purist" capitalists have argued that all of nature can generate value only if the commons is destroyed and all of earth is privatized, that is, privately owned to create true wealth. The destruction of the commons is fundamental to climate change, and it is integral to the bullying of animals and the bludgeoning of all of nature.

The schoolyard bully, of course, does not necessarily own property in the school. But he creates a de facto school order in which he is the only central property owner—in other words, the bully has the rights to control and deference. He views himself as the "natural" ruler of the yard and uses his power to impose that view on all the "weaker" kids. This is a kind of de facto social Darwinism, mirroring the structure of the larger capitalist world but without its codified legal form.

The second specific value in capitalist systems is growth. This notion, too, is rooted in both the philosophical and the structural models of capitalist ideology. Capitalism cannot be a static or stationary, no-growth system, at least as currently understood. The competitive structure requires that capitalists dominate and destroy their rivals by expanding production more cheaply, rapidly, and efficiently. Growing production means growing market share, and that weakens the competition. As in Darwinist evolution, the competition leads toward the strong destroying the weak; in the environment, this means humans dominating and exploiting nonhuman animal species and all of nature.[47]

Unlimited growth will foster climate change, at least as growth is conceived today. More and more production means extracting and using more and more finite resources, leading toward more energy use and increased emission of greenhouse gases. Even in a perfectly renewable energy system, the pressures of commodity growth on our finite planet would lead to environmental degradation.[48]

It may be possible to reconceive growth in ways that do not imply environmental destruction, but this would require two forces that are not part of US capitalism. First, it would require the growth of public goods—education, conversation, community—while ending the growth, at least in rich nations, of private commodities.[49] This is extremely difficult to accomplish in the United States because wealth is conceived as created only through private markets—and it cannot be created by government or public entities. In fact, as the famed economist John Kenneth Galbraith argued, the United States lacks a robust concept of public goods, and it does not recognize the public goods deficit that is the true deficit in American society.[50]

Second, growth that is not environmentally destructive, involving neither bludgeoning nor bullying, would require regenerative rather than extractive production processes.[51] Consequently, any extraction of natural resources would have to be structured such that waste is recycled and natural resources are regenerated to ecological balance after production is completed. This would be extremely difficult to accomplish in US capitalism because it would limit many forms of production that are cheap and meet the needs of short-term investors. Regenerative growth requires a long-term economic framework that accepts the true costs of extractive production—with all its environmental externalities—and moves toward a more ecologically balanced and steady-state model. Such a scenario would be impossible within the current US economic framework.

Growth, as conceived in the US model, and bullying are closely connected. Growth is entirely intertwined with the assertion and expansion of power, the bully's core goal. In the schoolyard, the bully's appetite for growth is not easily sated. He seeks, with weaker rivals, to control as much of the school as possible, and that may extend to control over the streets and the neighborhood. The same attitude toward the extension of power and appetite is even more obvious in the corporate bully, with companies constantly seeking to expand their global market share and take over as many rivals as possible.

The third core value of the US capitalist system is consumerism.[52] The system's survival depends on it, since if private consumer demand weakens, the entire US economy will falter; furthermore, if the people's appetite for consumption were to drop dramatically, the US economy would collapse into crisis. Some 70 percent of that economy is fueled by domestic consumer demand. Ever-expanding consumerism not only drives the economy, it also is a key factor in climate change and environmental bludgeoning and bullying. The more people consume, the more the planet is in peril.

Consumerism is thus essential to US capitalism, and it supports the unprecedented environmental damage wrought by climate change.[53] There are no alternatives in the US model, because public investment and consumption, with the exception of military or war-based investments and consumption, are viewed as illegitimate and as portents of socialism.[54] Public demand—investment and consumption by the government to expand education, health, or an environmentally clean infrastructure—is seen as an unsustainable aberration if it rises to any significant scale because wealth can only be created by the market, not the state. Consequently, the engine of growth and prosperity must always be the US consumer, who thereby bears the burden of both propping up the economy and fueling climate change.

We have already seen in chapter 2 how capitalist consumerism involves bullying. The corporate culture of consumerism leads to conspicuous consumption, a potent way of distinguishing powerful in-groups and weak out-groups. This dynamic has been widely noted in schools, where the in-groups bully the out-groups. The same is true in the larger society, as discussed in the last chapter, where high-consuming groups—buying mansions and lavish jewelry or yachts—cluster together and bully down the standing of those who cannot spend extravagantly.

Unfettered consumerism fuels the expansion that drives capitalist environmental bludgeoning and bullying. It requires more extraction, more growth, more intensive energy use, and more waste. It makes corporate bullying profitable, and it displaces public goods with unsustainable consumption of private commodities.

No discussion of climate change as environmental bullying can end without consideration of the fact that humans—not just other animals, plants, or natural resources—are ultimately also seriously threatened and hurt by environmental damage and climate change. Today, the humans most impacted are the poor, especially in developing nations, who may be described as being politically bullied through environmental bludgeoning and climate change brought on by the richer nations. This climate change and the capitalist bludgeoning of the environment that causes it (and also gives rise to subsequent bullying by authorities of weaker and poor citizens after the environmental bludgeoning has destroyed land or created droughts or floods) clearly show that environmental bullying is also an economic justice issue, reflecting global power and wealth inequalities. Of course, the poor in the United States and other rich countries are also vulnerable to the same fate, reflecting the great wealth and power inequalities in American society.[55]

The most vulnerable humans today are the poor, both in the United States and in developing nations. Money allows people options to move out of endangered areas, go to high ground, buy food or water when it becomes scarce, and live well even when large numbers of other less-affluent people are imperiled. Moreover, the most powerful elites design the policies that help lead to climate change and bully the poor after the environmental damage caused by climate change occurs.

This scenario played out painfully in New Orleans during Hurricane Katrina, a storm that scientists believe was worsened by the warming waters and stronger winds caused by climate change. The surging floods did by far the most damage in the Lower Ninth Ward, where poor people of color lived. Their homes were destroyed, their pets drowned, and many old and sick individuals died. A large number of residents had to flee their homes and suffer for days in the New Orleans Coliseum where police sent them, only to contend with insufficient water, food, and medical care in unhealthy, hot, and crowded refugee surroundings. Many poor people had to leave New Orleans permanently because the city did not budget money to rebuild their neighborhoods and kept residents from reentering their homes for months. Meanwhile, whites living in affluent New Orleans suffered little damage to their property or health; they were never forced to leave the city, and if they did so voluntarily, they returned quickly to their homes and businesses. The storm turned the city far whiter than it had been previously, as at least 200,000 poor people of color could not return, painfully symbolizing climate change as a form of environmental injustice.[56]

Nobody who saw televised images of New Orleans during the storm is likely to doubt that the poor were bullied by the authorities. Prior to the disaster, the Bush administration had repeatedly cut funding for the levees that could have prevented the flooding, denying urgent requests from the Army Corps of Engineers and thereby making clear that environmental and political bullying are interconnected. Elites created the conditions that condemned the city and its poorest residents. People without food or water standing on their rooftops waving flags for help in their flooded neighborhoods—often to little avail—vividly reflected the bullying elements among the police, local politicians, and national leaders as well as the indifference of agencies such as the Federal Emergency Management Agency (FEMA). Evangelist leaders claimed that the city's poor deserved the bullying, and then they piled on, arguing that God was punishing them for turning New Orleans into "Sin City."[57]

Internationally, the millions of people impacted today by climate change are mostly located in poor nations, such as low-lying Bangladesh, or very hot regions, such as Africa and the Middle East. Populations in these areas are suffering from drought, a lack of drinking water, crop failures, and the need to move to other areas, causing horrific new conflicts over land and water. Pentagon officials and other observers have argued that the mayhem in Syria, Iraq, and other nations has been exacerbated by climate change in that part of the world, and the same argument has been made regarding the genocides in Darfur and Rwanda.[58]

Rich nations are now bullying poor nations to restrain the growth that creates climate change, hinting at withholding development aid, foreign investment, and other funding as threats. But though we do need all nations to cut carbon emissions immediately and drastically, it is overtly unjust to put the burden on already poor people who did not cause climate change. The rich nations that created the crisis through fossil fuel–based industrialization must now pay to prevent looming catastrophe for all by establishing a massive global fund, supplied by taxation on the wealthy and on international financial transactions and carbon taxes, that can subsidize green development in poor countries. The biggest energy corporations and other carbon polluters in rich nations need to come up with a green fund along the lines of the Marshall Plan for massive public investment in a new clean-energy infrastructure in the richer and high per capita carbon-polluting nations, especially the United States.

As with all bullying, reducing environmental bullying is ultimately a question of justice. And our new bullying paradigm based on the sociological imagination recognizes that the problem is rooted in unjust societies organized around militarized capitalism. Reducing environmental and other bullying requires transforming economic and political systems that profit from injustice.

This is no academic matter, as some poorer and richer nations are beginning to assign constitutional rights to nature. In 2008, Ecuador created a new constitution specifying the rights of animals, as well as of plants, soil, air, and water. The constitution gives animals, plants, and even rivers and forests rights that must be enforced in the courts. The constitution states, "Nature or Pachamama . . . has a right that its existence is integrally respected as well as the right of the maintenance and regeneration of its vital cycles, structures, functions and evolutionary processes. Every person, community, people or nationality can demand from the public authority that these rights of nature are fulfilled."[59] The same principles were embraced by 30,000 representatives of civil society from many countries in a "people's agreement" crafted in 2010 in Bolivia at the World People's Conference on Climate Change and the Rights of Mother Earth.[60]

The concept of the rights of nature is also attracting attention in Europe and the United States. European organizations are working to define ecocide as a crime violating international law. In the United States, cities are taking the lead. In 2010, the Pittsburgh City Council passed an ordinance banning the extraction of natural gas and proclaiming that nature has "inalienable and fundamental rights to exist and flourish" in the municipality.[61]

Since 2000, Thomas Linzey, a US attorney, has specialized in helping American communities—many in rural Pennsylvania—develop local ordinances that ban corporate factory farms, fracking firms, and other polluting companies from operating in their cities. Although the corporations successfully got the state legislature to pass a law declaring such local actions illegal, more than 100 communities have banded together in a network to move forward anyway in order to defend community rights to ban corporations and protect the rights of nature in their locales.[62]

This, of course, sets up a potentially epochal debate about constitutional rights and who is entitled to them, while challenging the private property rights that have traditionally been viewed as central to the US Constitution. As climate change accelerates, survival will pit increasingly empowered environmentalists and ordinary citizens and communities against corporations that claim corporate personhood and the supremacy of their property rights over all other rights. These battles may determine the future of not only capitalism but also humanity and the survival of thousands of other species.

CHAPTER FOUR

Militarism as Bullying

The Superpower and the Schoolyard Bully

Today, in a world full of nations bristling with weapons that are far more potent than ever, we see rampant bullying by all the most powerful nations on earth: Russia in its threats to Baltic nations and incursions in Ukraine; Israel in its occupations of Gaza and the West Bank; Arab Shia and Sunni nations in their threats and vicious wars with each other; Pakistan and India in their mutual nuclear threats over Kashmir; and China in its intimidating military moves against Vietnam, the Philippines, and Japan. And the United States—today's overwhelming superpower—uses the Bush and Obama "doctrines" to explicitly defend America's right to threaten, strike from the air, invade, or occupy not just Middle Eastern countries but also any other nation on the planet it sees as dangerous or terroristic.[1]

A militarized society is a requisite element for a bully nation. If a country is highly armed and is a superpower wielding great military strength, it assuredly will bully weaker countries. After all, one prime motive for building up a powerful military is to threaten, intimidate, and attack other countries. The aim is to demonstrate national power, grab goods or territory, saber rattle to coerce weaker nations to obey, and satisfy feelings of superiority, including the satisfaction of simply being on top and scaring others into submission.

The grand game of nation-states in a militarized world (including terrorist self-styled states such as ISIS) is not so different from the games in the schoolyard. In this chapter, we show how the most powerful militarized nations—concentrating especially on the United States, the greatest superpower—bully in much the same way as the toughest schoolyard bullies, albeit on a grander scale.

Militarized bullying goes beyond foreign policy. In the United States, militarily equipped police forces and a huge prison system combine to perpetrate vast and violent militarized bullying against Americans at home. In this chapter, we look closely at the militarized bullying built into US foreign policy. In the next chapter, we will examine the epidemic of militarized bullying carried out by the "repressive apparatus" of the police, prisons, and other coercive arms of the state, directed especially against poor Americans and people of color.

As noted in the opening chapter, militarism in capitalist societies creates a double whammy, integrating two prime structural causes of institutionalized bullying. In chapter 2, we discussed the core ways in which capitalism causes bullying. In this chapter, we will look at how militarism contributes to the bullying forces within capitalism, intensifying the institutionalized bullying that arises in America's militarized capitalism.

THE SUPERPOWER AND THE SCHOOLYARD BULLY, PART 1

Bullying, we have shown, arises out of power inequality. When a nation (or a self-styled nation such as ISIS) uses superior military power to threaten, intimidate, or attack other countries in order to force them to do its bidding, it is engaging in "structural" or institutional bullying. The bully is not an individual person but the nation and its armed forces; the personality of the leaders do not have to be psychopathic or of "the bullying type," but the institutions require that they act in this manner.[2] President Obama was elected as a peace candidate and was seen as a rational, calm, and compassionate man even as he acted like his predecessors, including George W. Bush. Militaristic bullying is structural, and though the personality of the leaders may play a role, in the end they are subordinated to institutional imperatives, highlighting the weakness of the psychological bullying paradigm.

These observations apply in spades to an imperial superpower—a hegemonic nation with the most dominant military force in the world, where structural forces overwhelm the psychological predispositions of leaders. Bully nations may tend to produce macho leaders such as Andrew Jackson or Teddy Roosevelt, who glorify in aggression and war, but presidents with far milder personalities, whether Woodrow Wilson or Barack Obama, follow the same bullying script. This reflects the vital institutional interests of the military and other elites, whose power and profits cannot be left to hinge on personality.[3]

The United States has by far the most military power in the world, spending about $500 billion on the Pentagon in 2015 alone,[4] which is many times as much as all its potential adversaries put together (and this doesn't count much of the trillion dollar–plus cost of the wars in Iraq and Syria or other special appropriations for the CIA and nuclear power). Whenever such a huge inequality in military power exists, it creates the position of a structural bully. Even if the United States does not overtly threaten another country, its immense military superiority intimidates and constrains all other nations. Put another way, even if the state did not intend to do so, the inequality would have a bullying effect.

Neoconservatives since the turn of the twenty-first century, such as President George W. Bush and Vice President Dick Cheney, have ceaselessly advocated for the development of nearly unlimited US power in order to guarantee that other nations will never challenge America's dominance and threats. Their thinking has been codified in classic manifestos such as *Rebuilding American Defenses*, published in 2000 by the Project for the New American Century (PNAC), a leading neoconservative establishment organization founded by William Kristol and Robert Kagan.[5] This work proclaims that "at present the United States faces no global rival. America's grand strategy should aim to preserve and extend this advantageous position as far into the future as possible."[6] It calls for the United States to build the capacity "to fight and decisively win in multiple, simultaneous major theater wars."[7] This would necessitate a massive military buildup, including an increase in US "nuclear strategic superiority,"[8] and an overall military plan to "preserve and extend . . . the preeminence of US military forces" and "perform the 'constabulary' duties associated with shaping the security environment in critical regions."[9]

The argument for developing a surefire bullying power that no nation could even imagine challenging became an obsession of the US military and political establishment. Just nine days after 9/11, PNAC sent a letter to President Bush urging that " even if evidence does not link Iraq directly to the attack, any strategy aiming at the eradication of terrorism and its sponsors must include a determined effort to remove Saddam Hussein from power in Iraq. Failure to undertake such an effort will constitute an early and perhaps decisive surrender in the war on international terrorism."[10]

In other words, the United States had to invade and overthrow opposing regimes that had nothing to do with 9/11, including especially Saddam Hussein's government in Iraq because he had defiantly opposed US power moves for over a decade since the Gulf War. PNAC was not subtle about its view of the international arena as something similar to the schoolyard, where the bully must assert his own dominance over and secure the obedience of any challenger, no matter how weak: "The true cost of not meeting our defense requirements will be a lessened capacity for American global leadership and, ultimately, the loss of a global security order that is uniquely friendly to American principles and prosperity."[11]

President Bush followed through, vastly boosting military spending and invading Afghanistan and Iraq while beefing up US military power everywhere, showing his and Vice President Cheney's conviction that the international schoolyard was the property of the superpower.

The connection between superior military power and bullying is obvious, and the word *bullying* pops up spontaneously in the mass media and in our everyday conversation about military and world affairs, especially about adversaries such as Russia, China, Syria, Iran, and "terrorist" groups such as Al Qaeda or ISIS in any nation. Remarkably, though, the academic scholarship on bullying never analyzes the bullying carried out by militarily powerful nations against other countries. This reflects the dominance of the psychological microparadigm and spotlights its inadequacy. Great military powers bully other nations and transfer bullying values to their citizens through their violent cultures and through their warriors. Militarism creates long-standing bullying problems among both adults and children on the home front. This is true in all militarized societies, but it is especially severe in militarized capitalist societies.

Defenders of America's foreign policy will view the nation's military interventions as the opposite of bullying, since they see US forces as stabilizing the world order, fighting terrorism, extending civilized values, and defending the weak.[12] Or they will claim, as both Bush and Obama have, that the United States has the right—and the responsibility—to use its power unilaterally against others, in the name of self-defense or as its moral duty to police or protect the world and spread liberty.[13]

By contrast, many countries around the world view the United States as the planet's greatest bully, using its power simply to threaten and intimidate or attack other countries in order to get its way and establish its dominance. Polls show the people in the Middle East, Latin America, Africa, and much of Asia fear the United States as the biggest threat to their homelands and to peace. When Henry Kissinger said that "power is the great aphrodisiac,"[14] he was, in the mind of much of the world's population, reflecting their view of US leaders and the United States itself as the greatest bullies of all.

We argue that most powerful and militarized nations, especially superpowers and hegemons, typically accumulate and use military power to consolidate their own dominance. This is consistent with our definition of bullying as the use of superior power to establish control and domination. However, powerful, militarized nations almost always justify their own behavior, as noted earlier, in moral or religious terms, arguing that their use of military power is designed to protect, stabilize, or civilize rather than to dominate.[15] This may, in some instances, be part of the picture, as in the case of internationally coordinated attacks on ISIS, but as we view it, the norm is that powerful countries seek to defend, secure, and expand their power and dominance. Of course, such judgments will always involve subjective assessments of the motivations driving militaristic behavior.

The picture is complicated because so often hegemonic bullying nations such as the United States attack other nations or groups—for example, Iraq, Iran, ISIS, and Al Qaeda—that are also horrific bullies. Attacking less powerful nations, which often do their own forms of bullying, tends to create a cycle of vicious bullying, as was particularly vivid in the case of President Bush's 2003 invasion of Saddam Hussein's Iraq. The United States toppled the dictator allegedly to stop his bullying (and his alleged potential nuclear bullying), though it was also acting to secure oil and US power in a crucial region. But by overthrowing Saddam and dismantling his Sunni military and the long Sunni role in running Iraq, Washington created the conditions for the rise of groups such as ISIS and Al Qaeda in the Arabian Peninsula that did not exist in Iraq or Syria during the Saddam era. Some of the displaced and humiliated Sunnis became the nucleus of the new terrorist forces leading to ISIS, which by 2015, after its horrific terrorist attack on Paris, became defined in the West as the principal new global threat and enemy bully.

This is instructive because the US militarism that led to a war defended as an attack on a dictatorial bully, Saddam Hussein, in fact helped give rise to a more monstrous bully in the form of ISIS. Such is the cost of hegemonic bullying. Even when it is used to overthrow a bully, it promotes hegemonic power in regions that inevitably give rise to new occupations, wars, and terrorism. In the appendix, we look in more detail at ISIS and other terrorist and nonterrorist states, making clear that even though America has no monopoly on international bullying, it helps create or catalyze some of the states or terrorist groups that pose serious threats to itself as well as bullying threats to people and nations in their own regions.

These contrasting subjective beliefs about who is actually the bully help show the similarity between militarized bully nations and schoolyard bullies. As noted in chapter 1, there is always subjectivity about who bullies and what bullying is. Kids at school who are called bullies often say they acted justifiably because they were threatened or attacked. They may claim that they are more powerful and that the weaker kids are jealous. Or they may say that they are just keeping order and settling conflicts that get messy. Some bully kids (and their parents) say they are protecting themselves or the values of the school, punishing kids who don't live up to the right codes of behavior or who violate the school's values. Schools are inundated with arguments about who is the bully, whether the bullying was provoked or justified, and even what actually took place in a bullying incident. Ultimately, bullying is always partly in the eye of the beholder, whether in the schoolyard or on national battlefields.

Bullying or bullied nations make the same charges and countercharges as those lobbed by parents and kids in the school setting. Bully nations say they are using their military power properly, legally, and honorably, as noted, to defend themselves, keep order, protect values, and preserve a necessary hierarchy. The British invoked "the white man's burden." The Soviets invoked the ideals of communism. The United States invokes manifest destiny. Hegemonic nations claim to be punishing other nations that are not living up to civilized codes of behavior and that are savage and immoral. Comparing military bullies and schoolyard bullies, one is struck, as highlighted in this chapter, by the similarities rather than the differences between them.

THE SUPERPOWER AND THE SCHOOLYARD BULLY, PART 2

To understand military bullying, we need to move from the psychological paradigm to the paradigm of the sociological imagination. The latter highlights institutional bullying and the way in which it helps shape personal bullying. Since the United States is the world's military superpower, we will continue to concentrate especially on our own country, with the recognition that many other weaker nations—and some of the targets of US attacks such as Saddam Hussein or ISIS—are also horrific bullies.

But before turning again to the United States, let us look a bit more closely at the behavior and language of militaristic nations generally. Hegemonic or imperial ideology is a grander version of the code of the schoolyard bully. It arrogates to the bully—that is, the superpower nation—the right to control and to decide whom to attack and when. As in the schoolyard, this dynamic is based on the superior power of the bully or the right of the bully to make his own decisions, with the implicit view that the bully knows best. Nobody is in a position to contest him or disobey his orders. No permission slip is needed.

Bully nations model and exemplify on a planetary level the schoolyard bully formula. There are repeated threats, intimidation, and violence by the superpower nation against weaker target nations. The bully nation may offer all kinds of moral or strategic justifications for its behavior, but ultimately, it acts as it wishes because it has the power to do so, exactly as in the case of the schoolyard bully. The bullied nation, like the bullied kid, has one of two choices: to do what the bully wants or to suffer repeated threats and eventual attack.

The United States has been the dominant military power in the world since the collapse of the British and other European empires after World War II. American hegemony is widely discussed and debated, but nobody disputes the overwhelming superiority of US military power, sustained after the collapse of Germany and Japan and later the Soviet Union. Since the end of World War II, the United States has routinely used that power to bully on every continent, an argument documented most powerfully and meticulously in numerous books by Noam Chomsky.

Right after 9/11, Chomsky presented a talk entitled "United States, Global Bully," in which he said:

> For nearly 200 years the US expelled or mostly exterminated indigenous populations, many millions of people, conquered half of Mexico, depredated the Caribbean and Central America, conquered Hawaii and the Philippines (killing 100,000 Filipinos in the process). Since the second world war, the US has extended its reach around the world. But the fighting was always somewhere else and it was always others who were being slaughtered. . . .
>
> The world looks very different, depending on whether you are holding the lash or whether you have been whipped for centuries. Perhaps that is why the rest of the world, although horrified by the September attacks, nevertheless sees them from a different perspective.[16]

The post–World War II bullying Chomsky describes consists of interventions in large and small countries to secure US hegemony. These incursions include interventions in Nicaragua, El Salvador, Honduras, Cuba, and almost every other Central American nation, with the aim of installing or propping up dictators—themselves bullies using death squads and other forms of state terrorism—who were dependent on US backing to stay in power and in turn made their nations wards of the US state. This established friendly conditions for US corporate operations.[17] Conducted under the umbrella of the Monroe Doctrine, these interventions involved issuing bullying threats to any nation or insurgency in Central and Latin America that sought more independence from the United States. Such nationalism posed the greatest danger to the US bully because it raised the specter of democracy or popular control by mainly poor people all over the continent—an assault on the supposed right of American companies to create sweatshop conditions and appropriate resources and profits to send back to the United States. Nationalist resistance, whether by rebel groups such as the Nicaraguan Sandinistas or the Salvadoran Farabundo Marti National Liberation Front (FMLN) guerrillas, can be seen as a kind of assertion of rights that schoolyard bullies themselves never tolerate; they threaten and beat up kids who challenge their rights much as the United States beats up any nation or the democratic revolts staged by Nicaraguans, Salvadorans, Guatemalans, or Hondurans.[18]

Chomsky shows that the United States uses the same bullying dynamics on every continent to hold on to its global hegemony. But Chomsky, though he is the most cogent and comprehensive in his magisterial critique, is hardly the only one to document US bullying. One need only think of writers on America's militarism and empire such as Chalmers Johnson, Daniel Ellsberg, Steven Kinzer, and Andrew Bacevich, to name only a few. In his book *Overthrow: America's Century of Regime Change from Hawaii to Iraq,* former longtime *New York Times* bureau chief and international correspondent Steven Kinzer has documented fourteen military interventions and regime changes carried out by the United States in the twentieth century that fit the bully model.[19] These include the 1953 CIA overthrow of democratically elected Iranian president Muhammed Mossadegh, when he refused to submit to bullying over control of Iranian oilfields. They also include numerous US interventions in Central America as described by Chomsky—not only in Nicaragua, El Salvador, and Honduras but also in tiny Grenada and Panama, where these very small nations were forced to submit to US economic and political dominance in "our region." Another example is the 1973 overthrow of Chile's democratically elected president, Salvador Allende, who was killed after he refused to submit to American threats about ownership of mining companies and the design of the Chilean economy. In 1954, the United States ousted democratically elected Guatemalan president Jacobo Arbenz, who refused to back down from his plans to nationalize United Fruit's banana plantations. Arbenz's sin was that he refused to be bullied into acquiescing to

Guatemala's status as a "banana republic," a crime that spelled certain death for him.[20] After reading Kinzer's work, one Amazon reviewer wrote, "The United States may currently be the 'big man' on the international campus, but it ought not be the 'big bully' in the international school yard."[21] Kinzer's assessment of US foreign policy can be summarized as follows: power used and abused for selfish gain and corporate profit; the superpower threatening and invading nations on every continent; regime changes achieved; mission accomplished; no apologies and no permission slips needed.

Both President Bush and President Obama have claimed presidential authority to strike preemptively or preventively against any country in the world they deem a threat—with Islamic terrorism now defined as the central threat. Although Obama often uses the rhetoric of multilateralism, he, like Bush, has often acted without the permission of other nations or of the US Congress. Leading constitutional scholars, such as Yale Law professor Bruce Ackerman, have argued that Obama has exceeded Bush's executive power doctrine, claiming he has the constitutional authority to act entirely on his own to attack and wage wars solely on his own judgment. As Ackerman writes: "Mr. Obama is now taking the lead in an open-ended campaign, extending from Iraq into Syria, that could last years. If this isn't commencing 'hostilities,' what is?" Ackerman continues by noting that Obama "is acting on the proposition that the president, in his capacity as commander in chief, has unilateral authority to declare war. . . . In taking this step, Mr. Obama is not only betraying the electoral majorities who twice voted him into office on his promise to end Bush-era abuses of executive authority. He is also betraying the Constitution he swore to uphold."[22]

A schoolyard bully could only look on in envy as US military leaders are heralded as heroes by many of the same Americans who would harshly condemn the bully in the school. But in reality, both the school bully and the military leader bully at will, one on the microlevel and the other on the macrolevel.

NUCLEAR BULLYING

As the United States evolved into the most powerful militaristic empire in the world, it imposed ever-more perilous forms of bullying upon the rest of the world. A particularly dangerous form of militaristic bullying emerged at the end of World War II, as the world entered the nuclear age. In 1945, the United States used the first nuclear bomb to attack another nation, decimating Hiroshima to force Japan to surrender. Shortly thereafter, the United States exploded a second nuclear bomb over Nagasaki, killing and radiating thousands of civilians as a means to end the war rapidly. Many historians argue the bombing was done to prevent the Russians from reaching Japan before surrender, bullying Japan for immediate capitulation. Gar Alperovitz has found evidence that Japan was in the process of trying to negotiate a surrender when the bomb was dropped on Hiroshima.[23] But President Harry Truman proclaimed, "God told me to do it." In an interview on file footage, he defended his decision to the grave; he said, "That bomb caused the Japanese to surrender, and it stopped the war. I don't care what the crybabies say now, because they didn't have to make the decision."[24]

That was the only time in history when a nation bullied another nation by threatening to use nuclear weapons in war and then actually doing so. As a military bullying strategy, it is hard to think of a more brutal approach. It now survives as testimony to the horrific dangers of militaristic bullying in the era of weapons of mass destruction.

No other nation has carried out a nuclear attack on another country, but the United States has continued to play a unique role in nuclear bullying. The little-known but inconvenient truth is that since Hiroshima and Nagasaki, nearly every US president has threatened other nations with nuclear attack, justified under the banner of broad and evolving doctrines legitimating the use of nuclear weapons as a crucial dimension of US foreign policy.

The schoolyard bully can claim a right to monopolize turf, friends, or resources that will allow him to bully all the more. Others are not entitled to anything that might help them resist the bullying. A truly effective bully even controls the ideas that others are allowed to think; he certainly will not let anyone else question his right to bully. In 2015, the Obama administration "negotiated" an agreement to prevent Iran from developing nuclear weapons. Like many bullies, the United States gave Iran an "offer it couldn't refuse," supported by an implicit threat of invasion. Republicans and other opponents attacked Obama and his secretary of state, John Kerry, for conceding too much. However, there was hardly a hint of a debate within the mass media over whether the only nation to have used nuclear weapons—the nation that possesses more of these weapons than the rest of the world combined—has a right to dictate that another country cannot have access to them.[25]

As the military analysts Joseph Gerson and John Feffer have shown, nuclear bullying has been a key part of overall US military strategy since World War II. They observe that:

over the past six decades, the United States has used its nuclear arsenal in five often inter-related ways. The first was, obviously, battlefield use, with the "battlefield" writ large to include the people of Hiroshima and Nagasaki. The long-held consensus among scholars has been that these first atomic bombings were not necessary to end the war against Japan, and that they were designed to serve a second function of the U.S. nuclear arsenal: dictating the parameters of the global (dis)order by implicitly terrorizing U.S. enemies and allies ("vassal states" in the words of former national security adviser Zbigniew Brzezinski). The third function, first practiced by Harry Truman during the 1946 crisis over Azerbaijan in northern Iran and relied on repeatedly in U.S. wars in Asia and the Middle East, as well as during crises over Berlin and the Cuban Missile Crisis, has been to threaten opponents with first strike nuclear attacks in order to terrorize them into negotiating on terms acceptable to the United States or, as in the Bush wars against Iraq, to ensure that desperate governments do not defend themselves with chemical or biological weapons. Once the Soviet Union joined the nuclear club, the U.S. arsenal began to play a fourth role, making U.S. nuclear forces, in the words of former Secretary of Defense Harold Brown, "meaningful instruments of military and political power." As Noam Chomsky explains, Brown was saying that implicit and explicit U.S. nuclear threats were repeatedly used to intimidate those who might consider intervening militarily to assist those we are determined to attack.[26]

After Truman, the next president to employ nuclear threats was Dwight "Ike" Eisenhower. In 1954, just before the decisive battle of Dien Bien Phu in Vietnam between the colonial French forces and Ho Chi Minh's nationalists, it became clear that Ho's forces would win. To save the prospects for French control of Vietnam, Ike offered Paris two nuclear bombs. Fortunately, the French were wise enough to realize that nuclear bullying was unacceptable. They refused Eisenhower's bombs and subsequently lost the war, but they saved the world from another nuclear disaster.

Eisenhower made other nuclear threats. During the conflicts over the future of the small islands of Quemoy and Matsu off China, his administration let it be known that it was prepared to use nuclear weapons to preserve Taiwanese control of the islands and Taiwan's sovereignty. On February 20, 1955, Secretary of State John Foster Dulles announced the United States was seriously considering the use of nuclear weapons in the Quemoy-Matsu area.

The next day, President Eisenhower himself said that "A-bombs can be used . . . as you would use a bullet."[27]

This was all part of Eisenhower's New Look strategy, which emphasized the use of nuclear weapons to maintain Cold War superiority. The New Look doctrine stressed the fact that nuclear weapons were cheaper than conventional warfare. The Eisenhower doctrine incorporated a generic use of nuclear threats to pursue American power—a doctrinal approach to securing US hegemony through nuclear bullying.[28]

Successive presidents following Ike during the Vietnam era—including John F. Kennedy (JFK) and Richard Nixon—also issued threats of nuclear attack. The most famous nuclear bullying incident was the 1963 Cuban missile crisis, in which President Kennedy threatened the Soviet Union with a nuclear attack if it didn't withdraw the missiles it had secretly placed in Cuba. Kennedy's most hawkish advisers advocated an immediate nuclear first strike on the Soviets, and others advocated the view that if Nikita Khrushchev didn't withdraw his missiles, Kennedy should launch a nuclear attack on the Soviets. Kennedy himself made it clear that if the Soviets tried to break through the US naval blockade of its Cuba-bound ships, he would move toward war and the possible use of nuclear weapons. After an American spy plane was shot down over Cuba, a nuclear attack on the Soviets seemed almost inevitable; it was forestalled only by Khrushchev's agreement to remove the missiles. Many view this as a successful form of nuclear bullying by Kennedy. But in combination with the Soviets' own bullying move (putting missiles covertly in Cuba in violation of existing agreements), it created the greatest threat ever of global annihilation, with many analysts putting the odds of a nuclear war at that moment at one in three.[29]

After the missile crisis, the most dramatic nuclear bullying by the United States in this era was President Nixon's repeated threats to attack North Vietnam with nuclear weapons. Nixon concocted the "madman theory." He believed he could persuade Ho that he would actually use nuclear weapons against the North because he was losing control of himself and was increasingly possessed by the impulse to use nukes. Nixon threatened that he would bomb Haiphong harbor with nuclear weapons and flood much of the country.

During a 1972 spring offensive by the North Vietnamese, Nixon told Kissinger:

We're going to do it. I'm going to destroy the goddamn country, believe me, I mean destroy it if necessary. And let me say, even the nuclear weapons if necessary. It isn't necessary. But, you know, what I mean is, that shows you the extent to which I'm willing to go. By a nuclear weapon, I mean that we will bomb the living bejeezus out of North Vietnam and then if anybody interferes we will threaten the nuclear weapons.[30]

He continued on this theme when speaking with Kissinger a week later:

NIXON: I'd rather use the nuclear bomb. Have you got that ready?

KISSINGER: That, I think, would just be too much.

NIXON: A nuclear bomb, does that bother you? . . . I just want you to think big, Henry, for Christ's sake! The only place where you and I disagree is with regard to the bombing. You're so goddamned concerned about civilians, and I don't give a damn. I don't care.

KISSINGER: I'm concerned about the civilians because I don't want the world to be mobilized against you as a butcher.[31]

The nuclear doctrine became aggressive under President Ronald Reagan, as he greatly expanded military spending and argued for a defense shield that might make it more plausible that the United States could use nuclear weapons without fear of commensurate retaliation. Reagan believed that he could bully the Soviets into a full global retreat and then bankrupt them by forcing them to spend huge amounts on all types of weapons to keep up with his own madcap military escalation. Nuclear weapons also played a major role in Reagan's military strategy, including his embrace of a nuclear first-strike policy that Truman and Eisenhower had endorsed initially—and that was later embraced by President George W. Bush.

The *Bulletin of the Atomic Scientists* editorialized, "Not since the resurgence of the Cold War in Ronald Reagan's first term has US defense strategy placed such an emphasis on nuclear weapons."[32] Shortly after 9/11, Bush's nuclear bullying policy was laid out in his Nuclear Posture Review (NPR). As Joseph Gerson and John Feffer observe: "The NPR reiterated the US commitment to first strike nuclear war fighting. For the first time, seven nations were specifically named as primary nuclear targets: Russia, China, Iraq, Iran, Syria, Libya and North Korea."[33]

THE OBAMA DOCTRINE AND THE BULLY NATION

On September 23, 2014, President Obama made a speech at the United Nations in which he laid out more clearly than before the "Obama doctrine."

Not surprisingly, it had to do with his starting of a new war in Syria and Iraq, the latter having been subject to constant US military bullying over the previous twenty-five years. Referring especially to threats from ISIS, the extremist Islamic group taking over northern and western parts of Iraq and Syria, the president said:

> I know many Americans are concerned about these threats. Tonight, I want you to know that the United States of America is meeting them with strength and resolve. Last month, I ordered our military to take targeted action against ISIL [ISIS] to stop its advances. Since then, we have conducted more than 150 successful airstrikes in Iraq.
>
> First, we will conduct a systematic campaign of airstrikes against these terrorists. Working with the Iraqi government, we will expand our efforts beyond protecting our own people and humanitarian missions, so that we're hitting ISIL targets as Iraqi forces go on offense. Moreover, I have made it clear that we will hunt down terrorists who threaten our country, wherever they are. That means I will not hesitate to take action against ISIL in Syria, as well as Iraq. This is a core principle of my presidency: if you threaten America, you will find no safe haven.[34]

The last sentence is key and might be paraphrased as: "My most important belief as president is in the American right to militarily strike any nation in the world I choose, if I see it as a threat."

This is hardly a new idea; American presidents have been acting on it since the beginning of the nation. But it is illuminating in its framing. First, it screams out in the language of the bully: "I'm in control and can threaten any country anywhere. And I can do it without getting anyone's permission." The president's statement carries weight because, like the schoolyard bully, he has the power to carry through on his threats.

Second, the president makes clear that the United States views the entire earth as subject to its power. Any nation is a legitimate military target, based solely on judgments made by the president about threats it poses. This effectively makes the planet one big American schoolyard, with the United States its bully in chief.

Third, Obama's speech justifies US bullying based on the language of threats, in this case terrorist threats. Threats are the currency of the realm of bullies themselves, whose modus operandi (MO) is to threaten repeatedly and ruthlessly. Obama is essentially arguing that the world is full of bullies and wanna-be bullies, both nations and nonstate actors such as ISIS. It is the existence of other bully nations and organizations that justifies the US right to threaten and use military force.

Fundamentally, the president is arguing—and he is not entirely wrong—that the international system is a Hobbesian jungle. States and many nonstate groups are bullies who listen only to more powerful bullies. The only way to survive and prosper is to be tougher than anyone else and bully the others into submission. This is more or less the way schoolyard bullies see their world: to survive and prosper, you have to be the toughest dude on the block.

Elsewhere, the president also claimed authority to act without congressional authorization for the new long war that he foresaw. He declared that the 2001 and 2002 Authorization of Force agreements empowering George W. Bush to wage war after 9/11 gave him (Obama) the power to act. But he had earlier argued that these agreements no longer had legal validity for new wars. He thus essentially made the case that he could go to war without permission from the United Nations, America's allies, the US Congress, or the American people.[35] This is precisely the schoolyard bully's logic: I can act freely without authorization from anyone because I have the power to do so.

The development of drones offered a new technological means for Obama to carry out his threat globally, posing little risk to US lives but putting civilians around the world at great risk of being killed as "collateral damage." Drones give the United States the capacity to bomb any country in the world without declaring war. The rationale for using drones is typically to strike at terrorist groups, but in practice, drone strikes can be a means of bullying any nation to submit to US demands. First employed after 9/11 in Afghanistan, drones have been used extensively in Iraq, Syria, Yemen, and other Middle Eastern nations, as well as in Libya, Somalia, and other African states. The civilian casualties have been particularly significant in Yemen, where one strike in September 2012 killed twelve civilians in a town market, including a pregnant woman and a twelve-year-old child. After the attack, Yemeni civilians said, "We live in constant fear. . . . There is no assurance that we would not be the next target. . . . The US government should come to the region to see what targets it has hit."[36] Drones are proving to be a consummate weapon of a hegemonic bully nation such as the United States: in the US case, they are cheap; they save American soldiers' lives; they put civilians at risk; and they create fear around the world, exerting enormous pressure on national leaders globally to defer to US demands.

President Obama adds a strong moral discourse. Highlighting ISIS, the extreme terrorist group that beheaded Western journalists, he argues that the other bullies are often savage terrorists whereas the United States-as-bully is good because it is saving the world from their evil.[37] He is certainly correct that the nation-state system is full of bully nations and organizations, but his notion that the United States can be viewed as morally elevated while using the most powerful and lethal bullying as its "core principle" is hardly rational. One need only read the comprehensive report on CIA torture released by the Senate on December 9, 2014. The report, thousands of pages long, catalogs instances of chronic waterboarding, "rectal feeding," sleep deprivation, forcing detainees to sit and sleep naked on the floor in their own feces, slamming prisoners against the wall hard enough to break bones and sometimes kill, locking naked prisoners in freezing cells (some of whom froze to death)—making it clear that the United States was embracing the moral principles of its "savage" enemies.[38] The CIA's chief of interrogations said these techniques were all ways to wield "total control over the detainee,"[39] showing that torture is one of the most extreme forms of institutional bullying imaginable. The overall US imperial foreign policy mimics the implicit morality of the schoolyard bully, who essentially equates power with righteousness.

VIETNAM, MILITARISM, AND THE CULTURE OF BULLYING: CREDIBILITY, NEVER BACK DOWN, AND NEVER SHOW WEAKNESS

The Vietnam War remains one of the great illustrations of militaristic bullying. It tells us a great deal about the culture of militarism and the coin of the realm in international relations. It shows how militarized nations bully in world affairs, acting with the same values and practice as bullies in school.

The United States supported the French during their century-long colonial occupation of Vietnam, and it funded most of the French war against the anticolonial forces led by Ho Chi Minh in Vietnam after World War II until 1954, when he defeated the French at the decisive battle of Dien Bien Phu.

The United States then bullied Ho Chi Minh to divide his nation into North Vietnam and South Vietnam, installing a military puppet dictator, Ngo Diem, to run the South as a friendly regional base for America. President Eisenhower admitted that if the United States had permitted an election when Diem came to power, "a possible 80 per cent of the population would have voted for the communist Ho Chi Minh as their leader."[40] Washington gave Diem hundreds of millions of dollars in arms to fight and terrorize his own people, who hated his dictatorship. This kind of support for ruthless military governments created and propped up by the United States was a bullying staple of US foreign policy throughout the Cold War.[41]

In the 1960s, after authorizing the assassination of Diem, JFK sent 15,000 advisers to South Vietnam to keep the military government in power; Diem's brutality had made him an embarrassment. Shortly thereafter, Kennedy himself was assassinated and was succeeded by Lyndon Baines Johnson (LBJ), who declared war on North Vietnam after provoking an incident in the Gulf of Tonkin. Johnson built US forces up to about 700,000 by 1967, backed by overwhelming sea power. When this force failed to achieve victory, Johnson resigned and Richard Nixon took office, threatening Ho Chi Minh with using nuclear weapons on Hanoi and raining more bomb tonnage on the small country of North Vietnam than all the bombs dropped in World War II. This rampage, though unsuccessful, was as merciless a form of bullying as has ever been seen in the history of modern warfare, largely destroying Vietnam itself; one American general famously said about Hue, a major city, "We had to destroy it in order to save it."

As with the schoolyard bully, the United States was prepared to resort to any level of violence to bully the local population. As Gen. Curtis E. LeMay, the US Air Force chief of staff, put it, "My solutions? Tell the Vietnamese they've got to draw in their horns or we're going to bomb them back to the Stone Age."[42] This attitude became, in fact, the mind-set of the US commanders and soldiers. With Vietnamese guerrilla fighters embedded in the rural villages, the people of Vietnam themselves became the enemy, and victory would require bullying them into submission with ferocious violence:

Villagers would supply the NLF [National Liberation Front] with soldiers, food and assistance in the planting of land mines. What many U.S. soldiers feared most were land mines and then ambushes. Soldiers would become demoralized by weeks of mundane patrolling and then they would be hit unexpectedly by the explosion of land mines or an ambush. Enraged soldiers would go back to the nearest area they had just been through and brutalize the villagers in a racist fury. The effect of fighting a total war on an entire population was to create a situation where all Vietnamese people were seen as fair game to kill. The most famous case of this (but by no means the only one) was the My Lai massacre in March 1968, where Charlie Company, led by Captain Ernest Medina and Lieutenant William Calley, murdered over 350 unarmed women and children.[43]

An army psychiatrist reported later, "Lt. Calley states that he did not feel as if he were killing human beings rather they were animals with whom one could not speak or reason."[44]

This attitude became common among the American soldiers in Vietnam. One machine gunner, James Duffy, described another My Lai–type incident:

> I swung my machine gun onto this group of peasants and opened fire. Fortunately, the gun jammed after one or two rounds, which was pretty lucky, because this group of peasants turned out to be a work party hired by the government to clear the area and there was GIs guarding them about fifty meters away. But my mind was so psyched out into killing gooks that I never even paid attention to look around and see where I was. I just saw gooks and I wanted to kill them. I was pretty scared after that happened because that sort of violated the unwritten code that you can do anything you want to as long as you don't get caught. That's, I guess that's what happened with the My Lai incident. Those guys just were following the same pattern that we've been doing there for ten years, but they had the misfortune of getting caught at it.[45]

When Johnson resigned in 1968, it was obvious the United States was losing the war. But Nixon simply ramped up the threats and violence, refusing to accept defeat. Even though it was clear he would not achieve victory, he never relented in his use of ever more brutal force, saying repeatedly that the United States never backs down because to do so would jeopardize the security of the nation and the world. As President Johnson said in 1964, "Surrender anywhere threatens defeat everywhere"—precisely the schoolyard bully's philosophy.[46]

Historian Gabriel Kolko has clarified what Johnson and Nixon really meant. Kolko observes that both presidents were dedicated to US global dominance. Such control could never be compromised by shows of weakness. To back down would reveal the United States as a "paper tiger," and to let it be defeated by a leader of a poor nation such as North Vietnam would be a crushing blow to US power and stature.[47] In the parlance of the time, it would unleash a "domino effect," leading all the US-controlled nations in the region to rise up and challenge the paper tiger.

Kolko argues that what was really at stake in Vietnam was credibility. A nation's credibility is measured by the fear and respect it inspires in adversaries and among all other nations. To remain a superpower, the United States could only maintain its credibility by using whatever force was necessary to subjugate Vietnam and other nations that might rise up against it. If it backed down, others would be encouraged to rebel in the nationalistic spirit of the Vietnamese. As President Kennedy said, "Now we have a problem in making our power credible, and Vietnam is the place."[48]

This notion of never backing down and using all possible force would be fully understood by the schoolyard bully because it is precisely his own formula for maintaining his personal control and power. These, too, depend on credibility.

Another way of putting this is to show that the game of international relations is played like a game of chicken. In this old high school game, two students go out to a country road and drive their cars directly at each other. The one who drives off the road first loses. The one who doesn't blink and risks a head-on crash is the winner.

In Vietnam, the United States was playing the game of chicken against Ho Chi Minh and the Soviet Union. The game was all about credibility. The nation that "blinked" or backed down would lose its credibility. If it sought to retain power, it had no choice but to bully its opponent using whatever means were necessary, to ensure that all adversaries would themselves back down and accept the superpower's dominance and credibility. John Kerry put it this way, "Someone has to die so that President Nixon won't be, and these are his words, 'the first President to lose a war.'"[49] Summarizing the aims of the United States in Vietnam, Assistant Secretary of State John Mc-Naughton said in 1965, "U.S. aims: 70 percent—To avoid a humiliating defeat to our reputation as a guarantor."[50] In other words, win at all costs to ensure that nobody messes with your power.

The schoolyard bully plays the same game, with the culture of chicken and the pursuit of credibility comprising the operative value structure. The school bully retains power only by never backing down from a fight and never showing weakness. Any such display could forever destroy his credibility. And that could create a domino effect, rippling down the school corridor and yards and encouraging others to challenge or taunt the bully. Because this situation would be intolerable, it guarantees that the schoolyard bully, like the superpower, will never blink and will use all power necessary to conquer and crush any challengers in the yard.

The concepts of the chicken game and credibility give us a way of thinking about both the structure of the military international system and the culture of militarism. The system operates as a contest of power in which credibility is the central tenet. The aim of the game is to preserve credibility and all the power that it brings. This creates the core culture of bullying, whether among nations or in the schoolyard. The central values are power and credibility, requiring the bully to never back down or show weakness. Toughness and fear are the coin of the realm. The bully is the toughest and most ready to risk anything to dominate and win.

The Land of the Slave and the Home of the Bully

Race and Militarized Bullying

US militarized capitalism combines racial and class bullying, and militarized domestic police bullying is a mirror image of America's militarized bullying over other nations. Both forms of bullying by US elites have the same aim: to maintain control of subordinate races and classes, at home and abroad. American global power depends on global systemic bullying of a world mostly populated by poor people of color, the same category of people subject to the most brutal militarized bullying at home. As in the schoolyard, the US state bully uses meritocratic ideals to justify the violence and underlying bigotry of the racial and class hierarchies. The schoolyard bully says, "I have the right to control you because I am stronger, smarter and cooler." The US authorities—exercising power through the police or the military—use the same legitimating argument toward poor people of color at home and abroad, "We have worked harder; we have proved our talent; God has blessed us with the rights to impose our civilized order and values on you."

In this chapter, we offer a historical perspective on racial militarized bullying. We show that race has been integral to militarized bullying since the founding of the nation, employed both here and in other lands. Racial militarized bullying is part of the DNA of US militarized capitalism and has evolved from Native American genocide to slavery to Jim Crow to the twenty-first-century institutionalized racism integral both to the United States and the global corporate order. If genocide, slavery, segregation, and xenophobic exclusion of people because of their country of birth are not bullying, then the term may have little meaning.

"THE ONLY GOOD INJUN'S A DEAD INJUN"

From the very beginning, even while still a British colony, America planted the seeds of a militaristic empire that would be free to subjugate other peoples, especially peoples of other races, to its will. The United States began as an annex of Britain when white Britons crossed the Atlantic to take land from Native Americans. Because these individuals lacked guns, had no concept of private property, and did not follow Christianity, they were deemed racially inferior, weak, and uncivilized heathens. Like schoolyard bullies, the settlers felt free to do with the Native Americans and their land as they wished. At first, the British tried to enslave these people, but that proved impractical as the native population declined because of European diseases and because healthy individuals were able to escape into a land they knew better than the whites did.

The white settlers essentially reproduced British culture on this side of the Atlantic, but as they prospered, they developed their own industries, commercial networks, and resources; they then came to feel less and less need for the home [mother] country. The first of a series of British acts that led to the American Revolution was the Proclamation of 1763,[1] which restricted white settlement across the Appalachians. Whatever the British believed about the native people, in the short run Britain's offense was protecting them and their land from white settlers. Among the charges Thomas Jefferson made against the king of England (really Parliament) in the Declaration of Independence was that he "endeavoured to bring on the inhabitants of our frontiers, the merciless Indian Savages."[2] Once America became independent, whites moved westward, encroaching deeper and deeper into Native American lands. They felt completely justified in doing so because they had been endowed with a "manifest destiny" to stretch across the continent from sea to sea.[3]

A schoolyard bully makes "offers you can't refuse." When Mexico refused to allow white Americans to bring their slaves into Texas and then refused to sell their northern coast (what is now the state of California) for $30 million, the United States responded to the "insult" by declaring war and taking virtually half of Mexico's area by force. As a gesture of "generosity," Washington gave Mexico $15 million,[4] a figure the United States imposed.

The history of "how the West was *won*" is well known and need not be recounted in detail here. At the point of a gun and on the brink of starvation, the Native Americans were bullied into signing treaties and "voluntarily" ceding their territories to white authorities. Resistance would be met by the cavalry. If white settlers wanted the land for farming, if gold or other valuable minerals were found, or if railroads planned to move through the area, treaties that acknowledged territories belonging to Indians would be broken. As Lakota chief Red Cloud lamented: "They made us many promises, more than I can remember. But they kept but one—They promised to take our land . . . and they took it."[5]

Despite the harsh truths of what actually happened in the nation's earlier years, generations of Americans were raised on cowboy movies that depicted Native Americans as savage bullies who attacked innocent white settler victims, burned their farms and homes, pierced their hearts with arrows, and scalped their heads with tomahawks. Only brave heroes, played by the likes of John Wayne, could contain such sadistic barbarism and restore the natural order, with whites in their rightful place on top and native peoples on the bottom—the bullying hierarchy of power and rank.

Of course, from the whites' point of view, the danger of being attacked by Native Americans was real. However, the danger each side posed for the other was hardly equal or balanced. The desperate position into which white America actually bullied Native America is well expressed in Chief Joseph's surrender speech:

It is cold, and we have no blankets; the little children are freezing to death. My people, some of them, have run away to the hills, and have no blankets, no food. No one knows where they are—perhaps freezing to death. I want to have time to look for my children, and see how many of them I can find. Maybe I shall find them among the dead. Hear me, my chiefs! I am tired; my heart is sick and sad. From where the sun now stands, I will fight no more forever.[6]

"THERE AIN'T NO SINGIN' IN DEM FIELDS"

As early as the 1600s, when Native Americans failed to adapt to slavery they were replaced by Africans. It is estimated that 20 million Africans were seized from their homes in the slave trade and shipped across the Atlantic, with half of them dying during the "Middle Passage" before they could reach the Americas.[7] One survivor told of the experience of being human cargo on a Middle Passage ship:

I now saw myself deprived of all chance of returning to my native country. . . . The stench of the hold while we were on the coast was so intolerably loathsome, that it was dangerous to remain there for any time. . . . But now that the whole ship's cargo were confined together, it became absolutely pestilential. The closeness of the place and the heat of the climate, added to the number in the ship, which was so crowded that each had scarcely room to turn himself, almost suffocated us. . . . This produced copious perspirations so that the air became unfit for respiration from a variety of loathsome smells, and brought on a sickness among the slaves, of which many died—thus falling victims of the improvident avarice, as I may call it, of their purchasers. This wretched situation was again aggravated by the galling of the chains, which now became insupportable, and the filth of the necessary tubs [toilets] into which the children often fell and were almost suffocated. The shrieks of the women and the groans of the dying rendered the whole a scene of horror almost inconceivable.[8]

Once survivors reached the Americas, they were transformed into commodities to be bought and sold; they were stripped of their identity, their religion, their language, their culture, and their history. Some images of the era depict a benign slavery, with cheerful blacks singing in the fields, and certainly there were slaves who identified with their masters and saw their inferior position as natural and appropriate, just as there are schoolyard bully victims who identify with the bully. Yet even "nice" masters who regarded their slaves as "family" held latent bullying power. Whatever the owner's personality, slaves knew they were chattel, without rights, and if they became too "uppity," their master could always sell them to a more vicious owner or become more brutal himself.

Solomon Northrup, a free black man who was captured and forced into more than a decade of slavery, told his story in *Twelve Years a Slave*. He described the bullying that occurred on the not-so-benign plantations:

The hands are required to be in the cotton field as soon as it is light in the morning, and, with the exception of ten or fifteen minutes, which is given them at noon to swallow their allowance of cold bacon, they are not permitted to be a moment idle until it is too dark to see, and when the moon is full, they often times labor till the middle of the night. . . . The day's work over in the field, the baskets are . . . carried to the gin-house, where the cotton is weighed. No matter how fatigued and weary he may be—no matter how much he longs for sleep and rest—a slave never approaches the gin-house with his basket of cotton but with fear. If it falls short in weight—if he has not performed the full task appointed him, he knows that he must suffer. . . . It is an offense invariably followed by a flogging, to be found at the quarters after daybreak. Then the fears and labors of another day begin; and until its close there is no such thing as rest.[9]

Whites were also bullied by the slave system. For example, relatively benign masters were not permitted to educate their "property," to ensure that the slaves did not learn enough about life beyond the plantations to gain confidence and try to assert their independence. It was a crime to teach slaves how to read. It was also a federal crime to help a slave escape or to shelter an escaped slave. Beginning with the Civil War, the South would continuously attempt to assert "states' rights" and claim the North had used the federal government to bully Southerners into abandoning their culture, their way of life, and the basis of their economy, discarding a racial order that they were convinced was ordained by God or nature. However, prior to the Civil War when they exerted more control over the national government, Southerners, rather than asserting states' rights, had no compunction about using the federal government to bully Northern opponents of slavery into enforcing their "peculiar institution."

Despite claims that benign plantations existed, slavery was an economic bullying system that made its white upper echelon enormously wealthy.

In the upper South the selling of slaves became more profitable than the growing of tobacco. Slaves vary widely in value from fifty dollars to two thousand dollars depending on who they are, how old they are, but the valuable ones are very, very valuable. . . . Cotton became the key crop, the key cash producer in the life of the nation. For a period of time, there are more millionaires along a narrow band of land along the Mississippi River than in the entire rest of the nation combined. This is a terribly profitable crop that we're talking about. By 1840 the value of cotton exports was greater than everything else the nation exported to the world combined! And that made slaves the most valuable thing in the nation beside the land itself.[10]

JIM CROW LIVES

In the immediate aftermath of the Civil War, the Northern army temporarily occupied the South. White Southerners bitterly remembered this period, known as Reconstruction, as a time of destitution, insult, and degradation. Southerners saw their lives turned upside down as the North imposed an unnatural, alien order. The "outrages" the North committed included attempting to grant full citizenship rights to black former slaves and even permitting blacks to hold political office. Blacks and sympathetic white Northerners viewed Reconstruction as an effort to protect newly freed blacks from their former bullies, but white Southerners saw it as a time of being brutally bullied by greedy Northerners and their black lackeys. These diverse perceptions illustrate how subjective the concept of bullying can be.

When Reconstruction ended and the Northern army withdrew, the federal government would not permit white Southerners to restore slavery. However, a new bullying system was devised to restore the racial hierarchy and deprive blacks of most of their citizenship rights—segregation, nicknamed "Jim Crow." Segregation had a long series of rules; here are just a few of them: (1) black and white children had to attend separate schools, (2) blacks and whites had separate bathrooms and drinking fountains, (3) blacks could not be served in the same section of restaurants as whites, (4) blacks could not initiate handshakes with whites because that might imply racial equality, (5) blacks were to sit in the back of buses, and (6) black men could not approach white women.[11] In this way, the powerful white bully established written rules to ensure black subordination, much as the young bully establishes his unwritten code of conduct in the schoolyard.

Official white police forces in the South certainly embraced Jim Crow, but segregation was doubly enforced by violent private militias, especially the Ku Klux Klan (KKK). *Birth of a Nation,* often acclaimed as the greatest silent movie ever made, glorifies the Klansmen as heroes and ends with rows of hooded members preventing blacks from entering the voting booths at gunpoint. The movie implies that the Klan was composed of brave men who were needed to contain the vicious bullies invading the South—that is, the Northerners arriving during Reconstruction and their black minions, who had unrestrained lust for white women. If not stopped, these interlopers (savages) would bully white women into submission. The movie asserts that whites, both of the North and of the South, had to unite "*in defense of their Aryan birthright*"[12]—the exact term the German Nazis would use. The surest way to defend their Aryan birthright would be to lynch their enemies: from 1882 to 1968, a total of 3,446 blacks were lynched.[13]

After a long civil rights struggle, legal segregation was abolished. Yet as of 2011, "the median wealth of white households [was] 20 times that of black households," and the disparity has been rising dramatically since the beginning of the 2000s.[14] Today, racial profiling and harassment of blacks by the police are still routine practices, as demonstrated by the 2014 shooting of an unarmed black boy, Michael Brown, in Ferguson, Missouri;[15] the 2015 police choking of another unarmed young black, Eric Garner, on Staten Island, New York, who was shown on video screaming, "I can't breathe, I can't breathe";[16] and a horrifying series of other police killings of young unarmed blacks elsewhere in the nation. Such extreme police bullying, which involves these multiple murders leading to the rise of the Black Lives Matter movement, is only one of several forms of racial bullying that are routine in largely poor black neighborhoods. Blacks are profiled and stopped for minor violations while driving, and then they are often fined or jailed. (They may even be killed, as in the case of African American Sandra Bland, twenty-eight, who was stopped by police on July 7, 2015, after failing to use her turn signal in Hempstead, Texas. Sandra was threatened with a taser when she questioned the officer and then arrested; she died in Weller County jail under suspicious circumstances.)[17] They are harassed walking down the street while committing no offense at all. If they resist or question the officer, it is not uncommon for them to be bullied with verbal threats or physical violence. Black young men can be stopped by police just because they are wearing a hood or baggy, low-slung pants, which means parents have to worry about how their kids dress, slouch, or walk when they leave home for school or sports. Such routine bullying is an assault on the most basic rights of African Americans, especially the young black male, and it violates the elemental need for safety and belonging. No bully in the schoolyard could be more effective. The schools themselves have become a theater for police bullying of black students. In Richland County, South Carolina, a teacher called a deputy sheriff when a black student refused to leave the room. The white deputy sheriff pulled the student from her desk and dragged her across the classroom floor.[18]

The percentage of blacks executed in the United States since 1976 is almost double their share of the population: 34.6 percent versus 17.9 percent. As of April 2015, there were 2,257 Americans on death row, of which 1,189, or 52.7 percent, were black.[19] Black legal scholar Michelle Alexander proposes that the 2 million blacks in prison constitute a new Jim Crow segregation, perhaps more brutal than the original.[20] If felons are not allowed to vote, this becomes a new mechanism to assure black disenfranchisement, an institutional way to enshrine the racial bullying hierarchy.

Since the civil rights era, the black middle class has been growing, and there is even a black upper class, including an Afro-American president. However, as the data indicate, lower-class blacks may be worse off than before. As of March 2015, the black unemployment rate was 10.4 percent, more than double the white rate. And educated blacks were not exempt: 23.7 percent of unemployed blacks had attended college, 15.4 percent had graduated from college, and 4.5 percent held advanced degrees.[21] To ease the problem, there are education and job-training programs, but these will hardly be effective when jobs do not exist. When the velvet glove does not work, there is the iron fist. Largely to prevent the discontent within the urban black ghetto from overflowing and threatening capitalist institutions, most of them white, the police are on patrol.

Many leaders of the black liberation movement in the 1960s and 1970s, including Stokely Carmichael (renamed Kwane Ture) of the Student Non-violent Coordinating Committee (SNCC) and the Black Panther Party, referred to the police as the "internal army of occupation."[22] Today, the police are essentially engaged in "racial bullying" and acting as a military force. They are being provided with surplus military weapons, such as bayonets, M-16 rifles, armored personnel carriers, and grenade launchers.[23] They engage in training exercises with US Army Rangers and US Navy SEALs.

According to the Cato Institute:

> State and local police departments are increasingly accepting the military as a model for their behavior and outlook. The sharing of training and technology is producing a shared mindset. The problem is that the mindset of the soldier is simply not appropriate for the civilian police officer. Police officers confront not an "enemy" but individuals who are protected by the Bill of Rights. Confusing the police function with the military function can lead to dangerous and unintended consequences—such as unnecessary shootings and killings.[24]

Upper-class blacks are not exempt from racial bullying and racial profiling by the police. Distinguished Afro-American Harvard professor and millionaire producer of such Public Broadcasting Service (PBS) specials as *Finding Your Roots* (2012) and *The African-Americans: Many Rivers to Cross* (2013), Henry Louis Gates was arrested for "breaking and entering" on the doorstep of his own house in 2010.[25] The police officer on scene could not imagine that even a well-dressed, middle-aged black could live in such an affluent neighborhood as the section of Cambridge, Massachusetts, where Gates's house was located. To defuse the situation, President Obama invited Gates and the policeman to share beer with him on the White House lawn. But such situations are not so easily defused when they affect less-affluent blacks, such as Trayvon Martin of Sanford, Florida; Michael Brown of Ferguson, Missouri; or Freddie Gray of Baltimore, Maryland, all unarmed victims of either police or "community watch" violence.

"TERROR BABIES": GO BACK WHERE YOU CAME FROM!

Militarized racial bullying is also a huge part of the US approach to immigration. With the rise of Donald Trump as a leading Republican candidate in the summer of 2015, the Republican Party moved from any notion of immigration reform—permitting illegal immigrants to work their way toward citizenship—to militarization of the border and the forced deportation of "anchor babies" and their parents.[26] In the 2012 presidential campaign, Republican candidate Michelle Bachmann warned the country of "terror babies," whose pregnant mothers, usually Muslim, entered the country to give birth to babies who would have automatic American citizenship. The babies could be raised as terrorists and grow up to attack the country of their birth from within its borders.[27] Trump, Bachmann, and other Republicans were proposing a de facto policy that would result in the militarized bullying of immigrants crossing the border and of millions already living and working in the United States. The aim: to make crossing the border and living here so tortured that the immigrants would, as Mitt Romney had pronounced in 2012, choose to "self-deport."[28]

At least one conservative radio host contends that immigrants who did not leave in a few months would become "property of the state," that is, legal slaves.[29] They would be forced to work as "state assets," laboring at jobs for subsistence-level food and lodging without possessing any human rights. That host, Jan Mickelson, openly asked, "Well, what's wrong with slavery?" This signaled at least a lurch toward a return of Jim Crow, if not an actual slave racist bullying system, now extended from African Americans to encompass mainly Mexican illegal immigrants.

In the midst of the Republicans' xenophobic proposals, President Obama and the Democrats continued to defend "immigration reform," but the policies they advanced actually represented their own form of militarized racial bullying. The Obama administration deported more illegal immigrants than any prior regime,[30] and it took seriously the task of militarily "securing" the border. Obama provided border patrols with assault weapons and other military hardware, including surveillance drones; many discussed using the drones to shoot at Mexican border crossers, whom Trump had called "rapists."

The rise of Mexicans as a new prime target of militarized racial bulling calls up the image of Native Americans as well as African Americans. Native Americans were militarily bullied into giving up their land and sovereignty, a form of military conquest and genocidal exile and murder implemented to accommodate settler colonialism. Similarly, recall that Texas, California, and other southwestern states were once part of Mexico, conquered by the United States in the 1848 Mexican War and other conflicts. In militarily bullying Mexican immigrants to leave the country, the modern authorities are actually repeating a version of the Indian removal genocide; by telling people whose ancestral home had been Texas and California to "go home," they actually are saying, "Don't stay where your ancestors came from." The militarized bullying of Mexicans, with xenophobic Republicans shouting "Go home," is really a second merciless and brutal forced exile, this time compelling Mexicans to leave their native lands.

CHAPTER SIX

Marching to Bully

How the Military Trains Bullies,
Both Inside and Outside the Services

As we have demonstrated, American militaristic capitalism is a bullying system that draws upon bullying traditions found in, for instance, the Roman and British Empires. Our approach to the study of bullying is different from that of other investigators because we do not emphasize its psychological causes. But that does not mean we negate psychological and even biological influences. Clearly, a bullying society needs bullying personalities. There is no contradiction between focusing upon individual or psychological bullying and the study of institutional or structural bullying. Rather, both aspects depend on and reinforce each other. Elites depend upon institutions that build attitudes, values, and behaviors that make the rest of the population docile, willing to accept their subordinate position and to act and think in ways that maintain the status quo and enhance the wealth and power of the dominant people. This requires institutions that mediate between the elites and everyone else, conveying the appropriate attitudes and behaviors and making them normal and expected. Such institutions effectively transmit values and expectations. The next three chapters will look at various "transmission belt" institutions, starting in this chapter with the military itself along with its allied institutions.

Bullying is woven into the very fabric of the military. Using violence and aggression to impose its will on others is the fundamental purpose of the military—even if it presents itself as a defender, a paragon of moral virtue, and the protector of the weak. In the schoolyard, the weak who resist the protection of the bully face his full wrath. The military behaves in similar fashion. Consider the brutality that confronted people in Vietnam, Afghanistan, and Iraq who resisted America's protection or the lot of the colonial peoples who resisted the civilization offered them by white America or Britain.

Empires cannot survive without the military, whose role is to bully weaker nations into submission. No wonder, then, that President Obama promised, "So long as I'm commander in chief, we will sustain the strongest military the world has ever known."[1]

The United States openly views itself as the world's police force, morally ordained to impose its interests and values across the rest of the globe and justified in whatever it does, be that bombing villages, killing civilians, or overthrowing governments. America committed genocide against the Native Americans; raided Africa in search of slaves; seized about half of Mexico's territory; conquered Hawaii and the Philippines; and invaded Vietnam, Iraq, and Afghanistan. The victims may have viewed these acts as brutal bullying, and we shall see that they reflect the core values and dominance of the schoolyard bully. The US government claimed its actions were morally justified under the doctrine of manifest destiny or for several other reasons: for instance, it had an obligation to bring civilization to the savages; it was the duty of the strong to protect the weak; and it was a matter of self-defense on a global scale—all themes that, as we show shortly, also reflect the implicit mind-set of bullying kids. After World War II when the United States gave itself the world's sheriff's badge, it renamed the Department of War as the Department of Defense. The term *defense* may sound less aggressive than *war,* but war is sporadic whereas defense is permanent.[2] It can be argued that small countries such as Switzerland and Sweden need defense, but in dominant empires such as the United States, the military plays a very different role.

American capitalism revolves around the military. The Pentagon underwrites many of the largest corporations through weapons contracts, and it protects US-based corporations as they abandon American workers in favor of plants abroad and as they secure foreign raw materials and markets. America's militaristic empire cannot exist without people who support it and are even willing to kill and die in its battles. Accordingly, it must transmit militaristic values, which are essentially forms of violent bullying values, either through the military itself or through other institutions.

The words *civility* and *civilian* have the same root. Capitalism depends upon the armed forces, but militarism is in contradiction with the basic rules of everyday civil life. People generally agree that the most basic rule of common morality is "Thou shalt not kill." The armed forces must make killing acceptable—in fact, glorious and heroic—and have those values pervade the entire society. Other institutions, such as the National Rifle Association

(NRA), the Boy Scouts, professional sports teams, and even some schools, as we shall see in a following chapter, also convey these values, often through direct or indirect cooperation with the military.

Even before World War I, President Theodore Roosevelt—the president who used the "bully pulpit" to truly express bully values for all of society— insisted that elite universities such as Harvard had to enhance their football teams if America was to dominate the world. He declared, "We can not afford to turn out college men who shrink from physical effort or a little physical pain." The nation needed men with "the courage that will fight valiantly again the foes of the soul and the foes of the body."[3] The Boy Scouts, another leading proponent of military and bullying values in civilian life, promises that their alumni will be able to proudly declare: "America, here I stand my body strong to fight your battles! My mind trained to keep your democracy virile!"[4]

Military values appear to be inherently contradictory. The military needs individuals who are violent, aggressive bullies but simultaneously willing to submit to a chain of command and otherwise be docile and obedient. Militarism is caught in this dilemma: how do you build bullies but control them so they will only attack people deemed enemies and not turn against the very people who made them into bullies? In other words, bullies are fine as long as they are good guys who subdue bad guys. As the NRA's executive vice president, Wayne LaPierre, put it, "The only thing that stops a bad guy with a gun is a good guy with a gun."[5] This raises the question of how we can distinguish good guys from bad guys, especially if they both act the same way as gun-wielding bullies. Of course, this is not a problem that the ordinary soldier is allowed to worry about. As Alfred Lord Tennyson, poet laureate of the United Kingdom during the Crimean War, famously phrased it, "Ours is not to reason why, ours but to do and die."[6]

TRAINING FOR BULLIES

Now let us turn to the methods by which the military bullies its recruits into accepting Tennyson's charge. When you join the military, you are normally sent to boot camp for basic training, where the sergeants and the officers attempt to transform your entire identity. The majority of military personnel sit behind a desk or are engaged in technical pursuits, so we might ask why most must go through the training about to be described. Perhaps the answer is that the training constitutes institutionalized bullying; it reinforces military values, builds obedience, and leads soldiers to accept their place within a chain of command whether or not they will ever actually need a gun.

In recent times, most killing has not been done by snipers such as US Navy SEAL Chris Kyle, the hero of the immensely popular 2015 movie *American Sniper*,[7] who is credited with personally killing a record 160 Iraqis and Afghanis. Instead, most killing is done by unmanned drones or by tanks whose control panels look like video game consoles. These weapons require technical skills that are likely to be possessed by so-called nerds, many of whom have spent their childhood and adolescent years as bully victims. This reality expands in surprising ways the circle of military personnel whose careers involve bullying.

Physical strength is becoming less important in the modern military, leading to a broader range of potential military recruits and the infiltration of its bullying values into new groups. Today, women and gays are staffing the military, often going into combat. Until recently, though, military culture relied heavily on homophobia and masculine identity to bully the recruits into proving they would be worthy, obedient soldier bullies. For the most part, it still does, but these traditions are being challenged.

As it seeks recruits outside its traditional population, the military itself has become a battlefield in the culture wars we have discussed in other chapters (see especially chapter 9), with a war about bullying itself emerging within the services. Obama—a symbol of the commander in chief personifying some of the new internal conflicts in military culture—was perceived by many within the military as a liberal foe who attempted to institute new policies that they saw as violating fundamental military traditions and values:

> Obama is an unpopular president in the eyes of the men and women in uniform. . . . [He] oversaw repeal of the controversial "don't ask, don't tell" policy. Then he broke with one of the military's most deeply rooted traditions and vowed to lift the ban on women serving in combat. And the commander in chief has aggressively sought to change military culture by cracking down on sexual assault and sexual harassment, problems that for years were underreported or overlooked. . . . To his critics, his moves amount to heavy-handed social engineering that erodes deep-seated traditions and potentially undermines good order and discipline.[8]

Nevertheless, the military remains overwhelmingly committed to its traditional bully values. Despite the repeal of "don't ask, don't tell," the US

Marine Corps still relies heavily upon homophobia to intimidate enlistees into proving they are not "namby-pamby wimps" but belong among "the few, the proud":

> We're called faggots 10–50 times a day. "You think that's yelling? That's sweet, faggot." "Yeah, you would think that's a pushup, faggot," etc. . . . . "You stupid fucking thing. That's more wrong than two boys fucking." One captain, when giving an ethics class, and talking about how one mistake can change your life/identity told the entire company "you can be a bridge builder your entire life, but you suck one dick and you're a cocksucker till you die."[9]

The shortage of white enlistees has led the civilian government to attempt to attract more soldiers of color. When the United States invades Middle Eastern countries, it actively needs Muslim soldiers who would be sensitive to local cultures. This leads to pressure to promote multiculturalism in the military, yet racism and xenophobia, particularly anti-Muslim xenophobia, remain prominent in the repertoire of bullying techniques used by drill instructors (DIs).

> The one Indian looking kid in the platoon gets ripped by the DI's [every] day. . . . "[Name] are you a fucking terrorist?" "no sir" "well, if you were a terrorist, you wouldn't admit to it now would you?" "no sir" "so you're probably a fucking terrorist." "aye sir" "because you look like a fucking terrorist, why aren't you driving a fucking cab like the rest of your people?"[10]

Typically, the bullying practices used in basic training are many decades old. Repeated humiliation is standard. One recruit reports, "I had [to] stand in front of the mirror, point at the mirror and say, 'You're an idiot.' Then point back at myself and then say, 'No, I'm an idiot.' Forced to keep that up for 30 minutes."[11]

One of the first things that happens to a male recruit is that his head is shaved, something for which he must pay money. (Women recruits are exempt from this requirement.) This is intended to strip him of any personal identity, to reduce him to a cog in the larger military machine, indistinguishable from anyone else—to turn him into someone without personal desires or needs who will just blend in and do his assigned task. Paying for the haircut represents his consent and participation in the process. Further, in contrast to the expectation of civilian etiquette to maintain a soft voice, enlistees are expected to shout:

DI: From now on, you will speak only when spoken to, and the first and last words out of your filthy sewers will be "Sir." Do you maggots understand that?

RECRUITS: Sir, yes, sir!

DI: Bullshit! I can't hear you. Sound off like you got a pair.[12]

Challenges to masculinity are regularly used to spur males to prove they are traditional men who have the stuff—men who can simultaneously be tough and able to "take it" but not think on their own or question authority. It has long been standard practice to address male trainees as "ladies." In Stanley Kubrick's film *Full Metal Jacket*, we hear recruits being told: "If you ladies leave my island, if you survive recruit training you will be a weapon, you will be a minister of death, praying for war. But until that day you are pukes! You're the lowest form of life on Earth. You are not even human fucking beings! You are nothing but unorganized grabasstic pieces of amphibian."[13]

There are more women in the military today than during Vietnam, when the events in *Full Metal Jacket* took place. The United States now has a volunteer military; supposedly, recruits can leave if they choose. But drill sergeants still use bullying, not reassurance and support, to intimidate enlistees of either gender to keep them from bailing:

During one of [a female recruit's] first exercise routines where the drill sergeant was yelling at her, she started crying and said "I want to go home." Overhearing her, the drill instructor ran up to her and said "What did you say?" She said "I want to go home." He looked at her and said "Spin three times and click your heels." After she finished, he said "You're mine for the next 8 weeks Dorothy. Now give me 20!"[14]

As part of their training, soldiers are placed in near-death experiences, which some people might classify as torture. This is part of the toughening process whereby they learn to bully and accept being bullied:

Now, for the army at least, one of the first "hardcore" tasks you get in training is being sent to the gas chamber. Think a concrete box filled with "Ow, goddamnit it's in my eyes!" So, we march into the suck square, and they close the doors. We rip our masks off and breath in that sweet hookah from hell. . . . This shit burns your eyes, your nose, and especially your lungs—like you deep-throated Satan's member against your will. Anyway, everyone's puking, or crying, and they finally opened the doors to get out, so we stumble out.[15]

Actually, the United States uses napalm, Agent Orange, and nerve gas, but no other country has used poison gas on enemy combatants since World War I.

Although the primary purpose of basic training is to produce tough, violent, but obedient bullies, it is also intended to weed out people who are so unstable that they cannot be trusted with bullying power or who might turn their guns against their own leaders or fellow soldiers rather than against designated enemies.

> One of the senior drill sergeants held up a live round (live rounds are never, ever supposed to leave the range in basic training) and grabbed Private P. and brought him in front of the company. He was crying and the drill sergeants started screaming at him. We still didn't know exactly what had happened, and then the MPs came and took him away.... Turns out he had smuggled 6 live rounds, and he had written in his notebook his plan to kill his 3 platoon drill sergeants, our company commander and first sergeant, and himself.[16]

BULLYING AND VIOLENCE: BOTH ON MILITARY BASES AND IN CIVILIAN LIFE

Soldiers and veterans are trained to consider violence a legitimate response to a challenge and to believe bullying is fine as long as it's done by those on the right side. Under extreme stress, both while they are in the military and as they try to readapt to a civilian society that considers many military values taboo, these individuals often turn to violence—an extreme form of bullying—directing it either against other people or against themselves. Twenty-two veterans commit suicide every day.[17] Christopher Kyle, the hero of *American Sniper*, was killed on a shooting range by another veteran whom he was trying to help cope with his alleged post-traumatic stress disorder (PTSD).[18] At Fort Hood, Spc. Ivan Lopez killed three other soldiers and wounded another sixteen before killing himself.[19] A few years earlier at that same military base, Maj. Nidal Malik Hasan, an army psychiatrist, killed thirteen people, and he may have actually killed or wounded over forty. He fired 146 rounds.[20] Six years before Osama Bin Laden attacked the World Trade

Center, Timothy McVeigh, who had been awarded a Bronze Star in the army during the First Gulf War, killed 168 people—slightly more than the total number of Afghanis and Iraqis that Christopher Kyle killed—and he injured at least another 500 when he blew up the Oklahoma City Federal Building.[21]

Christopher Dorner was a former navy lieutenant, a specialist in undersea warfare, a rifle marksman, and a pistol expert who lost his job in the Los Angeles Police Department (LAPD). On February 3, 2013, he began a killing rampage, shooting his lawyer's daughter and her fiancé, firing at three police officers, killing one, and issuing a manifesto threatening to kill at least twelve more. The LAPD announced that the weapons training Dorner received in the navy made him a very serious threat.[22] On the same day that he went on his rampage, the Cable News Network (CNN) broadcast a long segment praising Clinton Romesha, a newly minted recipient of the Congressional Medal of Honor, as the "bravest of the brave," a soldier who directed the killing of over thirty Afghani "enemies" in a twelve-hour battle that left eight Americans dead.[23] We can ask what the difference is between Dorner and Romesha or between McVeigh and Kyle. If you kill enough, it seems, you may be awarded the Congressional Medal of Honor; in any case, bullying triumphs.

Military values are transmitted—often through bullying in civilian life— by schools, gun companies, and other institutions connected to or at least strongly influenced by the military, which aggressively seeks to spread its values into civilian culture. High school students may not have military experience, but they are recruited by military officers in their schools; many are inspired by the militaristic culture, with some turning into routine bullies and others into violent killer bullies. In a number of cases, students have taken guns to school and turned them on fellow students, teachers, and themselves. The killers were often fixated on military equipment, war stories, and the military bases near their schools. One of the most famous cases occurred at Columbine High School in Littleton, Colorado. After that event, Michael Moore made the film *Bowling for Columbine,* which showed that one of the Columbine shooters had lived on an air force base where a plane was displayed complete with a plaque proclaiming that it had killed people in Vietnamese villages one Christmas Eve. Moore asks: "Don't you think the kids say to themselves, 'Dad goes to work every day. He builds weapons of mass destruction. What is the difference between that mass destruction and the mass destruction over at Columbine High School?'"[24]

Both the military and its allies in the armaments industries have a strong stake in promoting a violent bullying culture where weapons are a norm.

Gun manufacturers know 50 percent of all sporting rifle owners in the United States are present or former veterans or in law enforcement. The industry is now actively working to increase that percentage, targeting veterans and their families with advertising campaigns, particularly those promoting the kinds of assault guns they used in the service. Manufacturers argue these guns are necessary both for the safety of the family and for having fun in civilian life. They highlight the fact that gun use is an integral part of America's constitutional and moral values and that it makes American society morally exceptional; all the while, they underplay the reality (one that they may not have thought through) that an armed population, operating under "stand your ground" laws, is one that is primed to bully. The gun industry's journal praised the social network of "America's modern veterans," which includes "hundreds of thousands of dads, brothers, uncles, wives, sisters, aunts, cousins and extended family and friends, who served or are serving in Iraq and Afghanistan. They are respected and admired. They carried firearms to protect our country. That factor, that imagery, has had a huge positive impact on how firearms are viewed in our country."[25]

The military does not work alone in causing the extreme bullying of gun violence. Gun violence is largely a response to poverty, but it also has roots in American culture. In the United States, possessing guns is deemed a fundamental right according to the Second Amendment, and as a result, gun bullying is enshrined in constitutional law. The gun culture is particularly rampant in the South and the West, where it evolved to keep blacks and Native Americans in their place. In fact, one of the motives for passing the Second Amendment was to establish patrols to capture escaped slaves.[26] Today, the South and the West have the highest rates of domestic gun violence, the largest percentages of their populations in the military, the most military bases, and the strongest support for military adventurism. Even a hundred and fifty years after the Civil War, white southerners still feel the sting of northerners destroying their "peculiar institution." In their eyes, they are victims of northern bullying. In much of the southern culture, the gun is more than an instrument—it is a badge of southern bullying identity:

"They're fixing to change this whole bidniss" as the man at the Charleston gun show had said—to take away the last vestige of Southern manhood. ... The gun show was the one place they could be themselves, like a clubhouse with strict admission and no windows. ... The gun show wasn't about guns and gun totin'. It was about the self-esteem of men—white men mainly—the dominant ethnic group of the South, animated by a sense of grievance ("the heart of the Southern identity," according to one shrewd historian)—who felt defeated and still persecuted, conspired against by hostile outside forces, making a symbolic last stand.[27]

McVeigh, Dorner, and Lopez can be called deranged or pathological, but pathological individuals do not develop in a vacuum. They live in a society, and American society has one of the highest murder rates in the world. Some societies stimulate people to kill more than others. The United States has almost eight times the murder rate of Switzerland.[28] A militaristic empire must inspire people to commit violence. It must reward the most extreme forms of bullying. It cannot guarantee that violent bullies on the battlefield will be nice, healthy, peaceful citizens on the home front. A society that routinely bullies other people cannot avoid having its own citizens bully each other. The military, the most violent bullying institution of all, can hardly expect to compartmentalize violent bullying. It will see it on its own bases, in the society from which it recruits members, and among its veterans as they return to civilian life. Treating violence and bullying as individual pathology cannot end it. This is a pathology that rests with the society, not the individual.

THE MILITARY AND THE PSYCHOLOGICAL PARADIGM

In recent years, heavy emphasis has been placed on providing psychotherapy for soldiers and veterans. Although this has been endorsed by the Departments of Veterans Affairs and Defense, it is somewhat problematic because psychology and the military have traditionally grown out of two very different cultures. As we have argued, the psychological paradigm is inadequate for addressing bullying among both adults and children because it looks at individual failings and does not consider larger institutional and social forces that have a stake in promoting bullying. This is even more true in the military than in other institutions, such as schools (which have been the focus of so much of the discussion about bullying). No other institution benefits more from promoting bullying than the military. Yet psychotherapists who work within the military would violate their professional ethics and risk their jobs if they suggested the real pathology, the real source of bullying and violence, rests with the institution itself. If the psychotherapists wear uniforms, as many do, they could face being court-martialed for insubordination if they offered that diagnosis or even allowed themselves to really think it.

As we have seen, the goal of military training is to make the soldier violent but not too violent, to turn the soldier into a "good guy with a gun" who only uses it against "bad guys with guns" or people who do not acknowledge that *we* are the good guys and *they* are the bad guys. A soldier has the paradoxical identity of a "good bully," being adept at using bullying methods for allegedly lofty ends. The public has been inundated with messages from the media that express shock over crime and violence on military bases and among veterans. We are supposed to be bewildered that people trained to be violent actually become violent. Army officials were disappointed by a psychological study they commissioned in the hope that it would better help them to predict who might turn violent against their fellow soldiers at military bases.[29] The report emphasized the reluctance of soldiers to report personal problems and the insufficient sharing of information among army agencies. The fact that their whole purpose is to train people to be violent did not seem to even cross the minds of the investigators or the army officers. The psychological paradigm has labeled as a disease an individual's failure to adapt after military service—especially after exposure to combat; after seeing gore, destruction, and death all around you; after being in dread of becoming a victim yourself or being bullied into becoming a perpetrator. In World War I, this ailment was called "shell shock." In World War II, it was called "battle fatigue." And since Vietnam, it has been called "traumatic stress disorder" or, among veterans, "post-traumatic stress disorder," or PTSD.

As we have seen in other chapters, the psychological paradigm takes society as a given, something beyond challenge to which the individual must adjust. There can be nothing wrong with the institution itself—in this case, the military institution. Increasingly, the military has been pressured to rely upon the psychological paradigm because the bullying built into classical training often backfires and because recruitment has become more difficult due to the fear that veterans may be left without support. The armed forces do this reluctantly, for psychology has tended to be considered a "liberal" profession on the opposite side of the culture wars. Meditation was a psychological exercise popular in the counterculture and antiwar movement of the 1960s and 1970s, but around 2010, the US Marines started adopting it as a technique to make their troops even tougher and more "mindful." According to Maj. Gen. Melvin Spies, "While teaching troops to shoot makes them a better warfighter, teaching mindfulness makes them a better person by helping them to decompress, which could have lasting effects."[30] If a marine were to adopt a mantra, perhaps it would sound like this: Oommm!!! Bomb! Bomb! Oommm!!! Boom! Boom! Oommm!!! Kill! Kill! Oommm!!!

Historically, career officers have often been hostile to psychological explanations for an individual's failure to blend into military culture, seeing it as a justification for "namby-pamby, wimpy cowardliness." During World War II, four-star general George Patton famously slapped soldiers diagnosed with battle fatigue. Upon seeing men in army hospitals with psychological illnesses, he issued this directive:

> It has come to my attention that a very small number of soldiers are going to the hospital on the pretext that they are nervously incapable of combat. Such men are cowards, and bring discredit on the Army and disgrace to their comrades who they heartlessly leave to endure the danger of a battle which they themselves use the hospital as a means of escaping. You will take measures to see that such cases are not sent to the hospital, but are dealt with in their units. Those who are not willing to fight will be tried by Court-Martial for cowardice in the face of the enemy.[31]

He ordered one soldier diagnosed with battle fatigue to return to duty, declaring: "You're going back to the front line and you may get shot and killed, but you're going to fight. If you don't, I'll stand you up against a wall and have a firing squad kill you on purpose."[32]

Patton provoked a serious controversy within the army when he did this. Other generals, including Eisenhower, wanted to recognize the legitimacy of alleged mental illnesses such as battle fatigue. Despite this historic debate, however, military psychotherapists usually try to blend in and dedicate themselves to the service, largely because the professional ethics of psychology say critiquing institutions is outside their domain. They are supposed to serve whatever institution solicits their talents.

The American Psychological Association secretly collaborated with the administration of President George W. Bush to bolster a legal and ethical justification for the torture of prisoners swept up in the post–9/11 war on terror.[33]

In conformity with professional ethics, if psychotherapists are working with active duty soldiers, their goal is to get them back on the front line; if they are treating veterans, their goal is to get them to overcome any remorse about those they shot or anything else they experienced while in the service.

Again, the problem is seen to rest with the individual, not the institution. If you are in the military, psychotherapists are there to help you adjust to what might be the most pathological institution of all, one in which the most sane response may well be insanity. The institution itself may be so insane that there is no sane way to function within it.

This was made clear—or at least as clear as something this muddled and contradictory can be made—in the World War II novel and movie *Catch-22*. A psychiatrist thinks that flying in combat missions is crazy and that he should prevent anyone from doing it. However, his professional commitment is to the military, and recognizing the insanity is really a sign of sanity. Therefore, he must force anyone who asks to be grounded to fly.

> DR. "DOC" DANEEKA [Air Corps psychiatrist]: Sure. Catch-22. Anyone who wants to get out of combat isn't really crazy, so I can't ground him.
>
> CAPTAIN YOSSARIAN [fighter pilot, main character]: Ok, let me see if I've got this straight. In order to be grounded, I've got to be crazy. And I must be crazy to keep flying. But if I ask to be grounded, that means I'm not crazy anymore, and I have to keep flying.[34]

Sociologist Jerry Lembcke sees a tendency to "psychologize the political," that is, to deny the sociological imagination in order to prevent any recognition that the problem may rest with the institution, not the individual. Using psychological labels can be a way of transforming rational responses to inherently irrational situations into diseases. We can infer that the way to cure the real diseases is to transform the entire society and possibly to abolish certain institutions:

> As a case of psychologizing the political, the construction of PTSD is a textbook case of how "badness" can be reframed as "sickness."[35] . . . In no sense did [the] neo-Freudian perspective on shell shock imply that the illness of veterans needing to be understood was not "real." Rather, it shifted the diagnostic gaze from causes external to the victim, like exploding shells, to causes that were internal to the mind and emotions of the veteran. What the patient was really afraid of was his own shortcomings.[36] . . . New stories about wartime atrocities that are couched as the failure of individual soldiers to meet the national standards, or reported as forms of personal "breakdown" are a kind of spin put on violations of human decency so as to shift the blame away from public policy and social norms.[37]

Soldiers and veterans certainly do act in ways that can be considered pathological. However, the response has, for the most part, been either to treat them as criminals who must be arrested, jailed, and maybe even executed or to label them as mentally ill and advocate for improved mental health services to help them rehabilitate and better adjust to society. Whether this is a society to which one *should* adjust is seldom asked. What are we to make of a country that spends more on armaments than the next ten countries with the largest militaries combined?[38] A country where the CEOs of the biggest corporations typically earn over three hundred and fifty times more than their average employee?[39] Unless we address the pathology within the society itself and consider the possibility that certain institutions are inherently pathological, we can hardly expect to contain individual bullying and violence.

CULTURE WARS: PEACE MOVEMENTS VERSUS MILITARISTS

The real search for a cure for bullying and violence should begin with movements to transform society. Individual bullies and their prey are victims of a society that encourages aggression, competition, violence, and bullying. Their personal problems are real. One sign of that pathology is that, under orders, they can be made to attack and bully or even kill other people with whom they have no direct contact and for whom they have no personal animosity. Enabling such individuals to adjust to pathological institutions will not solve their traumas. If we want to stop or at least control bullying, "rehabilitating" individual bullies and their victims by helping them to "adjust" to their situation could well be a self-defeating approach.

The psychological literature on bullying rarely considers peace movements, but perhaps they are the real antibullying campaigns, with the goal of ending the policies that encourage and reward bullying. These movements are neglected for two reasons. One is that they are not something psychotherapists are trained to look at. A second and perhaps more important reason is that elites have a stake in promoting bullying, violence, and competition, and as a result, they will strive to make these behaviors seem normal, even admirable, under some circumstances—particularly when they are directed against peoples whom elites deem enemies, not the elites themselves and their allies. Hence, we can expect to see conflicts over how to understand bullying and violence, which will manifest themselves in culture wars.

For decades—actually centuries—there have been peace movements to end the bullying brought on by war, the military, and their impact on the rest of society. Activists in such movements have been met by efforts to discredit them—to treat them as treacherous, cowardly enemies of the patriotic and valorous. Militaristic elites have considered the "peaceniks" as responsible for the suffering and death of frontline soldiers, troops who would achieve victory if only given the right support. This attitude is a way of deflecting responsibility away from the elites who forced the soldiers to face such traumas and transformed them into aggressive but compliant bullies.

The conflict between peace movement activists and their militaristic opponents can be called a culture war, one that is part of the broader culture wars and central to the fate of military and bullying values. The real antibullying movement is the peace movement and its allies in their efforts to end capitalist exploitation, the alienation of everyday life, and other forms of oppression that divide people who should be natural allies. Not surprisingly, though, given the control of the bullying discourse by psychologists, no "expert" on bullying has ever, to our knowledge, even suggested that the peace movement might be the front line—or at least a part—of the antibullying movement. To do so would require endorsing the paradigm shift in understanding bullying that we are offering here.

From the point of view of militaristic capitalist elites, one of the greatest dangers is that the peace movement could reach the frontline soldier. There is a risk that soldiers at the front may see their opponents as fellow victims, also bullied into acting against their will; they might come to feel they have more in common with the people they are ordered to kill than with their superiors. Early in World War I, at Christmas 1914, British and German soldiers heard people singing "Silent Night" on opposite sides of the trenches they occupied. They waved bottles at each other; climbed over the barbed wire separating them; shook hands; and starting drinking, singing, dancing, and playing games together. Had they continued, the war might have ended and both empires might have collapsed—an outcome that would have been decidedly detrimental to officers, aristocrats, and capitalists but possibly beneficial to ordinary people bullied into fighting for a cause they did not understand. The officers of each side threatened to court-martial their own troops for treason, an offense for which the soldiers could be shot by their own country's guns. Then the men were ordered to return to their trenches and resume killing each other, which they did. At that time, they succumbed to their own country's elite bullies, who were arguably their real enemies, not the fellow soldiers who wore different uniforms.[40] When Russian troops turned on their officers, the czarist regime collapsed. The war did end when, four years later, German sailors refused to leave port.

As the US government and capitalist class contemplated entering World War I, they had to manipulate popular sentiment to support the war effort and fight their battles. Opposition had to be suppressed. But songs such as "I Didn't Raise My Boy to Be a Soldier," which implied the war was little more than a pointless waste of blood—a ruthless bullying ritual—were popular; "I Didn't Raise My Boy" alone sold 700,000 copies:

> Ten million soldiers to the war have gone,
> Who may never return again . . .
> For the ones who died in vain . . .
> I didn't raise my boy to be a soldier . . .
> Who dares to put a musket on his shoulder,
> To shoot some other mother's darling boy? . . .
> It's time to lay the sword and gun away.[41]

When the United States finally joined the war in 1917, the population was enticed with patriotic rhetoric, designed to control the mass mind and make resistance to the effort simply un-American and unimaginable. Though a large percentage of the white American population was of German ancestry and though, prior to the declaration of war, few Americans harbored hostile stereotypes about Germans, the state and its allies in the media instantly transformed the German into the "Hun"—a savage and insatiable barbarian, intent on destroying all that was civilized, decent, pure, and holy. This campaign was largely effective, but there remained a sizable antiwar movement, which had to be controlled with a more direct bludgeon. Freedom of speech was abolished. The Alien and Sedition Act made it a criminal offense to speak against the war, to interfere with bond sales or enlistment, and to encourage draft resistance. Immigrants were rounded up and deported. Labor leader Eugene Debs was sent to prison for suggesting the masses were being bullied into killing and dying for the capitalists, their real enemies:

> The poor, ignorant serfs had been taught to revere their masters; to believe that when their masters declared war upon one another, it was their patriotic duty to fall upon one another and to cut one another's throats for the profit and glory of the lords and barons who held them in contempt . . . the working class who fight all the battles, the working class who make the supreme sacrifices, the working class who freely shed their blood and

furnish the corpses, have never yet had a voice in either declaring war or making peace. It is the ruling class that invariably does both. They alone declare war and they alone make peace. . . . You need at this time especially to know that you are fit for something better than slavery and cannon fodder.[42]

In 1920 while he was in jail, Debs received 919,799 votes for president of the United States (3.4 percent of the total cast), a sign of the antibullying cultural sensibilities during wartime and immediately afterward—and of the potential potency of the peace and justice movements in leading the fight against bullying values.[43]

Although there was an antiwar movement during World War II, it was relatively small.[44] Today, World War II veterans are commonly referred to, especially by the mass media, as "the greatest generation,"[45] an accolade coined by NBC News anchor Tom Brokaw because they rallied to the call to fight with little resistance and achieved a victory that assured American domination until another big war—Vietnam. Nevertheless, according to Brig. Gen. Samuel Lyman Atwood Marshall, 70 percent of World War II combat soldiers never fired a weapon.[46] Apparently, for the majority, the moral and psychological inhibitions against killing were too powerful. Marshall concluded that army training had failed to produce sufficiently compliant bullies, and he recommended reforms in training practices, as well as in school curricula and pedagogy—and cultural values and institutions. By his criteria, the changes were successful; in Korea, Vietnam, Iraq, and Afghanistan, the majority of troops shot their weapons. However, most of the actual killing was done by a tiny minority. In Vietnam, ordinary soldiers shot 25,000 bullets for every Vietnamese confirmed to have been killed, but a select group of specially trained snipers killed a "gook" for every 1.3 bullets fired. For the most part, these bullies were shunned, and they were "widely perceived to have the coldest hearts in the US military."[47] The sniper's perspective was given in a *Boston Globe* article: "'Back in Vietnam, our own people called us 'Murder Inc.,' says Jack Coughlin, a retired Marine sniper and author of 'Shock Factor: American Snipers in the War on Terror.' 'They thought we were psychopathic killers. But the whole point of our existence is to be there on overwatch to minimize the threat to our own men.'"[48]

The government, especially the Pentagon, and the corporations and many in the media certainly collaborated to make being the most violent bullies in Vietnam seem heroic and glorious. Dying in combat, giving his life for his country, was a fate a true American parent should want for a son. In the popular song "Ballad of the Green Berets," a dying Green Beret hopes his son will grow up to wear a uniform with silver wings just like his.[49]

During the Vietnam era, despite the best efforts of the Pentagon and the increase in combat soldiers who fired weapons, the consensus that had emerged since World War II—that soldiers were heroes who were to be admired and emulated—collapsed. It became apparent that the military's attempt to convey its bullying values throughout society had failed, at least temporarily. Hundreds of thousands of young men resisted the draft, sought asylum in Canada or other countries, or deserted.[50] Some antiwar rallies drew nearly a million participants. As the war came to a close, the peace movement reached the front line: many troops ignored orders to seek out the designated enemy and instead passed out marijuana joints.

The culture wars we referred to in other chapters were at their greatest intensity during the Vietnam era. As in World War I, the military establishment struggled to bully the antiwar movement into silence. Like Debs, acclaimed pediatrician Benjamin Spock and Yale University chaplain Sloan Coffin were indicted for encouraging draft resistance.[51] Meanwhile, the security apparatus tried to discredit the movement by sending agent provocateurs who would attempt, sometimes successfully, to intimidate pacifists into turning to violence.[52]

The divisions of the culture wars have given rise to two very different interpretations of the lessons of Vietnam. One side has understood it as proving that there are limits to American power and that a militaristic empire cannot bully and impose its will on another people with impunity. To the other side, it has shown that the greatest country in the history of the earth must never lose its will, must never hesitate or display signs of weakness, and must use its full might to guarantee success. According to those on this side, there is no alternative to victory, and America must always prevail. As the most powerful and the most moral nation on the planet, the only thing that can defeat America is Americans. In Vietnam, therefore, the troops were betrayed; to deny the valiant dead their victory is to allow them to die in vain. The other side—the so-called peaceniks—have interpreted this assertion as tantamount to claiming that the way to make sure they did not die in vain is to have more die in vain.

However, beginning with the Reagan regime in 1980, peace activists fighting post-Vietnam militarism often found themselves bullied into silence or irrelevancy. One consequence of this is that the wars in Iraq and Afghanistan, though unpopular, did not provoke a mass movement on US streets as Vietnam did.

Reagan spoke of the "Vietnam syndrome," a disease that sapped America of its confidence:

> For too long, we have lived with the Vietnam syndrome. This is a lesson for all of us in Vietnam. If we are forced to fight, we must have the means and determination to prevail, or we will not have what it takes to secure peace. And . . . we will never again ask young men to fight and possibly die in a war our government is afraid to let them win.[53]

According to many on the right during the post-Vietnam era, the troops were betrayed; they were "stabbed in the back" by protesters and politicians at home—an interpretation very similar to one Adolf Hitler used to explain Germany's defeat in World War I.[54] Hitler thought Germany was always good; Reagan and his followers thought America could never be wrong. Beginning with Reagan, the remnants of the Left and the peace movement were bullied into not questioning the overall purpose of America's militaristic empire. At best, they could say mistakes might have been made, but the nation's ultimate intentions—whatever the bullying techniques—were always magnanimous.

Today, as in World War I, there are some people who cannot be bullied into silence, such as Chelsea Manning or Edward Snowden, who showed the American people the Pentagon's own records in Iraq and Afghanistan along with its surveillance of millions of American civilians. But these very people have been bullied with threats of military prison sentences if they should be found within American jurisdiction.

To be listened to and be allowed to challenge an aggressive, bullying foreign policy in recent years, even if that means being threatened with arrest, it appears you need military credentials, which is an implicit sign of the continuing power of the military and the tenaciousness of its bullying culture. Chelsea Manning—born male and formerly known as Bradley Manning—was an intelligence analyst for the army in Iraq.[55] Edward Snowden was a system administrator for the Central Intelligence Agency and a counterintelligence trainer at the Defense Intelligence Agency.[56] Liberal CNN turned to generals to criticize the wars in Iraq and Afghanistan. Generals might question the wisdom of a particular policy, but they would never question the underlying purpose of the American military establishment. One opponent whose opinions were heard in the media was Cindy Sheehan, but she was a "Gold Star mother" who had lost her son in Iraq.[57]

Some people who were prominent figures in the peace movement shrank from their past in later years. For instance, John Kerry had organized Vietnam

Veterans against the War, but when he accepted the Democratic nomination for president, he began his speech with a military salute; then he announced he was "reporting for duty" and filled the stage with veterans, whom he referred to as "brothers." "Our band of brothers doesn't march together because of who we are as veterans," he pronounced, "but because of what we learned as soldiers. We fought for this nation because we loved it."[58] Of course, Kerry's opponent in the presidential race, George W. Bush, and the Bush campaign continually reminded the electorate of Kerry's cowardice and treachery.

To cure the Vietnam syndrome, there has been a campaign to make militaristic and bullying values pervasive and shove alternative perspectives onto the sidelines. Anyone who fought in any of the nation's wars is deemed a hero deserving of deferential esteem. The "MIA-POW: You are not forgotten" flag flies on public buildings everywhere. Bomber pilots such as John McCain, who spent time in a Vietnamese prisoner-of-war (POW) camp, are upheld as paragons of moral virtue. Films and other mass media outlets play a major role in the resurrection of this militaristic bullying culture.

The movie *American Sniper* presents Christopher Kyle as the ultimate heroic savior of all that is pure, holy, and vulnerable.[59] Other soldiers call him a "legend." Early in the movie, we see his father, who gave him a hunting rifle when he was eight years old, lecture Chris that there are three kinds of people: sheep, wolves, and sheepdogs. He warns, "We ain't raising no sheep in this house . . . and if you become a wolf," as he shows Chris his belt. This metaphor certainly summarizes much of what the public sees in the media. It does not apply just to the military but to domestic security forces such as the police as well. Turn on the television and you will find a police show conveying the idea that the more aggressive a cop is, the more heroic he is. We should not restrain him because there are lots of wolves out there and we need our sheepdogs to protect us sheep. Just as the military must not be grounded by hesitant, nervous politicians or peaceniks, the police must not be handcuffed by civil libertarians; otherwise, the wolves will run rampant.

In urban black ghettos, the police have been anything but handcuffed, although they certainly have *used* their handcuffs. In 2015, police violence against black young men created a national crisis, as highlighted by the protest movement known as Blacks Lives Matter. In the St. Louis suburb of Ferguson, a police officer fatally shot an unarmed black man who allegedly had robbed a store. After a grand jury acquitted the officer, massive protests erupted over a sense that black lives were not valued and that the police were in the ghettos primarily to protect capitalist institutions, not black lives.

Many of the demonstrators felt the police were in their neighborhood to intimidate and bully residents, not to improve the quality of life. The first concern of Missouri governor Jeremiah Nixon was to bring in the National Guard to ensure protestors did not threaten homes or corporate or government property: "More than 2,200 members of the Guard, he said, had been called for possible duty, and 1,200 were in and around the St. Louis region on Tuesday evening, protecting homes and businesses. A night earlier, 700 members of the Guard had been largely limited to protecting government buildings, including a police command post."[60]

Similarly, Baltimore was placed under a curfew as the National Guard was called up over violent demonstrations following the death of a black man while in police custody. Allegedly, the police had fatally injured his spine, and twelve days later, the Baltimore district attorney indicted six Baltimore police officers on charges ranging from second-degree murder and manslaughter to false imprisonment. It can be argued that beyond the horrific alleged police bullying, the rioters were themselves guilty of bullying, but it is clear that Maryland governor Lawrence Hogan wanted to protect business interests. He noted that "200 businesses were destroyed in rioting."[61]

Despite the bullying on the part of the police in real life, the media, with few exceptions, encourage us to applaud when we watch television programs that show fictional police, soldiers, FBI agents, and CIA personnel breaking into buildings and waving submachine guns. They are to be acclaimed as heroes, like Chris Kyle. Convinced that the sheepish public craves heroes, the former commander of the Green Berets, retired general William Boykin, praised Kyle and the movie about him:

> I think Americans are so fed up in terms of what they see as a lack of leadership in the Congress and the White House and every sector of our society that they are drawn to a movie like this because it shows a real hero, a real leader, a person who understands what their transcendent cause is, what's worth fighting, sacrificing and even dying for. . . . That's a very strong and powerful message, and I think it attracts Americans to it. . . . When you make heroes out of people that are clearly patriots . . . I think it's just too much for the left. But who cares? . . . A good sniper is irreplaceable. . . . A good sniper—who is really good at not just his marksmanship but is mentally switched on to understand the environment. . . . I hope they understand that veterans have paid a dear price, and I hope that translates into programs to hire veterans, to supports veterans and their

families. . . . I hope that it gets America fired up to want to have a strong military and to want to take care of our veterans.[62]

Movies such as *American Sniper* are intended to encourage the public, the sheep, to become sheepdogs or, if that's not possible, at least be grateful to the sheepdogs for protecting them from the wolves.

The question remains: who is the bully? Put another way, how do we distinguish the sheepdogs from the wolves? The military has found outlets throughout civilian society to drive home its values and answers. During the wars in Iraq and Afghanistan, we continually heard the mantra, "Support the Troops." You can drive down highways and see posters with that slogan, along with American and MIA-POW flags, yellow ribbons, and the names of veteran and dead soldiers hanging from the overpasses. The Boy Scouts organization features "The Ballad of the Green Berets" on its website and offers merit badges in firing rifles and shotguns (although it now requires Eagle Scouts to earn a merit badge in environmental science or sustainability). At major sports events such as the World Series or the Super Bowl, there is a call for a pause to honor the troops, as color guards from each of the armed services carry the flags of their branches onto the field. The entire stadium is expected to stand for the singing of "The Star-Spangled Banner" as fighter planes fly overhead. The message is clear: soldiers sacrificed for our country and therefore are worthy of unquestioned admiration and support. Time in the military is referred to as "service," something inherently unselfish. If you support the troops, you do not wonder if the cause for which they joined this killing, bullying institution was necessary, moral, just, or good for most of Americans or most of humanity. If they have sacrificed, it *must* be good, and we cannot allow their sacrifice to be in vain.

Of course, this campaign is an effort to discredit any potential antiwar movement and to make protestors seem like unappreciative bullies who want to impose their un-American agenda on the rest of the country—individuals who hold in contempt their country's values and institutions, especially its military. Stories abound about veterans returning from Vietnam being bullied and spat upon. Some veterans did feel shunned, both by protestors who saw them as "baby killers" and by self-described patriots who saw them as weak cowards who lost a war. However, according to Lembcke, there are no documented cases of Vietnam veterans being spat upon.[63]

In reality, most of those involved in the peace movement tried to make a sharp distinction between the wars along with the institutions, values, and leaders who promoted those conflicts, on the one side, and soldiers and veterans as individuals who were seduced and bullied by the warlords, on the other. The protestors may not have supported the cause for which the troops were dying and being sacrificed, but they sympathized with them as victims.

The "bravery" of the warlords is epitomized by Lord Farquaad in the animated film *Shrek*: as he is about to send out knights to slay a dragon holding the fair maiden and princess Farquaad hopes to marry, he declares, "Some of you may die, but it's a sacrifice I am willing to make."[64]

In World War I, the song "I Didn't Raise My Boy to Be a Soldier" and Debs's speech revealed a profound desire to save lives as well as compassion for the individual frontline soldier. During Vietnam, the slogan "Support the Troops; Bring Them Home Now!" was widely popular: if the troops were dying in vain, then having the war continue would just mean more would die in vain.

Demonstrators mourned the deaths of American soldiers in Vietnam. In 1969, during the March against Death that went from Arlington National Cemetery to the White House, every participant held a placard with the name of a US soldier killed in Southeast Asia. Each soldier's name was read aloud in front of the White House; it took two days to read all 45,000 of them.[65] In solidarity with conscripted soldiers during the Vietnam War, peace activists opened dozens of coffeehouses near military bases: "They were places soldiers could go for support and to get organized and were part of the huge groundswell of anti-war resistance in the military that saw mutinies, fragging of officers and a mass campaign against the draft."[66] Although these coffee shops closed down for a number of years after Vietnam, they were revived during the wars in Iraq and Afghanistan near bases such as Fort Hood, Texas. While there was a draft during the Vietnam War, opponents would go to selective service offices early in the morning and distribute leaflets to draft victims as they were about to board buses heading for the induction centers. By the time Nixon abolished the draft, there were more resisters than inductees.[67]

To undermine the opposition, leaders of the military establishment gave up their most powerful bullying tool, the draft, in 1973. That one tool had shown they truly ruled the society, for it enabled them to seize a citizen, against his will, and force him to do their killing and dying for them. In the absence of a draft, they had to find new ways to bully, to intimidate the civilian population into serving them. As we have seen, one technique was to malign the opposition, portraying opponents as treacherous bullies who were trying to undermine the greatest nation that ever existed on the planet. The history of the World War I peace movement has been substantially rewritten and almost erased from memory. There is a danger that the same may happen to the Vietnam antiwar movement as MIA-POW flags fly everywhere. For the foreseeable future, the military establishment and its allies will continue to attempt to control and indoctrinate the population.

The only thing that can reduce the effectiveness of these efforts will be an opposition peace movement, which must be prepared to face hostility in a militarized capitalist society. Martin Luther King led the way when he decided, "I could never again raise my voice against the violence of the oppressed in the ghettos without having first spoken clearly to the greatest purveyor of violence in the world today: my own government."[68] Like King, if we are to end bullying, we must speak out against the greatest bully of all.

CHAPTER SEVEN

Schooling for Bullies

Education and Bullying

Every society needs institutions that teach the next generation its values, traditions, and necessary skills. The family was the original school, but the school system as we know it is essentially a creation of industrial capitalism, and it was explicitly designed to develop a population that would maintain militaristic capitalism.

Children may automatically bully on their own without needing any adult influence. However, the bullying that occurs in school—the type of bullying that gets the most attention in the media—may be encouraged, intentionally or unintentionally, by the schools themselves. Schools have internal contradictions. They must teach both aggression and civility, and educators are apt to think of themselves as serving children, not militaristic capitalism. Recently, we have seen the growth of an antibullying movement in the schools, which may or may not have a sustained impact.

Before the mid-nineteenth century, formal schooling was mainly a luxury for the rich. British private schools (called "public schools" because they were an alternative to being taught at home by a governess) were expected to breed decorum, manners, and refinement among gentlemen, but the everyday experience within the schools would hardly seem like refinement. Although students were required to study formal subjects such as Latin, grammar, and mathematics, these were secondary in importance. The real lessons were embodied in the culture of the school, and it was there that "manly manners" were acquired—and often demonstrated through aggressive bullying.

One of the most memorable descriptions of this type of school appears in Thomas Hughes's disguised autobiography, *Tom Brown's School Days.*[1] At Rugby, Tom Brown's school, students' popularity depended upon how stoically they could endure bullying, "take their medicine like men,"[2] and then become bullies themselves when given the opportunity. Those who could not meet these challenges were apt to be labeled as "young mammy-sick." Younger students became "fags" to the older students: as such, they were virtually slaves who faced routine beatings, and they were expected to obey the older boys' every command, even doing their homework. In the British public school, younger students might accept the brutality and perceive this as a just system because they could anticipate that as they grew older, they, in turn, could bully their fags. The confidence that a bully victim could one day be a bully master was an upper-class privilege that most victims, outside the elites, could never achieve.

Hughes was convinced that brutality carried out in a "manly spirit" was not bullying. Rather, it was something that would produce "better men" in the future, precisely the type of men needed to maintain the British Empire and assert power and control over the native peoples in the colonies. This attitude was parodied by Bertolt Brecht in *The Threepenny Opera* when he showed former British officers reminiscing about their army experience:

> If we get feeling down we wander into town.
> And if the population should greet us with indignation
> We chop 'em to bits
> Because we like our hamburgers raw.[3]

SCHOOLING FOR MILITARISTIC CAPITALISM

Public schools in the American sense, that is, state-sponsored schools for the general population, became the norm in the United States in the late nineteenth and early twentieth centuries. As industrial capitalism matured, it needed workers conditioned to accept the bullying regimentation of the factory assembly line, individuals who could sit or stand still, work without questioning their assigned tasks, and gratefully anticipate the reward of a paycheck. America may envision itself as a melting pot, amalgamating people from diverse backgrounds into a common culture. But former black slaves and immigrants from southern and eastern Europe and, later, Latin America, Asia, and Africa had to be taught patriotism and capitalist values. To help achieve this, Andrew Carnegie established the Carnegie Foundation for the Advancement of Teaching. The industrialist confidently declared, "This true panacea for all the ills of the body politic bubbles forth—education, education, education."[4]

Like the British public (private) schools, America's true public schools taught formal subjects, but the form of the education, the pedagogical style, may have been the real lesson, not the content. There was a "hidden curriculum,"[5] more powerful than the official, overt curriculum. Unlike British public schools, designed to breed gentlemen, American public schools and even British state-run schools were developed to produce a labor force. With some exceptions that will be discussed shortly, students were typically expected to sit silently in rows and focus their attention on one authority figure: the teacher. The teacher conveyed facts that students were expected to spit back, having hardly reflected on their meaning.

In the modern school, the teacher, whatever her intentions, clearly acts as a bully as she carries out the imperatives of the larger bullying institution and conveys its values and expectations to her students. She may appear to bully gently, but she is expected to bring students to accept authority, seek her approval, and comply with her views and directions. As a reward for docility, students receive good grades, something directly parallel to receiving paychecks in the adult world. Ironically, the desire to get high marks can negatively impact learning:

> [First,] as motivation to get good grades goes up, motivation to explore ideas tends to go down. Second, students try to avoid challenging tasks whenever possible. More difficult assignments, after all, would be seen as an impediment to getting a top grade. Finally, the quality of students' thinking is less impressive. One study after another shows that creativity and even long-term recall of facts are adversely affected by the use of traditional grades.[6]

Grades teach that learning is not something intrinsically valuable but an external reward for learning information for a test and then promptly forgetting it. Moreover, students have to turn against each other, competing to see who can best impress the bullying authority. Students must act like bullied workers, not question authority, and let the rulers rule. Defiant students face a variety of sanctions from the adults, although they often are popular among their fellow pupils. They will receive poor or even failing grades, or they may be compelled to repeat a year. For punishment, they will be given detention and required to stay after school. Today, they will be sent to the school guidance counselor or school psychologist. In the past, they may have been spanked or hit. Corporal punishment in schools is now illegal in the Northeast, yet it is still practiced in the South.

An institution whose ostensible purpose is to promote education is not designed to instill a love of learning in most students. If anything, it produces the attitude that learning is something to avoid. From a corporate point of view, that may make sense because learning can lead to questioning. From the perspective of a military, which expects blind obedience, it makes even more sense. The No Child Left Behind Act (NCLBA) considers high schools that send their graduates to the army to be as effective as those that send them to college. It also requires schools that receive federal funds to actively assist the military in recruiting students: "The new NCLBA military recruitment provisions require high schools that receive federal funds to . . . provide, on a request made by military recruiters . . . the same access to secondary school students as is provided generally to post secondary educational institutions or to prospective employers of those students. Schools that fail to comply . . . risk losing federal funds."[7]

In high schools throughout the United States, there are over 3,000 Junior Reserve Officer Training Corps (JROTC) units, each proudly organized under a "chain of command."[8] In some high schools, students are bullied or coerced to join this group. In a Buffalo high school, one student was exempted from the requirement only after the New York Civil Liberties Union sued the school; other students in the school were still bullied to attend.[9] According to the federal statute authorizing the JROTC: "These programs will enable cadets to better serve their country as leaders, as citizens, and in military service should they enter it. . . . The JROTC . . . are not, of themselves, officer-producing programs but should create favorable attitudes and impressions toward the Services and toward careers in the Armed Forces."[10]

At the height of the Vietnam War, Frederick Wiseman filmed everyday occurrences at a Philadelphia high school. During an assembly, the assistant principal read a letter she received from a recent alumnus who had been a "subaverage student." When he wrote the letter, he was about to go on a bombing mission over North Vietnam, and he had left his GI insurance to the school in the event he did not make it back. He thanked the school staff for the values they had taught him, and he asked them not to mourn for him because he realized he was "only a body doing a job." Near tears, the assistant principal announced that when she received such a letter, she knew that "we are very successful at Northeast High School."[11]

Someone who accepted that he was "a body doing a job," who would "not reason why, just do and die" was a success for Northeast High School. He was bullied by the educators and military officers above him to proudly bully—that is, bomb—those below him. This is an attitude that the military expects high schools to cultivate, since it is crucial to military recruitment and success.

Right from its inception, the school system was replete with contradictions. To serve militaristic capitalism, children from diverse backgrounds had to be "Americanized." Families, especially immigrant or rural families coming from places where the family unit was more powerful, believed their children were theirs to raise as they saw fit, teaching them the family's values and culture. Schools whose purpose was to Americanize their children might have opposed this purpose. Many parents saw little need for formal schooling and indeed may have been hostile to it. Until the early twentieth century, the child may well have been more valuable as an economic asset, to help on the farm or bring money home from the factory. To end child labor and weaken the power of "un-American" families, schooling was made compulsory. The founders of the school system saw themselves as rescuing children from bullying families, but families often saw themselves as being bullied into giving up authority over their children.

That is not to say that children cheerfully went to the schools. Although some viewed school as an escape from the factory or an authoritarian family, many saw being forced to attend as being bullied by their parents, the state, or the school system itself. This remains true today. If young children enter school with enthusiasm, they tend to lose it as they advance to higher grades—evidence that schools may succeed in their real goal, which is to destroy, not build, a love of learning. According to one study, "The love of school diminishes with each passing year, going from almost 100 percent who love being in kindergarten to about a third who feel the same way about 9th grade."[12]

In preparing students for the labor market, schools typically teach that learning is work, not fun, and they take the pleasure out of learning. One year in the early 2000s, the state board of education required every fourth-grader in Massachusetts to write an essay on this topic: "A Dream Come True! It is snowing and there is no school. What would you do on that happy day?" The people who run the education system cannot imagine that any child would choose to be in school if she could be someplace else. Children may see teachers and school administrators as bullying enemies who could not possibly have their best interests in mind.

BULLYING TEACHERS

One popular book that resonates with children is Roald Dahl's *Matilda*.[13] It describes a sadistic principal named Agatha Trunchbull who hates children and runs a school so she can indulge in her greatest pleasure—torturing them. Young Matilda is rescued by a teacher, Miss Honey, who, although she is bullied by Trunchbull and terrified of her, strives to make children love learning.

Thus far, we have indicated that contradictions are embedded in the school system, but we have not fully discussed them. One contradiction is that teachers usually chose their profession not to make children hate learning but to bring them to love it. When Secretary of Education Arne Duncan asked teachers on the web why they chose to teach, he got responses such as the following:

> I want my students to love to learn! . . . I want my students to know that history is filled with ordinary people doing extraordinary things and students can do anything . . . create life long compassionate learners motivated to improve themselves and this country. And change the view of this profession. . . . [I] hope to create agents of change and instill in my students a love for learning and [help them] understand that their voices matter . . . promote a love of learning, guide them to think critically, and not just take tests.[14]

Many teachers are forced into imposing institutional expectations that they themselves oppose. Thus, they are being bullied by the school or grading requirements to bully their students and carry out institutional bullying, as noted in chapter 1, even though they may not personally intend to humiliate or dominate their students. High among administrators' criteria for judging teachers are classroom management (a corporate term) and maintenance of order and discipline.[15] Some veterans of the protest movements and counterculture of the 1960s and 1970s, many of whom were alienated from their own educational experiences, went into teaching to transform schools from bullying institutions that reinforced authority to "child-centered" places where children could explore, express themselves, develop their curiosity, learn to appreciate other cultures, and be creative. But if the real purpose of school is to provide a docile labor force for corporations and cannon fodder for the military, then child-centered education was not doing its job. In reaction, a "back-to-basics" movement emerged, beginning in the Reagan regime. Schools were to build respect for authority and patriotism; place more emphasis on memorizing facts than on independent thinking; and teach basic skills such as reading, writing, and arithmetic.

One of the original architects of the back-to-basics approach, Diane Ravitch, later denounced it for creating schools that served corporations, not children. "The reformers define the purpose of education as preparation for global competitiveness, higher education, or the workforce," she stated. "They view students as 'human capital' or 'assets.' One seldom sees any reference in their literature or public declarations to the importance of developing full persons to assume the responsibilities of citizenship."[16]

Another strong advocate of the back-to-basics movement was Lynne Cheney, wife of Secretary of Defense and Vice President Richard Cheney and herself chair of the National Endowment for the Humanities during the Reagan and George H. W. Bush presidencies. Alarmed that multicultural, child-centered education was undermining patriotism and support for military adventurism, she wrote sarcastically:

> As American students learn more about the faults of this country and about the virtues of other nations, . . . they will be less and less likely to think this country deserves their special support. They will not respond to calls to use American force, and thus we will be delivered from the dark days of the early 1990s, when President George Bush was able to unify the nation in support of war against Iraq, and be able to return to the golden days of the late 1960s and early 1970s, when no president was able to build support for Vietnam.[17]

The back-to-basics approach strove to impose uniform standards upon the curriculum. Teachers could be severely sanctioned or even fired for not upholding the very patriotic ideology Lynne Cheney demanded:

> Upholding the dismissal of a St. Louis teacher for allowing her students to use profanity in a creative-writing course, a court recently declared that the Constitution did not protect her "student-centered teaching method." . . . During the buildup to the Iraq invasion in 2003, an Indiana teacher lost her job for telling her class . . . that she had driven by an antiwar rally and honked her horn in support. . . . An Ohio teacher was dismissed for asking her students to select and read one of the American Library Association's most commonly banned books.[18]

One outcome of the back-to-basics movement was a demand for uniform accountability standards that could be measured by imposing a single test for entire school systems. The No Child Left Behind Act made federal school funding dependent upon students' test scores. Teachers now felt bullied into "teaching to the test." They could no longer encourage students' interests, creativity, independence, and joy of learning. In many school districts, the teachers themselves were tested. A good number of the most dedicated and creative teachers felt they were being driven out of the profession. Around 2010, half a million educators, about 20 percent of all teachers, were leaving or transferring annually, most often giving job dissatisfaction as the reason for their decision to leave.[19] Jonathan Zimmerman, a professor of education at New York University, laments: "If anything, the strong commitment to 'academic' goals has probably made teaching *less* academic—so far as the quality of learning is concerned—and more routinized than it was before. . . . We've created a system that is so firmly tied to scholastic achievement—as narrowly defined by standardized tests—that no serious scholar would want to teach in it."[20]

Today, teachers are being scapegoated, held responsible for everything that is wrong with the schools. The possibility that the root cause could lie with the organizers of the school system and their agenda is not open for consideration. Problems that lie beyond the scope of the school system, such as poverty, are not considered a legitimate excuse for poor teacher performance. The former superintendent of the Washington, DC, schools, Michelle Rhee, believes that student performance should be used as a stick to bully teachers:

> Poverty presents huge challenges in our schools. But expectations of academic success for a child should never hinge on the circumstances of his or her birth. . . . Too often, principals in low-income schools are forced to fill their vacancies with teachers excessed from other schools regardless of whether they are a good fit. These teachers may not be performing particularly well but have to be retained by the system because of seniority-based job protections.[21]

Ravitch now feels that the whole back-to-basics movement has become self-defeating, bullying both teachers and students and undermining the schools. She writes:

> Anyone who truly cares about children must be repelled by the insistence on ranking them, rating them, and labeling them. Whatever the tests measure is not the sum and substance of any child. The tests do not measure character, spirit, heart, soul, potential. When overused and misused, when attached to high stakes, the tests stifle the very creativity and ingenuity that our society needs most. Creativity and ingenuity stubbornly

resist standardization. Tests should be used sparingly to help students and teachers, not to allocate rewards and punishments and not to label children and adults by their scores.[22]

Elsewhere, Ravitch writes:

These approaches will narrow the curriculum and promote teaching to the test, which will rob children of the opportunity for a good education ... all have the potential to disrupt students' education, demoralize teachers, and shatter communities. What we need to improve education in this country is a strong, highly respected education profession; a rich curriculum in the arts and sciences ... CHILDREN NEED TIME FOR RECESS AND PLAY. And schools should have classes small enough for students to get the attention they need. ... We will not improve it by driving out experienced professionals.[23]

BULLYING BOYS

Bullying teachers into being agents of militarized capitalism, against their will, is certainly one contradiction within the school system. But in this section, we will turn to an even more fundamental contradiction. As we pointed out in previous chapters, capitalism requires not only a docile labor force but also independent and creative innovators who develop new technologies and techniques as well as manage the system. Even the military needs new weapons technologies and creative strategists. If all the schools produce is blind and bullied conformists, where will these innovators come from? Political economists Samuel Bowles and Herbert Gintis suggest there are two different school systems. One, found in poor neighborhoods, is designed to produce obedient workers and cannon fodder; the other, found in private schools and wealthy suburbs, is designed to produce creative, independent thinkers. In the affluent schools, students may be encouraged to explore, express themselves, and possibly even challenge the teachers and other authorities, thereby potentially threatening the bullying system underlying traditional schooling. As Bowles and Gintis observe, "U.S. education is not monolithic. ... [Some schools] provide the child with the freedom to develop 'naturally' with a teacher as guide, not taskmaster. Intrinsic interest was to motivate all work ... and the aim was to sublimate natural creative drives in fruitful directions, rather than repress them."[24]

Perhaps the two school systems can coexist in the same building, with honors sections and special needs or vocational sections. The sections may even coexist in the same classroom, with the teacher encouraging some "A" students to freely explore, while demanding silence or one-word answers from other, failing students.

Capitalist ideology claims it is a meritocratic system that provides equal opportunity but not equal results. People may be very different, but they should all be given a chance to exhibit and develop their full potential. Southern segregated schools actually denied capitalism whatever contributions talented blacks might have made. Similarly, authoritarian schools in poorer communities, which suppress all students' creativity and love of learning, would deny corporations and other powerful institutions the skills of students who would thrive in a more tolerant setting. So from an elite point of view, it would be wise to not treat all pupils the same way and to let curious students flourish and express themselves.

Teachers, who would feel alienated and frustrated in front of a class of hostile students, might welcome engaged pupils and be inclined to grant them special attention and privileges. This might, though, breed greater resentment among the other students, who would turn all the more strongly against the "teacher's pets," "brownnosers," and "nerds." Even in wealthier schools, which are more likely to foster independent thinking, there would be divisions among students. The militaristic capitalist culture beyond the school might make more athletic or aggressive boys or better-dressed girls role models whom their classmates would emulate, pushing the more academic types to the side, if they are not directly bullied. Some students might feel bullied into participating in the bullying culture because if they were to befriend the victims, they would risk being identified with them and becoming victims themselves.

Even if adults reward students who have not lost their curiosity, the student culture—certainly in the poorer schools and even in wealthier ones—reinforces the ideology that learning is something to shun. Some school authorities may officially condemn that culture while tacitly turning a blind eye to it or even reinforcing it. If nonelite schools are actually supposed to encourage children to avoid learning, then teachers and other school authorities have failed to convey that message to the children who still seek knowledge.

The burden for teaching the real lesson may fall on the student culture. The mechanism for transmitting it: bullying. In *The Bully Society,* Jessie Klein suggests:

At best, being smart, earning good grades, and showing interest in school work may place students outside the popular crowd, while at worst it can make them downright outcasts. A 2006 study of gifted children found that 67 percent of them reported being bullied by the time they reached the eighth grade and that many had been teased about their school performance. Rick, the school editor of his high school newspaper in a low-income northeastern rural area, said the kid who got picked on most in his school, Oliver, is "always reading. He loves books and you see him sitting in a corner reading and he gets made fun of for that. They call him 'fag' and 'Mama's boy.'"[25]

To avoid being labeled as a nerd, that is, someone who compensates for social failure through developing intellectual interests, many boys deliberately undermine their own academic performance.[26]

A PERSONAL ASIDE FROM YALE MAGRASS

I was the kid who got picked on most in my high school in a northeastern inner-city neighborhood. I certainly was a nerd, and I was called "fag." In the 1960s, homophobia was so pervasive that few could imagine anyone was really gay. (I was not.) The label was considered the ultimate insult and was used to sanction or bully anyone who violated certain male taboos, such as never appearing vulnerable.

Klein contends that since the 2010s and perhaps much earlier, schools have had "gender police,"[27] who determine what behaviors and attitudes are acceptable for each sex and use bullying to punish anyone who deviates too much from those standards. She asked her own students to characterize both capitalism and masculinity, with this result: "I asked my students to tell me what words they associated with capitalism. What qualities do you need to be successful in our society? The board filled up quickly: *competitive, aggressive* and *powerful*. . . . Later . . . I asked my students to list some words they associated with masculinity. The same list emerged—*competitive, aggressive* and *powerful*. Without intending to, my students had highlighted the link between masculinity and capitalism."[28]

In my high school, there was a clear hierarchy, and I was supposed to know my place. I may have been at the top academically, but I was on the bottom socially. The hierarchy was reinforced by both students and faculty, who were transmitting precisely the values the corporations and the military require. Even those who did not bully me directly found it entertaining to watch the bullying. When someone put his hand over my notebook, teachers, who considered me their best student, chuckled. When I left my seat to get back my Scholastic Assessment Test (SAT) scores (very high by the norms of the school), which another student had grabbed, the supervising teacher made me stay after school. When someone put my hand over a Bunsen burner in chemistry lab, the teacher asked me, "Where are you going to repeat chemistry next year?" Years later, I was invited to describe my experience before a group of handi-capped people—and even they reacted by saying that anyone who can be so bullied must deserve it. "Who are you to complain? You got legs," they said, and they asked me repeatedly why I didn't fight back.

British sociologist Paul Willis observes that many students, especially working-class boys, express their anger over the alienation, boredom, and tedium of school by bullying nerds. Boys whom American students might call nerds, Willis's British working-class students (or "lads") call "ear'oles." Willis notes, "[Attitudes toward the] 'ear'oles' are also expressed clearly . . . through phys-ical aggression. Violence and the judgment of violence is the most basic axis of 'the lads' ascendance over the conformists. . . . There is a positive joy in fighting, in causing fights through intimidation, in talking about fighting."[29]

Willis's lads must constantly show control. Like capitalists or armies, they are in a "thrive or be destroyed" competition. Although they themselves are bullied in the school system, they cannot let any other students intimidate them, certainly not nerds or ear'oles. They have to demonstrate they have a "killer's instinct."[30] Willis quotes one of them: "If you don't show your au-thority straight away when somebody starts to pick on you, like, they'll keep on all the time, like, all the kids if they know somebody you can pick on like, or at, they'll play on him for the rest of their life as long as they know him, they'll keep playing up. You gotta show you ain't gonna stand for it in the first place."[31]

Willis's students may be academic failures, but the fact that they can bully the nerds or ear'oles proves they are superior. Bullying becomes a weapon of preserving self-esteem in the context of failure. The nerds may have "book smarts," but Willis's lads have the intelligence that really matters, "street smarts" or "life smarts." Here again, we hear from one of the lads: "Guts, de-termination . . . we know more about life than they do. They might know a bit more about math and science which isn't important. It's important to fuck-ing nobody. That they've got to try and find out . . . they ain't clever in life."[32]

Even teachers do not have to be listened to because they also lack street smarts. As one lad puts it, "They do not know 'the way of the world,' because they have been in schools or colleges all their lives—What do they know telling us?"[33]

These working-class boys define success as making money, essentially the same way capitalists do, but most of them will end up working on a factory assembly line or in Walmart or McDonald's; others will be in the army or unemployed. So by their own criteria, how street smart or life smart are they really? They are rebelling against the confinement and regimentation of school and the stratification system that locks them into poverty and lack of status. Ironically, though, it is a rebellion that serves the very authorities against whom it is fought. With their intellectual interests destroyed, working-class youth compete against each other to show their indifference to school and to be "cool," often by becoming sports heroes and sometimes by being aggressive or even violent. They will strive for sex partners, alcohol, drugs, clothes, and cars that they cannot afford. To pay for these desires, they will take low-paying, low-status jobs at gas stations, McDonald's, and Dunkin' Donuts. The time and energy this absorbs makes their failure at school all the more severe. Many drop out of school altogether, but even if they graduate, they are typically trapped in low-level jobs like the ones they held in high school—if they are able to find work at all. Those working at the worst jobs are told that they are lucky and that they better not do anything to risk them. Romancing violence and aggression, many working-class youth consider joining the army the coolest thing they can do: maybe they can come back as war heroes. Their rebellion does not become an organized movement that threatens the elites, but rather, it becomes a culture that the rich and powerful can manipulate to their benefit. The ultimate result is that they become compliant workers and soldiers who can console themselves with recalling their success in bullying the ear'oles in the schoolyard.

Students from working-class ghettos or factory towns, like Willis's lads, may barely know of the existence of wealthy schools where adults encourage many students—not just a select few—to be independent, creative thinkers. All they know is that attending school is an alienating experience and that the school itself is a place where teachers and other adult authorities bully most pupils, except perhaps for a chosen few. They cannot understand why anyone would voluntarily accede to adult expectations and seem to want to learn. They assume such students are brownnosers, too timid to challenge the adults from whom they need favors and protection. Since they cannot fend for themselves, these students only deserve contempt. In wealthier schools, the nerds might be able to build an enclave for themselves where they can support each other and express their scorn for their bullies, even if they cannot confront them directly. Even there, however, they may be socially marginalized. The athletes and the aggressive dominate. It is not that social outcasts do not want to bully; they simply lack the power to do so. Klein points out that school shootings are often acts of revenge carried out by socially marginalized students, especially boys, who feel they have no other outlet for expressing their anger.[34]

As adults, working-class students who failed in schools suffer from a "hidden injury of class."[35] They see the college graduates, whom they had looked down upon as brownnosers or nerds, as successes, some of whom could now be their bosses—and they come to believe they deserve their fate. The myth of equal opportunity, of schools as "great equalizers," says they had their chance but "blew" it. Capitalist ideology teaches that if you fail, you ain't got nobody to blame but yourself. The successful had the stamina to endure boring, tedious, alienating schools, and they deserve to be where they are. Sociologists Richard Sennett and Jonathan Cobb describe the deference men who did not "make it" in school have toward the educated after they reach adulthood:

> "Well, they're educated people, they must know what they are doing" . . . "maybe there are things about this I don't know." . . . "The people in Washington must know something we don't know, and therefore they have some right to do what they are doing, even though from what we see it makes no sense" . . . the "higher knowledge" of those in power creates at once mystification of power and its legitimacy. The apportionment of mind and knowledge represents the divide between those who judge and those who are the receiving end of judgment.[36]

BULLYING GIRLS

Physical violence is obviously in the toolbox of most boy bullies. But though Klein tells us girl bullies do use physical violence,[37] their bullying usually is expressed through ostracism; ridicule; spreading rumors; text messaging; and posting messages on the web, Facebook, and other cyberspace venues. Reinforcing capitalist values, girl bullying is also about competition to establish a place within a status hierarchy, but it is not over who can be the most physically aggressive. Rather, it is about who is the wealthiest, the best dressed, or the most attractive to boys. This competition builds consumerism and enhances the coffers of corporations. Political economists Paul Baran and Paul Sweezy point out that corporate profits in mature capitalism require creating artificial needs that induce people to consume for consumption's sake.[38] Girls' competition over who has the latest fashion, the most expensive jewelry, the sexiest outfit, or the cutest case for their smartphone and even over who can have their bodies professionally made over fosters exactly the mentality corporations need. Carrie Goldman finds, "Over and over, young girls report being bullied because they have the wrong hair, the wrong clothes, the wrong purse, or . . . the wrong water bottle and back pack."[39]

In marketing, corporations such as Disney dictate what girls must want, and those who resist the trend face ostracism. "Girls are quick," Goldman says, "to throw out a member of the group who does not conform. . . . The Disney princesses, now a cohesive unit, are foisted upon young girls, in effect teaching many of them that a little girl who strays from the pink crowd is no longer welcome."[40]

Men may watch sports regularly, but few are serious athletes as adults. However, encouraging sports among boys builds competitiveness and aggression, two essential values in militaristic capitalism. What matters is that they learn these values; the way they acquire them is secondary. In other words, the form of the lesson is more important than the content. Similarly, anything that cultivates capitalist values in girls serves the same purpose. If bullying each other over boys, appearance, clothes, and other possessions fosters hierarchy, competition, and aggression, it helps mold girls for militaristic capitalism.

Until the 1970s, it was possible to support a family on one income, usually the husband's. This was true even in the working class, when factory jobs were more available and offered better pay. Today, although women of all classes are more likely to seek employment, working-class girls are being trained primarily to have babies for working-class boys or to become waitresses, maids, or store clerks. Like Willis's lads, they are not expected to be academically engaged or financially successful but to accept their place within a capitalist hierarchy that has clearly defined gender roles. They may compete with each other over who has the most attractive clothes, jewelry, and makeup, but they are far less able to do so than girls who attend wealthier schools. Furthermore, even if girls in wealthier schools have more opportunities to be creative and independent, the competition over boys and possessions in their groups may be just as intense, perhaps even more so.

As in the boy hierarchy, academic performance does not enhance a girl's status. In fact, she may deliberately downplay it in order to increase her popularity. As with boys, Klein observes, there are gender police among girls who impose standards of femininity. This situation may have served American capitalism in the immediate post–World War II years. During the war, women staffed the factories while the men fought overseas. But with peace came millions of returning GIs, who felt they had sacrificed for the nation and were now entitled to jobs, security, prosperity, and status. Had they remained underemployed, they might have turned their anger against militaristic capitalism. Women who might otherwise have competed with men for jobs were encouraged to leave the factories; marry the returning veterans; have their babies; move to the suburbs; decorate their houses; and buy, buy, buy. To prepare girls for the traditional housewife role, schools offered courses in home economics. In addition, the state helped establish vocational schools where girls learned to cook and sew.

Cultural values do not die easily. Although the nuclear family with a single male breadwinner may be vanishing, the distinctive gender roles it perpetuated may persist as an ideal. Boys and girls may be being prepared for a division of labor that no longer exists. Working-class women still face tedious jobs as store clerks, fry girls, or housecleaners—or unemployment—yet more girls than boys now pursue advanced education and enter the professions. Even if there have been changes in the curriculum, the school culture, as enforced by the students themselves, may reinforce obsolete gender differences, with the girls competing for boys by presenting themselves as attractive potential wives and mothers as well as supplemental breadwinners.

In the long run, sharp gender distinctions may be self-defeating for militaristic capitalism. The traditional division between gender expectations allows boys to be cool, detached, and analytical, but girls are supposed to be emotional, expressive, and artistic. Although we have seen boys risk being penalized if they are too interested in math and science, such interests are more acceptable for them than for girls. Girls fear being labeled math and science nerds, for they are considered unattractive and lacking in femininity. In a letter written to Carrie Goldman's daughter, she was told: "When I was younger, I got picked on by boys and girls. I went to space camp instead of cheerleading camp, and my mom liked to take me to the science museum instead of the nail salon. Guess what? Now I'm IN school to become a DOCTOR!"[41]

Goldman comments: "It is no wonder that kids taunt girls with boy interests. They are taught by society that girls should only stick to dainty things like flowers and princesses. Girls who play with science kits and solve math equations do not fit the equation and get labeled 'other.'"[42]

Bullying of girl nerds poses the same problem for capitalism that we saw with the deliberate miseducation of blacks and working-class students. At a time when America is at risk of losing its scientific and technological edge, corporations and other powerful institutions need to enhance the analytical, mathematical, and scientific skills of talented people of either gender. In recent years, we have seen a tendency to get girls more engaged in math and science. This may require reducing the bullying of girl nerds and may be a factor in the antibullying movement.

For the most part, though, competition among girls is not about who is the best student, certainly not about who is best in math and science. It is primarily about who is the most attractive to boys. However, if someone is too attractive, she may provoke hostility and bullying and be labeled as being loose or a slut. As in the boy hierarchy, academic performance does not enhance a girl's status. In fact, she may deliberately underplay her academic abilities in order to increase her popularity. Again as with boys, Klein observes, gender police among girls impose standards of femininity. As girls compete over boys, they must be careful not to get the attention of their rivals' potential boyfriends and be seen as invading other girls' turf.

Capitalism breeds competition and teaches that losers deserve their fate. Capitalists try to establish monopolies over markets, resources, and commodities. They are forever trying to expand and to destroy anyone who threatens their control. But capitalists who are too successful can gather enemies. They may provoke price wars or face antitrust lawsuits. Capitalism requires hierarchy, but competition means that hierarchy is under constant threat; consequently, even winners must be on guard and prepared to put any challengers in their place. Like high school boys, high schools girls are being acclimated to a capitalist culture and must compete both over possessions and over their place within a hierarchy. For high school girls, the most valuable commodity is popular boys, and the primary purpose of other commodities—clothes, jewelry, makeup, body makeovers—is to attract high-status boys. There is also a pecking order, with those on the top allowed to monopolize the most desirable boys, but that hierarchy is frail and must be protected. A girl who tries to usurp her place and appeal to boys who are above her station or who have been claimed as others' property or potential property is a candidate for bullying. She will probably be labeled a slut.

Klein learned about this from a girl named Kate: "They called one of her friends a 'slut' because they thought she was too confident with boys. Kate believes she herself became a target because she was 'too pretty' and too attractive to boys: the very qualities that had allowed her to become a member of this powerful clique caused her to be kicked out. . . . 'She can't sit with us anymore.'"[43]

In some cases, a so-called slut dating the "wrong boy" has had literally fatal consequences, as girls do resort to violence. Phoebe Prince, a fifteen-year-old Irish immigrant living in South Hadley, Massachusetts, committed suicide after being called an "Irish Slut" and a "whore" for dating a popular football player. The girls who bullied her felt she had not earned the right to compete with them for boys.[44] In another instance, Reena Virk, a fourteen-year-old girl from South Asia, was beaten and then drowned as dozens of bystanders watched. Two girls trapped her in a park "to teach her a lesson" after she had used one of their phone books to find the number of a boy whom she then called.[45]

As in capitalism, status among girls depends on possessions, not just boys. Of course, possessions help attract boys. Thus, consumerism and competition over boys converge. Klein learned about Lauren from thirteen-year-old Vanessa, who reported:

> When we were friends, she made me think of other things, made me act differently to my other friends. I started acting like her because I thought it was cool, but it made me feel terrible. . . . She would drone on about the places she went to—Alaska, Hawaii, Venice—and things she was getting; it made me feel bad—like I wasn't cool, since I didn't go anywhere. I just felt terrible—like she was much better than I was.[46]

When Vanessa didn't conform, Lauren physically attacked her.

It appears that dress codes are imposed on girls not only by other girls but also by teachers. In this way, teachers help bully girls into not appearing too slutty. As related by Klein: "They sent girls home for wearing a skirt that was too short or a strap that was too thin. A lot of teachers would pull a student out of class and they wouldn't be back. 'You need to come with me,' they would say. 'Your tank top is too revealing.'"[47]

Cyberbullying involving girls' gossip has become so routine that even celebrities treat it as an expected part of high school life. When nude pictures of Jennifer Lawrence were distributed on the web without her consent, she remarked in anger: "The internet has scorned me so much that I feel like it's that girl in high school that I'm like, 'Oh, you want to talk about her? Yeah, I'll do that!' Take my hoops off. I'm ready to go."[48]

Bullying of boys has been treated as cute and funny. So has bullying of girls. And though there always is a risk of trivializing the trauma, comedy can be a way of mitigating the pain of reality. Tina Fey decided to illustrate the torment of girl bullying by transforming a serious book about it, Rosalind Wiseman's *Queen Bees and Wannabees*,[49] into a comic movie entitled *Mean Girls*.[50] In it, Fey shows a culture among high school girls that is almost a microcosm of capitalism, complete with constant bullying and brutal competition over status, boys, and possessions to display. The movie takes place in a wealthy suburban high school where independent and creative exploration might be encouraged. Nevertheless, the main character, Cady (played by Lindsay Lohan), new to the school, is warned that joining the math team is "social suicide." Despite being an outstanding math student, Cady deliberately tries to fail calculus in order to impress a boy. In the cafeteria, there are clearly defined cliques with student-imposed rules about who can sit with whom. Cady is initially befriended by two nerds, who explain the various cliques and point out a table of girls they call the "plastics." (Nerds and social outcasts of both genders often have their own pejorative terms for popular "winners.") One of the nerds, Janis (played by Lizzy Caplan), who is perhaps motivated more by jealousy than by reality, harangues: "You're plastic. Cold, shiny, hard. . . . That's the thing with you plastics. You think that everybody is in love with you when actually, everybody HATES you!"

In response, the plastic girl tells Janis, "You know what! It's not my fault you're like, in love with me, or something!" Homophobia lives among the girls just as it does among the boys. Boys may call each other fags, but girls call each other lesbians, even if they do not believe they are really gay.

The plastics rule the school's social scene in Fey's movie. They, in turn, are ruled by Regina George (played by Rachel McAdams), the queen bee. The plastics actually welcome Cady as they explain specific rules, including how she must dress and wear her hair (with different styles required for different days of the week). They tell Cady whom she is allowed to associate with and that she must avoid her former nerd friends. Regina has even decreed that the queen bee is allowed to wear things forbidden for the other plastics. Gretchen (played by Lacey Chabert) laments:

> If you even knew how mean she really is. . . . You'd know that I'm not allowed to wear hoop earrings, right? Yeah! Two years ago she told me that hoop earrings were "her" thing and that I wasn't allowed to wear them anymore. And then for Hanukkah my parents got me this pair of really expensive white gold hoops, and I had to pretend like I didn't even like them and . . . it was so sad.

Among Regina's repertoire of bullying tactics is making parents fear their daughter is a slut. When she wants to get back at another girl outside the plastic clique, she calls the girl's home, knowing her mother will answer:

REGINA GEORGE: Hello, may I please speak to Taylor Wedell?
TAYLOR WEDELL'S MOM: She's not home yet, who's calling?
REGINA GEORGE: Oh, this is Susan from Planned Parenthood, I have her test results. If you could have her call me as soon as she can. It's urgent. Thank you.
[Taylor Wedell's mom faints.]

As part of her plot to degrade Regina, Cady gives her power bars that she says help in losing weight. They are actually high-calorie nutrition bars intended for gaining pounds. On learning what they really are, Regina feels fat. (In the movie, Rachel McAdams never looks heavy or unattractive.) Regina's ultimate revenge is to anonymously distribute pages of her "Burn Book," full of gossip and lies about students and teachers throughout the school. For example, math teacher Ms. Norbury (played by Tina Fey) is accused of distributing drugs. The school erupts into a riot. To restore calm, the principal and several teachers, including Ms. Norbury, have the students engage in various psychological exercises in which they are forced to express positive feelings and support for each other; for instance, they are told to fall into a crowd of students who must catch and hold them. The exercises result in a burst of good feelings among former enemies and a substantial reduction in bullying.

It is, of course, easier to reduce bullying among boys or girls in a movie than in reality. Militaristic capitalism is a bullying system that needs bullies and people resigned to being bully victims. It needs producers and consumers. Textile mill girls in the 1830s and 1840s may have been the original factory workers, and there may now be a new need for female producers; in the intermediate period, however, women were needed primarily as consumers.

They were expected to attract men, look pretty, have babies, and decorate houses. As we have seen, some schools offered courses in home economics that taught them the skills needed to meet those expectations. But the everyday culture within the schools, more than academic subjects, may actually have taught those lessons far more effectively. Girls were encouraged to police each other. Girls bullying girls established the limits on respectable behavior. Some girls would be bullied for being too masculine, too nerdy, or so attractive that they took the boys other girls wanted. If everyone knew her place, the social hierarchy would be preserved, both at the level of the school and at the level of the larger political economy.

THE PSYCHOLOGICAL PARADIGM IN THE SCHOOLS

Mean Girls has a happy ending. In movies, at least, psychological exercises reduce hostility and bullying. But as we have already pointed out, the psychological paradigm fails to consider how institutions may be served by bullying and thus have an interest in reinforcing and perpetuating it. Until recently, bullying was seen as a supposedly normal part of life. It was something to get over, and those who couldn't take it deserved it. Both adults and children considered it something to ignore or laugh over. In recent times, perhaps beginning with people questioning militarized capitalism in the aftermath of the Vietnam War, bullying has become recognized for what it is and accordingly opposed. Schools now develop antibullying programs. One reason for this may be that many veterans of the protest movements and counterculture of the 1960s and 1970s took jobs in the school system. We will discuss reasons for the growing opposition to bullying in greater depth in a later chapter. Yet we should note here that the treatment of bullying, even within the antibullying movement, has been overwhelming psychological.

Both bullies, who tend to be aggressive, and their victims, who have traits that attract harassment, are treated in the psychological discourse as having personality disorders. One common diagnosis for bullies and their victims alike is attention deficit/hyperactivity disorder (ADHD). These children may be given Ritalin or other drugs that are intended to alter their brain chemistry.[51] The assumption is there is something wrong with a child who cannot sit still for seven or eight hours. The child must adjust. There can be nothing wrong with an institution that makes that expectation. Rather than adapting the school to the child, the child must adapt to the school.

In the psychological paradigm, the main reason people bully or are bullied is related to their individual attitudes. If they thought and felt differently, bullying would not happen. Psychological approaches tend to ignore power. They see communication as the solution: when victims explain to bullies how being harassed feels, the perpetrators will understand the impact, feel remorse, and stop hurting them. But the truth is that bullies often intend to hurt their prey, and telling them they succeeded might only make them feel vindicated and reinforce their behavior. Of course, bullies may feign remorse in front of the school guidance counselor but act very differently when no adult authority is around.

We can see the psychological paradigm conveyed in books written for children. A typical example is *Bullies Are a Pain in the Brain* by Trevor Romain.[52] On the second page, this book reinforces the idea that bullying is normal and universal: "Everyone has been bullied at some point."[53] This declaration ignores the fact that for some children and adults, bullying is an occasional, dismissible event, but for others, it is a constant, life-defining torment. Nor does it address the fact that certain categories of people are far more likely to attract bullying than others. Romain says, "Bullies are people with problems,"[54] suggesting that bullying is purely a psychological condition. This assertion negates the reality that bullying is a privilege that comes with power, and it is beneficial to some people and institutions that have an interest in perpetuating bullying relationships. Romain reassures his readers: "No matter what a bully says, you're not a dork, wimp, teacher's pet, dummy, crybaby, jerk-face or knucklehead. And anything a bully says about your race, family, gender or national heritage simply isn't true."[55] Bully victims may not find this very reassuring and may question the sincerity of adult authorities who make such comments, when they themselves know they are from minority groups or are gay, clumsy, physically weak, handicapped, socially outcast, vulnerable, not conventionally attractive, introverted, bookish, or dependent upon adult protection.

Like the psychological paradigm in general, Romain's approach is contradictory. Despite saying that bullies' insults are always lies and that no one deserves bullying, he implies that some people's posture and manners invite it. Apparently, it is all a matter of attitude: change your attitude, walk with pride, and you won't be bullied. "Bullies go after people who appear anxious, sensitive, quiet, or cautious," he writes. "Like ants are attracted to candy, bullies are drawn to people who are somewhat shy . . . [so] work on appearing more sure of yourself. Stand up straight, look people in the eye, talk with a firm voice, and hold your head high. If you act more confident, you will start to feel more confident."[56]

Romain advises that if all else fails, one should run[57]—but bully victims are often not very athletic and may not be able to run as fast as their tormentors. Another recommendation he makes is to tell an adult authority,[58] but that dismisses the possibility that both bully and victim may have legitimate reasons not to trust authority figures. It also ignores the possibility that bullies might interpret going to the authorities as a sign of weakness, a violation of an implicit code among students, and an invitation to further harass the victim. Like most followers of the psychological paradigm, Romain believes the real source of someone's bullying problem ultimately is in his or her head. Events in the external world, the larger society, hardly matter: just change your attitude and things will take care of themselves. However, people who have constantly been harassed and are continually told they are inferior may have good reasons for having low self-esteem, and they are hardly in a position to develop proud, self-confident personas. Beyond that, therapy for individual bullies or their victims will not end the problem. Schools designed to serve a bullying society such as militaristic capitalism ultimately will reinforce bullying, not cure it. We can't say what will end bullying, but we *can* say that as long as we live in a bullying society, bullying will persist.

CHAPTER EIGHT

The Heartless World
All in the Family

The family is probably the oldest institution in human history, much older than capitalism. It is a residue of medieval feudalism and even older societies. It has a life of its own and does not perfectly blend into capitalism. Unlike other institutions that transmit bullying values, including schools, the military, the media, and sports, the family is not the creation of the corporation or the state. As a refuge from corporations and other dominant institutions, it has been called by historian Christopher Lasch a "haven from a heartless world."[1] But it has also acted since ancient times as the heart of a heartless world in itself.

The extended family—parents, children, grandparents, aunts, uncles, and cousins—has lost most of its power, and some critics consider the nuclear family—parents and children living alone—an endangered species.[2] The instability of the modern family may stem from its being assigned a role for which it was not designed and which it is not equipped to fulfill, that is, compensating for the emotional support and the sense of psychological security that have been undermined by capitalism. As an institution that transmits values, the family may be even more contradictory than the school. It is the alleged sanctuary of love, security, support, and affection, but it is also a repository of conflicts from the outside world, a place where hostilities can be expressed, and a theater of bullying and competition for a place within a pecking order.

Early capitalists tried to circumvent the family altogether. In the 1830s and 1840s, the first textile mills in Lowell, Massachusetts, recruited girls from local farms, separated them from their families, and had them live in company-owned dormitories. There, they were fed and provided minimal recreation as a relief from their seventy-hours-plus workweek; they were also given books, and they even worshipped in company-owned churches. The factory owners tried to completely replace the family and directly control their employees' emotional, psychological, and social lives. Eventually, the owners found this system too costly to maintain, especially as the women organized for higher wages and shorter workweeks and when the Civil War made cotton scarce and drove their prices up.[3] As capitalism matured, members of the 1% came to accept the family, but they still tried to control it and manipulate it to serve their own ends. Because employees needed to support their families, they did not risk losing their source of livelihood by defying their bullying bosses.

The family is *not* a capitalist institution. It is ancient, although it blended well into feudalism. Early industrial capitalists experimented with abolishing the family. Immediately after the communist revolutions in Russia and China, the new regimes made even stronger attempts to eliminate it. Early Israeli Zionists, who wanted to create "new Jews," also tried to replace the family with the kibbutz. However, in all cases, the family proved to be too resilient. Today, capitalism is stuck with it, and it therefore tries to manipulate the family to benefit the corporation and the state. The bullying that occurs *within* the family would go on with or without capitalism or, for that matter, socialism. Because the family has interests independent of capitalism, corporations and the state try to assign powers that historically were the domain of the family to other institutions, such as schools, the media, and the military. Since the family is unreliable as a tool for transmitting capitalist bullying values, due to the contradictory family pressures discussed earlier, whole professions, among them social work and psychology, were created largely to police it.

The family bullies and is a conservatizing institution. It cannot be abolished, but it can be tempered and used to convey values that serve militarist capitalism. It can also serve as a safety valve that provides relief from the alienation that militaristic capitalism produces; as such, it can prevent anger from becoming too dangerous and explosive.

The irony is that capitalism—even as it relies upon the family to help instill bullying values—has coerced the family into giving up much of its traditional bullying authority, while also weakening the patriarch who historically ruled and bullied the family. Parents, especially fathers, now often feel themselves bullied by their alleged subordinates, including their children and perhaps their spouses. Grandparents, who were once considered the rulers of the extended family, are now put on the back burner, although part of the reason for this development may be that more people now live long enough to be considered a burden by their relatives. These changes have been sources of great resentment and generational conflict, weakening traditional patriarchal bullying but at the same time expanding the number of family members who seek to empower themselves against everyone else.

People for whom capitalist institutions, including work, have been heartless often seek a haven where they can be loved, respected, and powerful. Many expect their families to give them psychological gratification, but families are not fully equipped to do so. People may seek the bullying authority they imagined their parents or grandparents had, though that may be a nostalgic myth. Unfulfilled outside the family, parents may try to tighten their hold on their children. With their traditional bullying authority eroded, they seek a new bullying strategy. Ironically, infantilizing their children, indulging them, and preventing them from growing up and leaving home becomes a way to bully them. With access to school, the media, and friends, children have outside resources. It is not clear who needs whom more. Children can fight back, even counterbully. It is debatable if wives ever gave husbands the deference traditional patriarchal ideology said they were entitled to. But now, with the rise of the feminist movement and with more women becoming as educated as men and having professions outside the house, the control exerted by husbands is even weaker. Wives often bully husbands, just as husbands often continue to bully wives.

THE PRECAPITALIST FAMILY

Before capitalism, the family was the primary economic institution, and within the family, adults and children were bullied into accepting their places in a fixed hierarchy. If there was love in the family, it was secondary. Primogeniture meant younger siblings had to submit to older ones, and children had to submit to parents who controlled them even into adulthood. Under some circumstances, as we will see shortly, parents could even legally kill their children. Traditional family authority encompassed all the classic elements of a bullying culture: hierarchy, submission, and obedience.

In the *Wizard of Oz,* young Dorothy tells us that "there's no place like home! . . . If I ever go looking for my heart's desire again, I won't look any further than my own backyard."[4] In earlier stories, however, there was little pretense that the family was where you would go to find love and affection. In the Bible, siblings often hated each other, tried to destroy each other, and sometimes killed each other over shares of family wealth and position within the family hierarchy: think of Cain and Abel, Esau and Jacob, and Joseph and his brothers.[5] According to legend, Rome was founded by two brothers, Romulus and Remus, but in a dispute over where to locate the city, Romulus murdered Remus and anointed himself king.[6] And as Shakespeare's play *Hamlet* begins,[7] Hamlet learns from his father's ghost that his uncle, now king, had assassinated his father to gain the crown.

Throughout history, when aristocrats and monarchs held real power, siblings would plot against each other, sometimes killing or waging wars against one another to determine who would inherit the manor, the title, or the throne. Aristocratic families, especially royal families, often gave absolute legal authority to the husband. Henry VIII felt free to divorce three of his wives and behead two others for adultery, even as he consorted with an unknown number of mistresses.[8]

Before the Industrial Revolution, the family was the primary economic institution. Its emotional function hardly mattered. Adults and children typically worked on the family farm or in the family business, nominally controlled by the patriarch. Whether family members loved each other or hated each other, the institutional and legal relationships would not change. Children were economic assets whom parents could exploit or bully for their labor. With children serving as unpaid workers, big families were desirable, especially because it was assumed a large percentage of the offspring would not live to adulthood. Primogeniture was the rule, with the oldest son inheriting most or all of the family's wealth and authority. Until the mid-nineteenth century, husbands in Britain and the United States had complete control over all the family's wealth, including anything the wife earned or inherited before the marriage.[9] Under British law, the royal children of the oldest son override their adult uncles and aunts. Even in 2015, two-year-old Prince George, followed by his baby sister, Charlotte, would inherit the throne before their thirty-year-old uncle, Prince Harry, who in turn would receive the crown before his fifty-four-year-old uncle, Andrew, the Duke of York. Primogeniture meant the family fortune could not be divided. Younger siblings would be bullied into never leaving the extended family unit and thus were dependent upon their parents or older siblings well into adult life.

Primogeniture, with a bullying hierarchy built into the structure of the family, was hardly unique to the West. Chinese Confucianism taught that virtue was maintaining order and harmony through fixed positions, which empowered the aged at the expense of the young. The family was a sacred entity bound by tradition, and ancestors were worshipped. Five obligations specified who was supposed to submit to whom. Three of them focused on the family: son to father, younger brother to older brother, and wife to husband.[10] The obligations continued for life; even as adults, younger siblings were supposed to defer to and accept bullying by their parents and older siblings.

As in many, if not most, other cultures, including the precapitalist West, marriages were not a personal choice but were arranged by the parents, who would try to maintain control for life. Love, affection, and romance hardly entered into the equation in choosing marriage partners. Indeed, husbands and wives often met for the first time on their wedding day. In China, the bride could be a little girl, whose birth family would force her to live with her husband's family. Despite the official male dominance within traditional China, this young bride would be at the mercy of her mother-in-law. These mothers-in-law were notorious for turning the girls into virtual slaves, whom the older women would beat if they disobeyed. The child bride could look forward to someday brutalizing her own daughter-in-law and ruling her own household.[11]

In the West, a child who defied parental authority and bullying could also face severe consequences. According to Deuteronomy:

> If a man has a stubborn and rebellious son who will not obey the voice of his father or the voice of his mother, and, though they discipline him, will not listen to them, then his father and his mother shall take hold of him and bring him out to the elders of his city at the gate of the place where he lives, and they shall say to the elders of his city, "This our son is stubborn and rebellious; he will not obey our voice." . . . Then all the men of the city shall stone him to death with stones.[12]

The next chapter of Deuteronomy firmly establishes that daughters are the property of their parents, commodities to be sold to other men—and this was written in a society where, compared to capitalism, relatively few things were commodities. As a commodity, the daughter had to retain her value by remaining pure and unused—a virgin. She did not own her body; until they sold her, her parents did, especially her father. If she lost her virginity without her parents' consent, she was damaged goods with no worth, and she should be killed:

> If any man takes a wife and goes in to her and then hates her and accuses her of misconduct and brings a bad name upon her, saying, "I took this

woman, and when I came near her, I did not find in her evidence of virginity," then the father of the young woman and her mother shall take and bring out the evidence of her virginity to the elders of the city in the gate. And the father of the young woman shall say to the elders, "I gave my daughter to this man to marry, and he hates her; and behold, he has accused her of misconduct, saying, 'I did not find in your daughter evidence of virginity.' And yet this is the evidence of my daughter's virginity." And they shall spread the cloak before the elders of the city. Then the elders of that city shall take the man and whip him, and they shall fine him a hundred shekels of silver and give them to the father of the young woman, because he has brought a bad name upon a virgin of Israel. And she shall be his wife. He may not divorce her all his days. But if the thing is true, that evidence of virginity was not found in the young woman, then they shall bring out the young woman to the door of her father's house, and the men of her city shall stone her to death with stones, because she has done an outrageous thing in Israel by whoring in her father's house. . . . If a man meets a virgin who is not betrothed, and seizes her and lies with her, and they are found, then the man who lay with her shall give to the father of the young woman fifty shekels of silver, and she shall be his wife, because he has violated her. He may not divorce her all his days.[13]

THE FAMILY TRANSITION: THE EROSION OF TRADITION AS CHILDREN CHALLENGE PARENTAL AUTHORITY

The family historically bullied its members to be docile, justifying this practice through tradition. Capitalism, which needs 99 percent of the population to be submissive to authority, replaces tradition with progress and therefore undermines an institution it tries to use to convey its values. Parents may attempt to bully their offspring, but millions of children now have the knowledge and outside resources to resist. Despite this, many children do accept parental authority and feel their parents have the right to discipline, even spank, them. The traditional family is giving way to a capitalist family that empowers children but retains many bullying elements of parental authority.

As capitalism developed, the family was transformed but this transition took over two centuries to unfold and may still not be complete. When capitalism emerged, most economic activity shifted from the home to the factory, the office, and the store.[14] Less time was spent with the family; adults worked in businesses, and children learned in school. Outside influences infiltrated the family and overrode its authority. Tradition lost its value, eroding a classical way of transmitting bullying.

According to Tevye of *Fiddler on the Roof,* tradition is the cement that binds society, especially the family, together. On the one hand, tradition establishes a hierarchy with fixed roles, assigned places, and a chain of command, specifying who can bully whom. On the other hand, it also provides a sense of stability, meaning, purpose, direction, and even love. "Because of our traditions, every one of us knows who he is [FATHER, MOTHER, SON, DAUGHTER] and what God expects him to do. . . . Without our traditions, our lives would be as shaky as . . . as . . . as a fiddler on the roof!"[15]

Karl Marx, writing over fifty years before *Fiddler on the Roof* was supposed to have taken place, had no such faith in tradition or the family and actually praised capitalism for undermining both:

[It] has put an end to all feudal, patriarchal, idyllic relations. It has pitilessly torn asunder the motley feudal ties that bound man to his "natural superiors." . . . It has drowned the most heavenly ecstasies of religious fervor, of chivalrous enthusiasm, of philistine sentimentalism, in the icy water of egotistical calculation. It has resolved personal worth into exchange value. . . . In one word, for exploitation, veiled by religious and political illusions, it has substituted naked, shameless, direct, brutal exploitation. . . . The bourgeoisie has torn away from the family its sentimental veil, and has reduced the family relation to a mere money relation.[16]

One of the contradictions of capitalism is that it can use the ideology of the traditional family to reinforce its need to have the 99 percent submissive to authority, but it undermines the traditional family. Capitalism prefers progress to tradition. Profits depend upon technological innovation, changing consumer tastes in style and fashion, and ever more subtle forms of population manipulation and control. In the old-fashioned family, the authority of parents and grandparents rests on the assumption that the old are wise— simply because they have lived longer, and the past is a good predictor of the future. That presupposes a stagnant society in which each generation will live essentially the same way as the one before. Families assert the right to arrange marriages because they claim they know what their children need; they can predict how they will live as adults better than the children can themselves. The family bond is permanent. It is not to be broken by children growing up, moving out, and establishing a life of their own.

However, in a rapidly changing society, children may sense what is appropriate for their generation more than their parents and grandparents do. The knowledge of the old can become obsolete, quaint, and maybe even comical. This certainly happened when science replaced religion and capitalism replaced feudalism during the American, French, Russian, and Chinese Revolutions; in the cultural revolutions of the 1920s and 1960–1970s; and when improved birth control led to changing sexual mores. It also happens when family members move continents or oceans away from each other, either to escape oppression (perhaps the oppression of the family) or to seek the opportunity promised by the capitalist dream, whether real or myth. As Marx implied, the one freedom capitalism does provide is escape from the rigid bonds of tradition, family, and caste.

Another force that can undermine the authority of the older generation is new technology, especially when the young are more comfortable with it than the old. The young find computers, smartphones, remote controls, and the Internet perfectly natural facets of everyday life, whereas the old struggle to adjust to them and may never succeed in doing so. In fact, they often have to ask their children or grandchildren for help. The cable company provides a code that parents can use to prevent children from watching programs the parents do not approve of, but children may use their "techno-smarts" to turn the tables on them: Magrass's son, for instance, used the code to prevent his parents from watching their choices, while he looked at whatever he wanted. What is progress for one side can be degeneration for another. In some households during what remains of the family meal, children spend their time on their cell phones, text-messaging with their friends.

For a while, America was evolving into a society not divided by families but by generations, with the young living in college dormitories or apartments with roommates and the old living in retirement communities or nursing homes. But in recent years, this tendency has been reversed by the economic collapse, as people in their twenties and even thirties have moved back to live with their parents because they can no longer afford to live on their own.

In the traditional family, parents were right by virtue of their being parents: they were right because they were right. They had a wisdom that children could not understand and dared not question. These ideas persist, at least implicitly, today. When Magrass's students are asked how their folks would react if they did something their parents didn't like, they almost always begin their response by saying, "If I did something wrong." Apparently, most of these students believe that "something my parents didn't like" and "something wrong" are synonymous. Decades ago, it was axiomatic that it was the duty of parents to bully their children. They were to impose discipline, authority, obedience, and control, and the failure to do so was considered neglect and weakness. One of the most common punishments was spanking—using direct physical violence. In the classical spanking, the parent would place the child over her knee, pull down his pants, and hit him repeatedly with a stick or a strap. It was a clear statement that the parent owns the child's body. The child is entitled to no privacy and must lie down or bow beneath the parent. The strap or the stick embodies an abstract authority, perhaps the family itself. It implies the parent is acting through more than personal anger, which would be suggested if a hand were used. Many social workers now regard something that was once considered appropriate discipline as child abuse. Today, spanking is illegal in over thirty countries—but not the United States.[17] A majority of Magrass's students report they were spanked, with a significant number saying they had to lie bare-bottomed across the parent's knee.

THE FAMILY AS A BATTLEFIELD IN THE CULTURE WARS

Capitalism can use the family to convey its values, but at the same time, it undermines the family's authority and its capacity to transmit bullying. The bullying power of the family is further weakened by schools, social workers, and other state agents, who have been called "coastal elitist liberals." They— the cultural liberals—are perceived as trying to take away parents' control over their children, including their bodies and sexuality. Through media and education, the cultural liberals also expose children to ideas that contradict family authority. This is actually part of a broader culture war between liberals and conservatives, with capitalists on both sides of the divide, that we discuss in other chapters. Defenders of traditional family authority ally with right-wing, procorporate politicians, mostly Republicans, to restore the traditional family. The future of the family as a transmitter of bullying will depend upon who wins this culture war and whether changing economic forces weaken or strengthen the family.

The debate over whether spanking is desirable discipline or parental bullying is part of the larger culture wars, as we discuss elsewhere. The cultural liberals claim to want to "liberate" children and let them be free, creative, independent thinkers, which is something many parents, of course, also want for their children. But cultural liberals see disrespect for hierarchical authority, including family authority, as a virtue. They were at their height during the 1960–1970s' counterculture, New Left, and student movements. In chapter 7, we heard from Lynne Cheney—a fierce critic of cultural liberalism—about the need to undo the damage the cultural liberals did to militarized capitalism.

Cultural liberals' embrace of free expression extends not only to politics but also to lifestyle. This leads to a sense that the young should control their own bodies, something that would further erode parental bullying power. People such as Lynne Cheney fear the liberals have gained undo influence within schools and certain parts of the state. Former Republican senator and presidential candidate Richard "Rick" Santorum charges the government is using schools to undermine families: "The government has convinced parents that at some point it's no longer their responsibility. And in fact, they force them, in many respects, to turn their children over to the public education system and wrest control from them."[18]

But as we have seen, some within the corporate elite are skeptical about the family as a conveyor of bullying values; capitalists are internally divided and fall on both sides of the culture war divide. The capitalist liberals would have the family monitored by schools, psychologists, social workers, and other state agents, who tend to be cultural liberals and use, at least rhetorically, the language of freeing children. These professionals might support guaranteed family incomes and parental leave from work so parents could have the time and money to raise their children—a prospect that is not attractive to the corporate elite who are cultural conservatives or indeed to most other cultural conservatives.

Although these policies might seem to strengthen the family, cultural conservatives, allied with the corporate 1% on this issue, have labeled liberal professionals as enemies of the family and dismissed them as "coastal elitist liberals" who want to bully parents and prevent them from raising their children as they see fit. The conservatives say the liberals are contemptuous of family, tradition, and religion. According to Tim La Haye, former California chairman of the Moral Majority and author of Battle for the Mind[19] and Battle for the Family,[20] they use education to undermine wholesome values: "The higher a person has advanced in education, the more likely he is to be atheistic."[21] Evangelist Tony Perkins, president of Family Research Council (FRC), believes politicians may try to outlaw spanking in an effort to undermine parental authority and religion:

A new bill in Massachusetts is daring parents to discipline. After trying unsuccessfully to outlaw spanking in 2005, state legislator Jay Kaufman is taking a new crack at the spanking bill. In January, California tried their luck at a similar bill but parents were so outraged with the idea that the leaders dropped it. Odds are the Kaufman plan will be just as unpopular. In a CBS poll, only 23% of Americans supported such a ban and why should they? It completely undermines parental authority and I think we will agree government does enough of this as it is. Now obviously no one wants to turn discipline into child abuse but the problem isn't whether a child is spanked but how. There are plenty of laws on the books to prevent physical abuse and this is not one of them. Instead it is an effort by the politically correct to demonize parents who paddle. Proverbs 25:15 says "The rod of correction imparts wisdom but a child left to himself disgraces his mother." God gave children to parents for a reason and it is their responsibility, not the state's, to raise them.[22]

Perkins's predecessor at FRC, James Dobson, holds a PhD in psychology, but unlike most psychologists, he has endorsed spanking as a way to build obedience to authority in the family, the school, and the corporation.

A spanking is to be reserved for use in response to willful defiance, whenever it occurs.[23] . . . Two or three stinging strokes on the legs or buttocks with a switch are usually sufficient to emphasize the point, "You must obey me."[24] . . . By learning to yield to the loving authority . . . of his parents, a child learns to submit to other forms of authority which will confront him later in his life—his teachers, school principal, police, neighbors and employers.[25]

Capitalism may need progress and innovation, forces that undermine tradition and the family, but it also needs a compliant, obedient workforce, which is something that reinforcing tradition and the family can help provide. These two seemingly contradictory needs have been melded together in the "family values" ideology that has been adopted by the core of the cultural conservative movement. Santorum embraces the capitalist ideal of limited government with low taxes—a government that does not interfere with the corporation, the church, or the family. "I believe in capitalism," he proclaims,[26] observing that "capitalism actually encourages morality."[27] Elsewhere, he states, "You can't ignore the reality that faith and family, those two things are integral parts of having limited government, lower taxes, and free societies."[28] He exhorts people, "Defend the church. Defend the family. . . . Defend them against a government that wants to weaken them."[29]

With spokesmen such as Perkins, Le Haye, Dobson, and Santorum, the cultural and religious conservatives claim to adopt so-called family values. They endorse two seemingly contradictory ideas. One is the notion that the family is an independent entity with a life of its own, whose interests override those of the individual. The other is the capitalist principle that you are on your own and the master of your own fate. We see these two principles blurred together in a simultaneous belief that a young woman's body is the property of her family whose members can bully her as they see fit—a position we found in the Bible—and that the young woman is responsible for what she does with her body and must face the consequences of her actions—an idea consistent with capitalist ideology.

Many of the staunchest Protestant, evangelical "right-to-lifers" oppose welfare, family leave, and government services for parents of young children because they fear they limit parental authority and bullying (although Catholic opponents of abortion are usually more accepting of social services). Forcing a pregnant daughter to carry an embryo to term illustrates how cultural conservatives expect parents to bully their children: if you get pregnant with a child you can't afford, that is your problem, but abortion is not an option. Being forced to raise a baby is part of an appropriate punishment for promiscuity. Some evangelists would call it the wages of sin. Michael Huckabee is a former Baptist preacher turned Republican governor of Arkansas turned presidential candidate turned talk show host on Fox News. He is convinced female promiscuity leads to poverty and misery unless the government intervenes—though that contradicts the capitalist and biblical principles of self-reliance:

> Most single moms are very poor, uneducated, can't get a job, and if it weren't for government assistance, their kids would be starving to death and never have health care. And that's the story that we're not seeing, and it's unfortunate that we glorify and glamorize the idea of out of wedlock children.[30] . . . If the Democrats want to insult women by making them believe that they are helpless without Uncle Sugar coming in and providing for them a prescription each month for birth control because they cannot control their libido or their reproductive system without the help of the government, then so be it.[31]

Birth control and abortion would allow the daughter to hide what she is doing from her parents. They remove control of her body from parental authority. She can play and not pay. Teenagers may be sexually active, but they fear the consequences of their parents finding that out, although parents today may be more accepting than in the past.

Of course, some religious parents and other opponents of abortion are motivated by their faith and moral code. There is an irony here. Supporters of abortion often endorse the right of children, especially daughters, to act independently of their parents. Yet people who believe fetuses are children can argue that abortion is the ultimate statement that children are the property of parents and thus that abortion is an extreme form of bullying.

Conservative parents frequently reacted with horror over pregnant daughters, severely bullying them, long before the recent culture wars. We see an example of this in the movie *Wedding in White*.[32] It takes place during World War II, before legalized abortion and the development of the birth control pill. Upon learning his daughter is pregnant (she was raped), a father reaches for his belt for one last spanking before marrying her off to a man as old as he is.

The movement to restore traditional values is largely a reaction against a sense that the family is being bullied into surrendering its authority or perhaps being forced to adopt what is considered politically correct. Professionals who are seen as cultural liberals—social scientists, psychologists, and social workers, often acting as agents of the state—specify how parents may raise and discipline their children. With government funding, Planned Parenthood has given teenage girls access to birth control and abortions without their parents' consent or even knowledge. Experts and professionals may think they are protecting children from being bullied by their families, but parents are told by cultural conservatives that they are being bullied into forfeiting control over their offspring.

STRUCTURAL FORCES ERODING THE FAMILY

Even as capitalism tries to use the family to convey its bullying values, it builds other institutions that challenge the family: schools, media, and professions such as psychology and social work. Feeling less in need of the family, the young develop their own generational culture and network of friends, all of which makes them feel even more independent. The student movement of the 1960s and 1970s was a rebellion not only against militaristic capitalism but also against the family. It is ironic that, in a weakened economy, people who grew up after the sixties and seventies often feel less of a generation gap between themselves and their parents.

We saw in the schooling chapter how compulsory education provokes hostility among some immigrant families—who are seen as prime recruitment targets by cultural conservatives—for exposing their children to alien values, cultures, and lifestyles. Around the same time schooling became mandatory, child labor laws eliminated the child as an economic asset, denying the family whatever income supplement, however meager, the child might provide. Portuguese students at the University of Massachusetts–Dartmouth report that in previous generations, Portuguese immigrant parents would routinely pull their children out of school to send them to work the minute they turned sixteen, no matter how high or low their grades were. In the current generation, this is rare, as evidenced by the fact that so many attend this and other colleges.

Some immigrant parents and other parents without advanced education find culturally conservative values attractive. Although immigrants are not ardent cultural conservative warriors, the values of many of them conform to the conservative movement. Some immigrants and other conservatives see work not only as a source of income but also as a disciplining mechanism whereby you learn that you must submit to authority: don't challenge your boss; don't challenge your parents. Schools certainly teach obedience and submission, but some schools, especially universities, also teach independent, creative thinking. That is dangerous to employers of low-level workers and to parents who fear the bonds of the family are eroding. As Magrass became involved in the 1960–1970s' student movement, his father, who spent his life as a clerk to the rich owner of a trucking company, lamented, "I think a college education is highly overrated; all it does is give them wild ideas. If they had to go to work like we did, they wouldn't have time to worry about what's wrong with the world." Despite his resentment, however, he felt compelled to pay his son's college bills. The student movement of the sixties and seventies was not only a reaction against militaristic capitalism; it was also an assault on the family. Even as parents were trying to stop the deterioration of the family, their children were trying to accelerate it.

MORE FORCES WEAKENING FAMILY AUTHORITY

In the 1960s and early 1970s, children were free to rebel because it was a time of relative prosperity when they did not really feel they needed their parents.

They could move out to college dormitories or off-campus apartments and feel independent, even if it was only an illusion because if things went wrong, Daddy and Mommy could pay the bills. Ironically, their independence from their parents depended upon their dependence. Since that time, college costs have risen much faster than the rate of inflation, and the overall economy is weaker. As a result, parents have a much harder time paying those college bills, assuming they wanted to in the first place. For students of this later generation, the consequences of breaking with their family may be more dangerous. Many will stay close to home, both physically and emotionally. Another irony is that because the family is in a more precarious position, its bonds are tighter, for people need each other all the more. Despite children being more of an economic liability than an asset today, aging parents may eventually become dependent upon them financially. As of 2010, a semiprivate room in an average nursing home cost $74,820 a year,[33] substantially more than the 2014 median family income of $51,939.[34] And because nursing home expenses are so high, nearly 10 million adults take care of aging parents, with 25 percent of the adult population either providing financial support or physically caring for their parents.[35] The family appears to be growing more tightly bound together, even if its long-term prognosis is dubious and its ability to transmit bullying values is weakening.

To be sure, there are momentary glitches when the family seems to be resolidifying. But most critics agree that the family is being undermined by outside forces. Both conservative family advocates and liberal psychologists and social workers deplore "peer pressure," likely meaning that children listen to each other rather than to adults. Friends become another outside influence that undermines the control of the family, and children may come to identify with their own generation more than with their elders. Although children certainly bully each other, peer pressure weakens the bullying power of both parents and school officials. Peers thus become a common enemy against which family and school unite. One of the reasons why the psychological paradigm focuses so closely on child-to-child bullying is that it is allied with adult authority. In fact, psychologists are an adult authority. The goal of psychology is adjustment—to induce conformity and to bring children to think and act as adults expect. Hence, the psychological paradigm may actually be a tool of bullying rather than a remedy for it.

The media—including television, movies, music, and the Internet—comprise an additional source of alien information that invades the family. Often, peers introduce each other to the media. At the same time, there are campaigns to "protect" children from the media, to ensure they don't learn things adults don't want them to know and to keep them from being exposed to alternative values and ways of thinking. Of course, much information on the media is false, and users of any generation must learn to separate the wheat from the chaff; still, there is a fear that the media can teach children things their parents and even teachers don't know and thus make the young all the more difficult to bully.

A HAVEN FROM CAPITALIST BULLYING OR ITS EMBODIMENT?

Capitalism can use the family both as a means for transmitting bullying values and behaviors and as a haven that absorbs the hostility and alienation that otherwise might be turned against the capitalist system. If the family worked the way it should, it would be a microcosm of the larger capitalist society, complete with rulers (parents) and subordinates (children). But often, it becomes a place where people who have been denied respect and authority in the outside world can try to compensate, not necessarily successfully, by demanding respect from and exerting authority over their children and possibly their spouses.

Capitalism reduces the majority to "employees," making them things that are to be used. For most adults, their primary activity is "alienated labor," wherein they are bullied into serving larger institutions. This is true not only for manual laborers and service workers but also for professionals who have some degree of autonomy. Survival depends upon submission. Demand too much independence and you may find yourself on the streets. The home becomes the sanctuary where working parents expect to be able to assert themselves and where everyone feels supported and loved—away from the brutality of the outside world, especially the world of competition and work, the rat race. But this does not always happen; the realities are contradictory. As Marx observes:

The worker therefore only feels himself outside his work, and in his work feels outside himself. He feels at home when he is not working, and when he is working he does not feel at home. His labor is therefore not voluntary, but coerced; it is forced labor. It is therefore not the satisfaction of a need; it is merely a means to satisfy needs external to it. Its alien character emerges clearly in the fact that as soon as no physical or other compulsion exists, labor is shunned like the plague. External labor, labor in which man alienates himself, is a labor of self-sacrifice, of mortification. . . . As a result, therefore, man (the worker) only feels himself freely active in his animal functions—eating, drinking, procreating, or at most in his dwelling and in dressing-up, etc.; and in his human functions he no longer feels himself to be anything but an animal. What is animal becomes human and what is human becomes animal.[36]

When the world of work, the primary focus of life outside the home, is stripped of fulfillment and meaning, when all it leaves is alienation, the 99 percent might turn against the system that produced this situation. To prevent this, capitalism needs a safety valve, a place where people can seek purpose and vent their anger. The family has been assigned this role. It serves capitalism both as a conveyor of values and as a place to seek relief from capitalist tedium and powerlessness. Of all transmission institutions, it is perhaps the one least under the direct control of the corporation or the state. Other transmission institutions teach militaristic capitalist values in a more obvious way. By contrast, the family replicates capitalist values through subterranean means. Capitalism simultaneously reinforces the family and undermines it. Historically, it stripped the family of its original purpose—to serve as a locus for economic production—and then gave it another function for which it is not naturally equipped—to function as a refuge for emotional support. Accordingly, it becomes contradictory: the family is both a tool of capitalism and an antagonist to it, a place where people get bullied and a place where they seek relief from bullying.

Consciously or unconsciously, parents bring home their experiences from the outside world. In the family, people reduced to employees may try to find the power they have been denied in their places of work. They may attempt to bully their children, demanding obedience and submission. Many parents try to construct a microcosm of capitalism in the family, with a class structure featuring rulers (parents) and subordinates (children). Even when parents indulge their children and give them love, affection, and material luxuries, they control the resources, just like capitalists control the means of production. In creating this microhierarchy, parents, like schools, are preparing their children for an adult world where, beyond certain limits, you must not challenge authority (or if you do, you face dire consequences). Students report that one of the most significant values their parents try to teach—in fact, demand—is "respect," by which they often mean children accepting their subordinate position within a fixed hierarchy and deferring to adults, especially their parents, whom they recognize are always right. Parents insist that their children must respect other adults as well. The children may call their parents "Mom" and "Dad," but they must not assume equality and familiarity with other adults by calling them by their first names. Instead, they must address them as "Mr.," "Mrs.," or "Ms.," unless they have special titles such as "Doctor" or "Professor."

CHILDHOOD FOREVER: BULLYING THROUGH LOVE AND INDULGENCE

Unable to find meaning and purpose in the outside world, parents often seek these qualities through their children, which gives the children bullying power. Giving and withholding love also becomes a weapon for bullying. Parents may tell their children they want the best for them but at the same time fear the children will become independent. As parents lose their direct coercive power, they may turn to a subterranean weapon—indulging the children and thereby infantilizing them so they can never leave the nest. (Of course, some parents do want their children to leave.) Indulging actually serves capitalism because it encourages consumerism even as it operates as a disguised mechanism for possessing and bullying children in the name of love.

Parents may not receive the respect they desire because outside influences, which we have already discussed (peers, schools, media), give children the resources to feel free to defy their parents. As the family declines and people cannot find meaning, purpose, and community within capitalist institutions, some parents actually need their children more than the children need them in the long run. As we pointed out in chapter 2, power often rests in the hands of whoever is capable of exiting. Children grow up and leave. If parents cannot find emotional fulfillment in the work world, they invest their psychological needs in their children. They live through them. Some parents construct an imaginary world where they fantasize the family having an integrity it does not possess. Often, they try to reconstruct a time when their family was intact and had real power, although this may be based on a romantic image of the past rather than historical reality: "When I was your age, we wouldn't talk that way. We had RESPECT." In the 1970s' television series *All in the Family,* Archie Bunker (Carroll O'Connor) sentimentally reminisces: "Whatever happened to the good old days when kids was scared to death of their parents?"[37] He is bitter that he is not receiving the respect and authority he once gave his father and now feels entitled to enjoy himself as the current head of the family. But his memory of his childhood may be based more on a nostalgic reconstruction than on reality. Archie remembers something that an outside observer might call parental bullying or abuse as the epitome of love.

> Don't tell me my father was wrong. Let me tell you something, a father who made you is wrong? Your father, the breadwinner of the house there? The man who goes out and busts his butt to keep a roof over your head and clothes on your back you call your father wrong? Your father, that's the man that comes home, bringing you candy. Father is the first guy to throw a baseball to you. And take you for walks in the park holding you by the hand? My father held me by the hand, hey, my father had a hand on him though I tell you. He busted that hand once, and he busted the other on me to teach me to do good. My father, he shoved me in a closet for seven hours to teach me to do good, 'cause he loved me, he loved me. Don't be looking at me. Let me tell you something, you're supposed to love your father 'cause your father loves you. How can any man who loves you tell you anything that's wrong?[38]

Parents and children, husbands and wives all need each other to affirm one another, to protect, to give love and security, and to provide a sense that there is a home where things are all right despite whatever happens in an often brutal outside world. Love makes things right, and as Archie says, the mere fact that someone loves you makes that person right. Right is not merely a matter of having wise ideas or acting appropriately; it is being motivated by love and caring. Love also gives power. Again, power is in the hands of the people who can leave. The more family members need each other and the more they love one another, the more power they have over each other. Withholding or giving love can be a form of bullying. After all, you really don't care how your enemies feel about you; their emotional power over you is limited. Yet you strive to win the love and admiration of those you love. You will do what they want. One of the most traumatic experiences in life is realizing that your love is not reciprocated. One weapon children and parents, husbands and wives use against each other is accusing the other family member of not loving them. Of course, love exists in the eye of the beholder, and acts that the giver may claim are done in love may be perceived very differently by the receiver. As Archie points out, parents may view discipline and even physical punishment as acts of love. The children may or may not agree. There is a fine line between love and possession.

Even if, in the long run, the family is in decline, the process is not linear. When the economy is weak and the overall social fabric is deteriorating, family members may need each other more than ever. Sentimental memories of family affection and bonding during the Great Depression are legendary. This is probably what Archie was remembering. During crises, when children are bullied by peers or rejected by people their own age, they often turn to their parents. Derber's students at Boston College do not report a generation gap like the one that received so much attention in the 1960s, with slogans such as "Don't trust anyone over 30."[39] Rather, many say their parents are their "best friends" and give them the understanding no one else will. They report that they send extensive text messages to their parents or engage in long cell phone conversations with them almost daily. Their parents give them advice and certainly exercise financial control. Many insist that the hard-earned money they spend on their children's education should not be wasted on majors such as sociology that won't bring lucrative salaries, and they expect the students to forgo concern for frivolities such as "social justice" and instead focus on something more practical, with a well-paying career trajectory.

Students at the University of Massachusetts–Dartmouth report their parents want the "BEST" for them, and undoubtedly, that is what they heard their parents say. However, *best* is never defined, and few students seem to have thought about what it means. For some, it means *success,* another undefined term, but that usually refers to success in the capitalist sense—making money. Another meaning students may give to the notion of "best" is *good values,* yet another vague term and one they have a difficult time defining. When pressed, they tend to say their parents preached "family values," which suggests they wanted to ensure their children could never break their ties to their parents and other relatives. Such parents may say they love their children, but they are really bullying them. They are trying to control how the children live and think and may set them "free" when they are "mature" enough, which means when they will carry the parents' values and worldview inside them, wherever they go. In George Bernard Shaw's play *Major Barbara,* a mother assures her son, "I have always allowed you perfect freedom to do and say whatever you liked, so long as you liked what I could approve of."[40]

For all their rhetoric of wanting the best for their sons and daughters, the possibility that the children could actually do better than they have and no longer need them can be frightening to parents. The comic book *How to Be a Jewish Mother* begins with this warning: "Fail to master these techniques and you hasten the black day when you find your children get along without you."[41]

In the movie *My Big Fat Greek Wedding,* an immigrant father tries to reconstruct on the American continent a large, ethnic, extended family network, something that would transcend generations. He is terrified that his thirty-year-old daughter, Toula (played by Nia Vardalos, author of this semi-autobiographical script), who had worked as a waitress in the family restaurant, might acquire the independence to escape the family bond; this implies that "the best" for his family would mean the daughter perpetuating it into the future.

> GUS [the father, crying]: Why you want to leave me?
> TOULA [the daughter]: I'm not leaving you! Don't you want me to do something with my life?
> GUS: Yes! Get married, make babies! You look so . . . old![42]

To maintain their hold over their children, some parents try to infantilize them. Infantilizing may seem like the opposite of bullying. It usually involves indulging the children—giving them material things, food, entertainment, and attention and providing an environment so comfortable that they will never want to leave. However, its real purpose is to guarantee the children never acquire independence and leave the parents with an empty nest where they have no further purpose in life. It serves the parents at the expense of the children. Of course, some parents find their children so difficult to get along with that they hope they move out; others even throw their kids out themselves.

In another movie, *Failure to Launch,*[43] the parents (played by Terry Bradshaw and Kathy Bates) decide that it is unhealthy for their thirty-something son (Matthew McConaughey) to live with them. They hire a combined therapist-prostitute (Sarah Jessica Parker) to seduce him into leaving. But their real motive, conscious or not, is to ensure he never leaves. The mother irons and folds his laundry with precision. She makes him elaborate gourmet breakfasts, lavishing his pancakes with strawberries and whipped cream. When the son does move out, the parents must confront the emptiness of their lives; they realize the son was the bond holding them together and that they must relearn how to get along with each other—a task the son had helped them avoid for years.

Children, especially indulged children, are the ultimate consumer good. The more people consume, the more profit for corporations. Political economists Paul Baran and Paul Sweezy have argued that as capitalism matured, encouraging consumption became a more serious problem than maintaining and enhancing production. Though children may no longer produce wealth for the family, they certainly consume it. According to the US Department of Agriculture, in 2010 it cost, on average, $226,920 to raise a middle-class child from birth to age eighteen.[44] That figure excludes the cost of a college education, which can easily exceed another $200,000. Whole industries—devoted to producing toys, certain kinds of clothes, music and entertainment, theme parks—are almost completely dependent upon parents indulging their children. Thus, December holiday gift buying virtually sustains the entire retail industry. In December 2013, shoppers spent $600 billion.[45]

THE NEW DEMOCRACY OF FAMILY BULLYING

Capitalism needs the family to convey bullying values and behaviors. The fact that the family bullies is more important than who bullies whom. Husbands can bully wives, wives can bully husbands, parents can bully children, or children can bully parents. Bullying can be violent or verbal, conveyed through taunting and sarcasm. Husbands and parents who try to bully can be counterbullied by being mocked by the very people they try to control. They can be forced to either accept their powerlessness or lose the people they love. The father was the main bullier in the traditional family, but bullying is dispersed in the contemporary family, ironically leading to bullying by all family members.

 Fathers and mothers both have a stake in controlling and bullying their children, even well into their adult lives, yet there is also substantial jockeying for power between husbands and wives. Occasionally, it ends in violence, but usually it does not. As we have shown, the family is both a sanctuary of love and an arena of bullying where parents and children, husbands and wives each try to dominate one another. It transmits, perhaps inadvertently, the bully values and behaviors needed in the larger militaristic capitalist society. From the point of view of militaristic capitalism, it may be less important who wins or who ends up bullying and being bullied. What really matters is that family members try to bully each other and divert their anger from the larger society. In most cultures, the official ideology says the man is in charge, and indeed, he usually represents the family to the external world. Husbands may nostalgically yearn for a time when they allegedly bullied wives and when parents, especially fathers, bullied children. But wives and children now have the resources to fight back, and the father can end up being the bullied one, forced to accept a situation he cannot control or else lose the people whom, behind it all, he loves. Feeling powerful, sometimes wives or children will initiate the bullying; again, their power to bully may stem from genuine reciprocated love.

Some husbands are brutal bullying tyrants. They can be violent, even to the point of killing their wives or girlfriends. According to the Centers for Disease Control and Prevention, one-third of US women have experienced domestic violence at some point in their lives, and 60 percent of such incidents occur in the home. Overall, more than 38 million women will experience violence by an intimate partner during their lifetime,[46] and on average, three women are killed by an intimate partner each day.[47] Some 3 million men also face physical attacks.[48] Some male violence may result from anger over being denied the bullying power the traditional patriarchal ideology says they are entitled to enjoy. The Lifetime Network, billed as "Television for Women,"[49] regularly broadcasts movies, based on true stories, about men who abuse or even kill their wives or girlfriends, have affairs with other women, or commit other crimes. In one show entitled "The Familiar Stranger," a wife discovers that her husband, who she thought committed suicide after being charged with embezzlement, actually fabricated his own death and is living well under a new name. In "Sins of the Preacher," a minister husband appears to be in deep mourning over his wife's suicide, but he actually killed her. In "The Girl Next Door," a police officer protects a woman from a violent partner; the officer gets the woman to fall in love with him and then asks her to kill his wife, all so he can avoid a messy divorce.

A number of cases of husbands and boyfriends killing wives and girlfriends have gotten national and even international attention. Charles Stuart jumped off a bridge when he realized he would be caught after claiming his pregnant wife had been killed by a black robber who shot both her and him while they were sitting in their car. Allegedly, he killed her for the insurance money.[50] In South Africa, Oscar Pistorius, who had won Olympic medals as a sprinter despite having had his legs amputated, was convicted for fatally shooting his girlfriend through the bathroom door while in an uncontrolled rage.[51] Professional athletes have received a lot of attention for nonfatal violent attacks on wives and girlfriends. Football hero Ray Rice of the Baltimore Ravens, for example, was suspended for knocking his wife unconscious. Incidentally, the rate of reported violence against wives and girlfriends among professional football players is about four times the national average for men of comparable income.[52] There are also cases of women who brutalize men, and some of these incidents receive international publicity. Jodi Arias was convicted for stabbing her boyfriend twenty-five times, shooting him in the head, and almost cutting his head off.[53]

The majority of family bullying is not violent. When you actually look at the dynamics inside the home, it is not always clear who is in charge. Even in the most stereotypical patriarchal societies, wives can override husbands. Toula's mother offers this advice in *My Big Fat Greek Wedding*: "Let me tell you something, Toula. The man is the head, but the woman is the *neck*. And she can turn the head any way she wants."[54] We cannot be sure whether this metaphor reflects power or compensation for powerlessness. If the mother really thought she had the power, wouldn't she call herself the head, since that is where the brain, the command center, is located?

Patriarchy might not be the best way to describe the traditional family because the mother, like the father, has a stake in its preservation. This would have been especially true in the past, when the home was her domain and she was less involved in the outside world. Today, as capitalism undermines the family, the traditional housewife may be especially threatened because she is left without a role. Of course, in recent times, far more women have advanced degrees and professional careers. Sociologist Arlie Hochschild suggests today's wives may have their feet in two worlds—the home and the office.[55] As the family changes, mothers, like fathers, have reasons to fear losing control of their children. Some women feel a need to assert bullying power, and their husbands can feel the impact of it. Capitalism may not have a direct stake in whether husbands or wives bully more, but nonetheless, it is the driving force behind the destabilization of the family. As capitalism transforms the family, both sexes will react. This will produce more anxiety and possibly more bullying or at least different forms of bullying. And if bully victims feel empowered, they will fight back. So we will see bullying by both sexes and all generations.

In *All in the Family*, the wife, Edith (Jean Stapleton),[56] ultimately rebels against her domineering husband. Losing his bullying power, Archie's only real defense is to eat at his favorite bar instead of at home.

ARCHIE: Edith, that was an order.
EDITH: I ain't taking no orders. . . . I can be a Sunshine lady if I wanna be. And I wanna be. And I am.

ARCHIE: You are in trouble, Edith. You are in big trouble.

EDITH: No, you are. 'Cause I ain't getting your dinner on the table until you take back what you said.

ARCHIE: What I said goes. And you don't gotta get no dinner on the table for me 'cause I'm going down to Kelsey's.

EDITH: Oh no. You ain't gonna slam this door in my face because this time it's gonna be your face AND I'M GONNA BE THE SLAMMER.

When they are not fighting, Edith makes her motive for putting up with Archie quite clear: "I wash your clothes and iron your shirts and make sure they're all folded in the right drawers . . . I LOVE YOU, Archie. That's why I do all those things for you."

The official ideology of the Jewish shtetl in late czarist Russia where *Fiddler on the Roof* takes place is extremely patriarchal. As the play begins, Tevye tells us he has "the final word at home," and he can pick his daughters' husbands. Furthermore, only men can read the holy books. Capitalism was fully developed in America and Western Europe when the events in *Fiddler* occurred, but it was an embryo that was about to be aborted in Russia at that point. As the czarist regime deteriorates, the Jews are scapegoated, and Tevye sees his world collapse. Although his people have faced brutal bullying under the czar and although the collapse of the czardom might be good for the Jews, political instability undermines the institutions of the shtetl, including the family. Tevye reacts angrily as he realizes he does not have the authority he thinks he is entitled to: "Tradition! Marriages must be arranged by the papa. This should never be changed."[57]

Reluctantly, Tevye accepts two of his daughters' choices of Jewish husbands, but even though he proclaims himself "the master of the house," he fears his wife's reaction: "What shall I tell Golde?" He may fantasize about having control, but his wife and daughters sometimes ignore and even mock him. When his son-in-law Motel the tailor gets a sewing machine, the entire town comes to see it. Just as Golde leaves Motel's shop, she sees Tevye approaching it:

GOLDE: Oh, you're finally here. Come, let's go home now.

TEVYE: I want to see Motel's new machine.

GOLDE: You can see it some other time. Let's go home now.

TEVYE: Quiet, woman, before I get angry! Because when I get angry, even flies don't dare to fly!

GOLDE [sarcastically]: I'm very frightened of you. After we finish supper I'll faint.

TEVYE [angrily]: Golde, I am the head of the house! I am the head of the family! And I want to see Motel's new machine NOW!

[He opens the door a crack, peeks inside, then closes it.]

TEVYE: Now, let's go home.[58]

Tevye and Golde's marriage was arranged. For twenty-five years, they almost never thought about love, but through all the fighting, they ultimately realize they do love each other.

When Tevye's third daughter, Chava, marries a gentile, he refuses to accept it—but he is powerless to stop it. Despite all the claims he makes about the power of tradition, the authority of the family is purely voluntary by Tevye's time. As much as he may want to, he cannot bully his daughter. All he can do is lose all relations with her. He gains nothing. "Chava is dead to us!" he declares. "We'll forget her." He is tormented by his decision, and his daughter laments it, but she lives her life.

In *My Big Fat Greek Wedding*, Gus, the father, recognizes he no longer has the power to arrange marriages, but he invites Greek men to the house in hopes his daughter, Toula, might be interested in one of them. However, she loves a white Anglo-Saxon Protestant (a WASP). All Gus can do is grumble about his declining authority and the changing sex roles. As much as he may want to, he cannot prevent Toula from being exposed to the outside world. "Didn't I say is it mistake to educate women?" he asks. "But nobody listen to me, now we have a boyfriend in the house! Is he a nice Greek boy, oh no no Greek, no Greek, an Xeno!"[59] (Here, he uses the Greek word for stranger or non-Greek.)

Bullied into accepting the WASP fiancé, Gus pays for an elaborate wedding. He does, though, preserve some Greek traditions, including announcing the parents' gift at the wedding reception, which turns out to be the house next door to his. This may appear to be a very generous gesture and the opposite of bullying, but in reality, it prevents Toula and her husband from establishing a life on their own and escaping the family watch. Despite her complaints, in the end Toula feels loved, comforted, protected, and secure: "They're my family. We fight; we laugh and yet wherever I go, whatever I do, they will always be there."

Television and movies have long portrayed bullying in the family, even though just who is the bully and who is the victim may be ambiguous. In the

1950s' comedy *The Honeymooners*, Ralph Kramden (Jackie Gleason) is a bus driver who feels disrespected and exploited at work but dreams of another life where he can be free and in charge. He continually envisions entrepreneurial schemes—all of them disasters. Lacking recognition in the outside world, he tries to crown himself "king of his castle" and bully his wife, Alice (Audrey Meadows), but she feels free to dismiss him.

> RALPH [to Alice]: Let's get something straight right now, right here and now: a man's home is just like a ship. And on this ship, I am the captain. I am the captain of this ship, do you understand that? You are nothing but a lowly, third-class seaman. That's all you are. Your duties: get the mess, swab the deck, and see that the captain feels good. That's all you have to do. Remember, you're nothing but a lowly third-class seaman. I'm the captain. [He notices that Alice is leaving, and he stops her.]
>
> RALPH: Where are you going?
>
> ALICE: Seaman Kramden, third class, is retiring to the poop deck until this big wind blows over.

Despite all the bickering, the Kramdens often embrace in the end, with Ralph adoringly assuring Alice, "Baby, you're the greatest!"[60]

More recently, America watched Ray Romano's semiautobiographical situation comedy *Everyone Loves Raymond*.[61] Raymond and his wife, Debra (Patricia Heaton), live across the street from his parents, Marie (Doris Roberts) and Frank (Peter Boyle). For most of the series, Ray's older brother, a 6'8" New York cop named Robert (Brad Garrett), who is even more trapped in the family network than Raymond, lives with their parents. Debra, who is always belittled by Raymond's parents (especially Marie), chose the house where they live even though her husband warned her it was not a good idea. Marie challenges Debra's housewifely skills, badgering her for not keeping her home as clean as Marie's and, more seriously, for failing to prepare delicious meals for Raymond as Marie has always done. Although Raymond is married and self-supporting, Marie regularly cooks for him in a deliberate attempt to undermine his marriage and make him dependent upon her. Debra is furious when Raymond agrees his mother is a better cook, and Raymond is afraid to do anything but placate her.

> DEBRA: I don't get why you couldn't see my side of this? You're so busy defending your saint of a mother that you made me out to be some

kind of ungrateful nutcase! Well who's the nutcase now Ray!? WHO'S
THE NUTCASE NOW!?!?

RAY [responding to Debra]: The meatballs are not exactly like my
mother's, and I am saying to you: We have a house . . . we have a car
. . . our student loans are paid off. You should be able to sleep!

Despite his 6'8" height, Robert constantly complains about being unnoticed. He is jealous of his younger brother, who he thinks got more of their
parents' attention, even though he, not Raymond, lives with them. Here's
how Robert describes his situation: "I'm a cop and live with my parents. I'm
on a constant diet of human suffering."[62]

In one episode, Robert has an opportunity to apply for a job he really wants
with the Federal Bureau of Investigation (FBI). To emphasize his dependence
upon her and to seem helpful, Marie (who is so proud of her housekeeping
skills) tries to iron his favorite suit but destroys it. Because of his problem in
finding an appropriate replacement, Robert is late to the interview. Despite
the emphasis on machismo and control in the law enforcement culture, Marie calls the interviewer and explains why it was his mother's fault that Robert
was late. Robert does not get the job. Marie then goes to see the interviewer
and openly admits that she deliberately subverted his application because
law enforcement is dangerous and causes a mother to worry too much. She
wants to keep forty-something-year-old Robert as her baby, unable to escape
from her or rebel against her.[63]

In the last few pages, we have seen how television and movies can display
the inner dynamics of everyday life and show us, often through humor, a reality that it is sometimes taboo to discuss directly. Humor may deliberately ex-
aggerate in order to focus attention. There are male and female perspectives
that lead to different ways of seeing the bully and victim. Most of the male
scriptwriters we cited are reacting to declining patriarchal authority. Female
scriptwriter Nia Vardalos also sees a growing ambiguity in roles and hierarchies as father figures respond to wives and children usurping their power.

As the family declines and the outside capitalist world produces ever
greater alienation, people turn to the family for relief. Consequently, husbands, wives, parents, and children make increasing demands on each other,
which can result in more bullying and anger rather than love and support.
There is probably no more bullying within the family today than in the past,
maybe less, but family bullying dynamics appear to have taken a different
form. Everyone seeks bullying power: husband, wife, parent, and child.

Traditional patriarchal family ideology provided a clear bullying hierarchy, and though it may never really have existed in the form rhetorically extolled by patriarchal champions, it certainly is in the process of breaking down. As roles become more ambiguous, husbands seek new ways to assert authority, but wives feel empowered to counterbully. Meanwhile, children now have more access to outside resources and can resist parental bullying. The old lose their purpose and may try to maintain it by keeping their offspring as perpetual children.

There is resentment and anger between the generations, for parents cannot get along with their children but nonetheless want them under their watch. A popular bumper sticker suggests that if you live long enough, there is hope for revenge: "*Get even. Live long enough to be a burden to your children.*"[64] This bumper sticker actually references a romantic image of a lost time when children took care of their parents. Ironically, at that time relatively few people lived long enough to lose their competence. Today, as more people live to an advanced age, the nursing home has replaced the family, although there are indications that the "good old days" of adult children having to take care of their aging parents are coming back. Another bumper sticker makes it clear that children have the final power: "Be kind to your children. They'll choose your nursing home."[65]

Although there is love in the family, it is not and never has been a haven of unlimited love. It has always, at least in part, been a theater of hostility, competition, and bullying. Capitalism undermines much of whatever support there once was while simultaneously making family members more psychologically dependent upon one another. In coming years, the family may prove to be in irreversible decline, or it may have a renaissance or even assume a new form. It may also deteriorate with nothing else emerging to bind people together, provide an emotional sanctuary, and offer a refuge from bullying. The result would be ever greater alienation and angst. No matter what, we could see increased bullying. A stronger family will revive the bullying forces within the family unit, whereas a weaker family could result in more isolation, leaving people all the more vulnerable to bullying. What the prognosis is, we cannot say.

CHAPTER NINE

The Antibullying Movement
The Cultural Contradictions of the Bully Nation

Despite—or perhaps because of—the bullying scourge discussed in this book, an antibullying consciousness is emerging in America. This is a new development in American history, evolving on a large scale only since the 1990s. It is surprising because the systemic forces causing bullying are getting stronger. But it is also potentially hopeful because it may reflect a growing revulsion against bullying in certain sectors of the population. This could change the conversation—and perhaps help change values and behaviors as well. Bullying has always been with us and will remain so, but the extent to which society rewards or condemns it can change, reducing the scale of suffering.

What are signs of the antibullying surge? Bullying has become a focus of discussion across America, especially in schools. Since the late 1990s, forty-nine of fifty states have passed antibullying laws (the exception is Montana).[1] National Anti-bullying Month (October) was designated in 2006, and there are also antibullying weeks and days.[2] Schools, workplaces, and governments are enacting codes of behavior and extensive legislation seeking to reduce bullying and protect vulnerable target populations, such as the disabled, minorities, gays, and women. Bullying politicians, among them Donald Trump and New Jersey's governor, Chris Christie, have been called out. There is the federal Congressional Anti-bullying Caucus devoted to bills addressing bullying. Movements against bullying have arisen among parents, students, workers, and many other groups. Moreover, a new culture of antibullying is taking shape in plays, songs, novels, blogs, and other venues.[3]

One of the early signs of the emerging antibullying sensibility was the emotional national reaction to the gruesome murder of a gay student at the University of Wyoming in 1998. Matthew Shepard died six days after being attacked by two other young males in Laramie, Wyoming, on October 6,

1998. He had been taken to a remote area in a car and tied to a fence, then robbed, pistol-whipped, and tortured, his skull fractured after being ruthlessly beaten. During the few days he survived in intensive care, people held candlelight vigils for him all over the world. Since then, the Matthew Shepard Foundation has reached 300 million people in its efforts to memorialize the young man; end the bullying against the lesbian, gay, bisexual, and transgender (LGBT) community; and build a new culture devoted to peace and diversity.[4]

The foundation is dedicated to quelling hate and bigotry of all forms, and Shepard's name is now seen as an iconic symbol of a new antibullying movement. That movement extends beyond the core mission of protecting gays and is advocating for new antibullying conversations and laws to protect all marginalized groups.[5]

In this chapter, we will consider why this antibullying movement is taking place and whether it might help reduce both personal and institutional bullying. Is it addressing the root causes of individual and structural bullying that we discuss in this volume? Does it portend the beginning of a truly deep change in the values and institutional power structures of our militarized, corporate society? Does it have legs?

A few initial qualifications are in order. First, the rise of antibullying protests is not a sign that bullying is diminishing in America. As noted earlier, it may instead reflect the spread of bullying, evoking disgust among millions of Americans who are beginning to think about the scale and trauma of this problem. The antibullying sentiment is, at this stage, largely rhetorical, starting a new American conversation but without reflecting any clear record that bullying has declined. Nor has it transformed—or even put on the radar screen—the structural and institutional forces that we have argued lie at the heart of the bullying problem.

This situation partly reflects the newness of the movement. All change efforts start with attempts to put new issues on the table and raise consciousness. Over time, those seeking change may deepen their analysis and move beyond rhetoric into serious critiques and movements for structural change. But in the case of bullying, much will depend on how widespread and resonant the antibullying surge is in the population. Those supporting an antibullying culture are, we believe, only a small slice of the entire population. They are deeply divided from other sectors that tacitly endorse the bullying culture, reflecting the larger culture wars that increasingly polarize the nation.

Moreover, the antibullying movement appears to be constrained by the microindividual paradigm of bullying that we have critiqued. It stresses personal bullying and mainly involves conversations and policies that deal with young people and the schools. Its discourse, in other words, is largely captured by the psychological and therapeutic view of bullying; as a result, it fails to reflect the sociological imagination and our macroparadigm that sees bullying as a product of structural forces, carried out by institutions such as corporations and militaries. The exception is the concern with cultural hierarchies associated with gender, sexual orientation, and race, as discussed widely in the case of Matthew Shepard and more generally in the scholarly literature on psychological bullying. These "identity" issues are connected to critical macropolitical power systems. But as with the gender and race movements themselves, the new antibullying discourse does not call attention to militarism and capitalism as root causes of bullying.

None of these limits, however, mean that the antibullying discourse is insignificant. It is genuinely new, and it challenges deeply held values and practices in American society. It appears to resonate widely and has been embraced by millions of adults concerned about their kids being bullied, as well as by many kids themselves. And institutions such as the schools that have become ground zero for the individual and youth bullying problem—as discussed in chapter 7—seem, in some of their practices, to be taking the new discourse seriously.

The antibullying movement reflects emerging contradictions in capitalism and militarism growing out of new values, technologies, and competitive trends. And it also reflects developments in the culture wars themselves. In the rest of this chapter, we will look at these causes of the antibullying surge and end by assessing its potential to reduce the bullying scourge.

THE NEW CONTRADICTIONS OF CAPITALISM

Capitalism has always been driven by basic contradictions. One is the wage paradox. To make more profit, each capitalist will set wages as low as possible, which is one of the bullying forms endemic to our economy—and a rational move for each individual employer. But when all capitalists reduce wages at the same time, creating a collective bullying of the workforce, they also endanger capitalism itself, for the workers will not have enough money to buy the goods that generate profit. This is the contradiction Henry Ford feared in 1916 when he paid his workers an amazing (for the time) minimum of $5 a day, telling his scandalized fellow capitalists that this was the only way that workers would be able to buy his cars.[6]

The contradiction that we want to highlight here is different; it might be called the "bullying paradox." As shown in chapter 2, capitalism is a system of competition that requires the bullying of many actors on the capitalist battlefield. Capitalist competition is a form of social Darwinism in which the toughest survive. The fundamental value is dominance—of the market, of competitors, of workers, and of society itself. As capitalists see it, the "makers" must control the "takers," leading to all the forms of capital bullying described in earlier chapters, involving the subjugation of workers and competitors. It produces a bullying culture of conformity and obedience to capitalist authority, with the mass of workers and poor people being bullied to adopt a feeling of inferiority and to submit because the rich are superior to them.

But capitalism has also always required, as noted in chapter 7, a contradictory set of values linked to innovation and competitive advantage. These values require challenges to authority and a willingness to think outside the box. Such a willingness to rebel against established ideas, products, and technologies is key to winning the competition because it is one way in which capitalists can beat their rivals, allowing them to innovate more quickly and efficiently with better products. The rebellious spirit clashes with a bullying culture and requires a new corporate culture that rejects the dominance and obedience of the bullying culture. This is one plausible explanation for the antibullying surge emanating from within the corporate system itself.

Capitalism has always depended upon a culture of conformity and submission to authority—but it also needs a parallel culture marked by innovation and the rejection of traditional authority. Most workers historically have been bullied into submission; only a small number have been encouraged to be "creatives," or individuals who innovate and do things their own way. Without innovation, there can be no new products and techniques, but innovative workers are independent and hard to control. The culture of the innovators is not a bullying culture: though it may be competitive, it encourages fresh and critical thinking and a willingness to challenge authority and existing ways of acting—a kind of occupational "disobedience" that is out of sync with the bullying culture.

This bullying paradox in capitalism, though always present, has become a much more serious problem for the system in recent decades. The transition to a high-technology, knowledge-based economy has shuffled the deck in terms of the types of values and workers that maximize competitive advantage. In postindustrial economies, more grounded in knowledge than in low-skill manufacturing, the need for creatives has expanded dramatically, as creative thinking has become the key to market success.[7] A much larger percentage of the labor force, even in the manufacturing sector, must learn computer skills and use creative thinking on the job.[8] A high percentage of workers need advanced education and are expected to adopt an autonomous and critical mind-set, an attitude that conflicts with the emphasis on dependency and dominance in the bullying culture and traditional capitalism. This new set of corporate values may help explain the rise in antibullying sensibilities today among significant numbers of both workers and managers.

Nonetheless, a large percentage of today's jobs, especially in the lower-paid portion of the service sector, continue to require conformity and submission. Whether among data entry clerks or fast-food workers or nurse's aides or cashiers at big box stores, the culture of service sector work resembles the traditional authority system of a hierarchical capitalist economy. McDonald's and Walmart workers are subjected to the same "scientific management" that existed a hundred years ago (whereby their every move is micromanaged by supervisors), and they face extreme regimentation. They must learn to embrace submission and obedience to the authority of their bosses and the rules of the company.

Two other examples help illustrate other variants of the new bullying paradox. In Silicon Valley, creatives are major players in a world of technical prodigies and innovators, resisting any kind of established authority and espousing a culture of creative discovery as the only game in town. But of course, this is *not* the only game in town. Silicon Valley is intensely competitive, and it plays a tough capitalist game with venture capitalists and entrepreneurs and creatives, all constantly engaged in struggles for control and dominance.[9] The new technical genius is integrated with financial and competitive hierarchies that are not so different from traditional capitalist authority.[10] Silicon Valley both fuels the antibully surge and reinforces some of the toughest capitalist bullying in modern society.

Another example is depicted in the widely acclaimed 2014 film *Whiplash*,[11] about the ruthless measures employed by demanding music teachers—and many other mentors—in cultivating excellence. A bit reminiscent of the approaches used by Asian "tiger mothers,"[12] who are outraged if their children dare to bring home an A-, the bullying techniques in the film are used by great mentors to produce world-class technical excellence; the teachers drive their brilliant students and performers with unrelenting demands that cultivate creative skill while almost crushing the rising geniuses. Here, we see creatives enmeshed in a culture of out-of-the-box innovation and technical perfection, on the one hand, and a culture of dominance and abuse, on the other. This melding of bullying and antibullying cultures may be a model of what the new knowledge-based economy will emulate—encouraging both antibullying and bullying at the same time.

The capitalist bullying paradox today is thus highly tangled and complex, and it can help explain the continuation of large-scale bullying as well as the antibullying surge in the economy and larger society. With regard to antibullying, competitive success in the new knowledge economy demands that a larger percentage of workers reject bullying values. Although these workers may add more innovation and technological value to a firm, they also create a culture of autonomy that clashes with the firm's need to have its authority accepted. The many workers who are trained for submission and obedience in lower-ranking jobs are simultaneously exposed to two cultures in the company, one emphasizing creativity and the other conformity. In a sense, the culture wars are brought into the company, which finds it must create and straddle or meld bullying and nonbullying cultures in order to succeed.

Before moving on to the culture wars themselves, it is worth noting that military companies—those that produce most of their goods for the Pentagon—and the military itself are increasingly experiencing their own bullying paradox. Military technology is very sophisticated and requires a growing number of creative and innovative thinkers. The electronic revolution in warfare has made intellectual power as important as brute strength both in military companies and in the military. Military contractors and the military itself are under pressure—as a condition of "national security" and sustaining American dominance of the world—to cultivate technological innovation demanding so-called nerd skills rather than jock skills. Yet both military companies and the military remain institutional bastions of hierarchical authority, and they continue to cultivate obedience and dominance as central values.[13]

Although the infantry still needs to train hardened bullies who will enter villages in Iraq or Syria and "destroy them in order to save them," the weapons controls inside a tank resemble a video game or a more complex computer, which is likely to appeal to nerds. As in the corporation, creating new weapons and strategies requires innovation, with all the challenges to authority that can entail. This may be especially problematic in a culture as grounded in blind obedience to authority as the military. The bullying traditionally used to breed unquestioning cannon fodder may no longer serve to build the skills the military needs today.

This has led to an especially complex contradiction in the culture of the military sectors, as discussed in chapter 6. On the one hand, these sectors continue to require an unquestioned acceptance of authority and violence, the core pillars of military institutions. Some top generals may get PhDs and meditate in the Pentagon, but they still wage brutal wars. Meanwhile, the drill sergeant is still a bully, and the culture of boot camp or basic training is still a bullying culture.

On the other hand, the "new military" is a high-tech machine requiring its own immense cadre of creatives. They introduce a wild card into the traditional military, since they are expected to exhibit original and innovative approaches to their work and upset the applecart in their take on military weaponry and strategy. The military creatives may be the most surprising group of all, for they have an affinity for the antibullying sentiments in the larger society.

THE CULTURE WARS: IS A NEW COUNTERCULTURE—IN THE SPIRIT OF THE ENLIGHTENMENT AND THE 1960s—CHALLENGING THE POWER ELITE BULLIES AND THE SCHOOLYARD BULLIES?

In this section, we want to look more closely at the groups of Americans who are active in or sympathetic to the antibullying movement. This effort is partly speculative, since the documentation of antibullying proponents is not well established, though we have scholarly and media reports of people and organizations involved in helping promote antibullying values. Still, it is an initial step in assessing the popular base that might move the nation toward less bullying.

But we need to indicate one other initial limitation here. The current antibullying sentiments are largely reflecting the view of bullying found in the micropsychological paradigm, which focuses on kids and schools. They do not adequately reflect the sociological imagination and the macroparadigm that concentrates on adults, institutions, and the structural bullying built into a militarized capitalist society. Any genuine movement to reduce bullying has to take seriously this larger perspective—a central message of our book. In the final section of this chapter, we will highlight the implications for a movement that recognizes the interconnected plagues of both personal and structural bullying and seeks to change institutions that fuel the bullying scourge.

Let us begin, though, with the antibullying movement today, with all its limitations. Beyond its neglect of institutional bullying caused by the military and the corporate system, this movement is also limited by the fact that it does not reflect the attitudes and opinions of the overwhelming majority of Americans. It is not building a new national cultural consensus. Instead, it is a cultural shift taking place in important but limited sectors of the populace, being part of a deep cultural polarization in the nation rather than uniting it under a new cohesive antibullying worldview. We suggest, as a first approximation, that antibulliers are more strongly represented in the following groups or organizations:

- Marginalized groups that are traditionally bullied, including gays, the disabled, girls, nerds, and ethnic or racial minorities
- Urban populations rather than rural ones
- Intellectuals, including students and faculty in higher education
- Feminists and other groups advocating challenges to traditional gender and sexual identities and rights
- Social service workers
- Teachers
- Artists
- People who oppose the death penalty and long prison sentences
- People supporting strong gun control
- People from the East and West Coasts
- People who do not embrace fundamentalist religious doctrines
- People who support the redistribution of wealth and power away from the rich
- Political progressives advocating for the powerless and poor—and for a more socially just, environmentally sustainable, and peaceful society
- Animal rights activists

We suggest that those supporting more traditional bullying cultures and values are disproportionately drawn from the following groups:

- Whites
- Males
- Rural rather than urban communities
- Gun owners and those strongly against gun control
- People from the South and the West

- Jocks and anti-intellectuals
- Death penalty supporters
- Fundamentalist religious communities
- Military, police, and prison workers
- People advocating for "traditional family values"
- People opposing gay marriage and equal pay for women
- People who are strongly prowar
- People who strongly support large corporations
- Antifeminists and antigays
- People who oppose the redistribution of wealth
- Opponents of benefits for the poor and workers
- People who oppose environmental regulation and animal rights
- People who don't believe in human-caused climate change

These lists are just illustrative samples. Although they might seem to be deliberate caricatures, since there is obviously a great deal of cultural diversity in all the groups within each list, they nonetheless give us a rough starting point for an analysis of the cultural wars surrounding bullying and antibullying. Individuals falling within the second list, for reasons related to social values, regional differences, wealth, or military position, tend to be more strongly associated with values of power, dominance, toughness, machismo, hierarchy, competition, conformity, control, and violence than those in the first list. Individuals in that first list, we shall argue, are more likely to reject these traditional values of a bullying culture.

There is also a familiarity in the division of the two lists, for they look something like the red and blue political maps we see on Election Day. Moreover, for those familiar with the conversation about American culture wars, these two lists help to define leading protagonists on either side of the culture war battlefield.[14]

In this section, we want to look more closely at antibullying sentiments in the context of the history and fever of America's culture wars. Though it has not been widely discussed in these terms, the antibullying culture, in our view, is part of larger countercultures that have challenged the ruling cultures and elites in Western militarized and capitalist societies, especially in the United States. If we look briefly at the history of culture wars—and what has intensified and changed them in recent decades—we can learn more about the meaning and prospects of the antibullying movement.

The media tend to report on culture wars as a recent phenomenon, tied to fights over gender, sexuality and sexual orientation, family values, and religion. American cultural warriors are now doing battle over homosexuality and gay marriage, abortion, traditional family values, guns, and the role of religion in politics and society.[15] They also tend to expand their battle over cultural issues to related socioeconomic and political issues, such as capitalism, inequality, climate change, militarism, and the dominant role of the United States in the world. In political terms, one side of the culture wars asserts values related to the acceptance of traditional family, sexuality, religious, and capitalist authority, whereas the other side challenges these established authority structures and seeks more egalitarian, feminist, gay-friendly, secular, sustainable, and cooperative values. One side ultimately accepts dominance based on traditional hierarchies, and the other opposes not only the existing power structures but also the very legitimacy of steep power inequalities and hierarchies.[16]

The cultural wars are on fire today, but they are not new; indeed, they have a long history. A brief historical survey offers a useful context for looking at the rise of countercultures that have confronted dominant cultures, as well as the way in which the antibullying movement may be part of a current counterculture with deep historical roots. Culture war history helps us understand the depth and breadth of the values contested within the current discussion of bullying. It puts on clear display the difficulty inherent in creating an antibullying counterculture that targets some of the most deeply ingrained values in America's militaristic and capitalist systems.

Two prior historical epochs of cultural wars provide useful insights—and they show that even though countercultures can weaken or destroy earlier established bullying systems, they can also create new bullying of their own. One example is the earliest of the modern Western cultural wars: the period in the seventeenth and eighteenth centuries when the European Enlightenment emerged to take on the Catholic Church and traditional religious authority. The Enlightenment took many different forms in different centuries and nations, but it generally involved challenges, based on reason, science, and human rights, to the medieval order, which was based on religion, tradition, and fixed social hierarchies. Historian Jonathan Israel argues that until the eighteenth century, Western civilization rested on faith, tradition, and authority.[17] The Enlightenment was a counterculture that served up a revolutionary challenge to the medieval religious culture, offering a new vision based on reason, science, and democracy.[18] In its most radical form, inspired especially by the great seventeenth-century Dutch philosopher Benedict de Spinoza, it advocated revolutionary cultural and political changes that would be familiar to those following the current culture wars: "democracy; racial and sexual equality; individual liberty of lifestyle; full freedom of thought, expression, and the press; eradication of religious authority from the legis-lative process and education; and full separation of church and state."[19] The French Enlightenment's philosophes, great cultural figures such as Voltaire, Jean-Jacques Rousseau, Denis Diderot, and Montesquieu, offered up their own variant of this countercultural surge to enshrine reason, science, critical thinking, and democracy as values to replace absolutist religious and politi-cal authority.[20] Together, they became one of the legitimating forces behind the French Revolution and its overturning of the ancient aristocratic and religious order. Unfortunately, we must remember, the French Revolution degenerated into violent bullying during the Reign of Terror and ended in the creation of another monarchy under Napoleon.

Nevertheless, the Enlightenment emerged as a counterculture in a great culture war that continues in new form even today. In the seventeenth and eighteenth centuries, this new counterculture burned with a revolutionary zeal, contesting the basic values that had dominated Europe since the Middle Ages. The Enlightenment thinkers were seen as heretics and were often per-secuted for attacking the religious and political dogma of the day. They were questioning dominant values that lay at the heart of the Catholic Church and the landed aristocracy.[21]

Although they expounded new values of critical thinking, human rights, and equality, their real accomplishment was complex and contradictory.[22] On the one hand, the Enlightenment thinkers planted the seeds for revo-lutions that challenged fundamentalist medieval truth and church absolut-ism, speaking of democracy, rationality, and skepticism of authority. They helped dismantle the medieval culture of bullying. But they also helped put in place modern capitalist and military systems that fostered new kinds of structural bullying, even as they rhetorically embraced the culture of science and skepticism.

In rhetoric and philosophy, the Enlightenment thinkers rejected claims to an unquestioned authority or dominance based on birth or divine right. This set them up to be in conflict with the established religious and political authorities, and it created a great culture war between the church and the Enlightenment theorists. At stake was the very idea of medieval authority and dominance, with church leaders claiming infallible authority and divine power and the Enlightenment thinkers challenging the legitimacy of any in-fallible truth or of absolute power and dominance (although autocrats of the era, such as Catherine the Great, would reinstitute absolutist rule in the name of the Enlightenment, a practice we discuss later).

What is the relevance of these historical trends to bullying? In today's terms, we might argue that the Enlightenment was testing the heart of the form of bully culture established in the Middle Ages and in the medieval church. It philosophically rejected the church's claim to absolute truth. The Enlightenment's weapons were reason and persuasion, and it rejected medieval ideas of fundamentalist religious doctrine or the absolute power of theocracy. The Enlightenment encouraged skepticism in regard to all claims to authority.[23] It posed a profound challenge to a bully institution or a schoolyard bully, since it rejected the bully's world of absolute domination. It claimed that the only legitimate authority had to be based on the human rights and consent of the governed. The bully had no legitimacy within the Enlightenment counterculture to dominate and bully people into submission.

But the Enlightenment was a complex system whose legacy did not destroy structural bullying but instead established new forms of it. As it helped demolish medieval fundamentalism and church absolutism, it also laid the groundwork for modern capitalism, which, as we have demonstrated all along, establishes its own structural and personal bullying—particularly the militarized capitalism of the United States. True, the culture of capitalism is based on a rhetoric of democracy and scientific rationality, but in practice, it has produced its own hierarchies and repressive systems to sustain itself. Further, the Enlightenment actually provoked another counterculture in opposition to its embrace of science and reason: the romanticism that claimed real truth could be discerned through feeling and intuition. And in turn, that romanticism led to modern right-wing movements, such as fascism, that were as violent and bullying as the medieval forms.

How successful, then, was the Enlightenment as an antibullying movement or counterculture? Certainly, one has to marvel at its accomplishments. It helped delegitimate the centuries-old medieval religious world of infallible authority, as well as the divine military authority and power claims of the aristocracy. It promoted ideas of human rights, science, and equality that have become leading ideals in Western rhetoric.

Nonetheless, we need to point out three serious failures. First, despite the fact that Enlightenment principles have had striking success in changing the rhetoric of modern Western cultures, they have *not* translated into contemporary economic and social institutions that destroy power hierarchies and ensure equality or human rights. The Enlightenment ended a highly unequal system, feudalism, that was based on caste and that considered inequality a virtue. However, the replacement system, capitalism, was also highly unequal, although it was based in class and masked itself as bringing equality. Rhetoric is not reality, a point we will return to in a moment.

Second, the limits in reality have to do partly with the fact that the older values of church and aristocracy were challenged but hardly defeated. The Enlightenment did not destroy the old values but set the stage for an ongoing culture war between religion and science, authority and democracy, reason and violence. That war of values continues in the modern culture wars.

Third, the new institutional orders created by the Enlightenment were decidedly not models of egalitarian and peaceful societies. Today, the church and fundamentalist religion continue as powerful forces, and elite capitalists have replaced elite aristocrats. The new capitalist systems, backed by the most powerful military forces ever created, embraced Enlightenment values, but they have not put many of them into practice. As it changed ruling classes, the Enlightenment also changed ruling epistemologies, or ways of thinking and knowing. It replaced a religious epistemology, in which truth was established through authority and tradition, with science, which valued questioning and progress. But scientists evolved into a class of professional experts who sometimes intimidated or bullied many in the population into not questioning them by claiming they had a monopoly over objective truth.[24] As shown throughout this book, new leaders put new bullying into place, and both old and new forms of bullying have remained pervasive.

This takes us to a second and more modern culture war that burst out with spectacular fireworks in the United States in the 1960s—and continues today in new forms. Like the Enlightenment, this modern culture war attacked the established bullying culture but also created its own bullying practices, showing how difficult it is to move beyond bullying in social relations of any form.

The New Left of the 1960s was a counterculture composed mainly of secular youth, empowered by affluence and a mixture of an Enlightenment-style skepticism of traditional religious authority and a romantic embrace of emotion and spontaneity. The young people who forged this new culture challenged racism, sexism, and the political influence of US capitalist and military power. Motivated by the injustices of segregation and the wanton, unjust violence of the Vietnam War, American youth took to the streets and helped launch a cultural revolution that confronted militarized capitalism's ideas of truth and power and redefined America itself as a bully nation.[25]

At the heart of the 1960s' student-led culture was the slogan, "Challenge Authority!"[26] The ethic of challenging authority was an intellectual broadside directed at the US form of Western capitalism and militarism that legitimated itself partly by claiming to represent Enlightenment values. The sixties' counterculture argued that militarized capitalism had broken down medieval authority and absolutism but created its own fundamentalist and bullying ideologies of war and money, presenting them as objective truths.

Among the key contributions of the 1960s to the culture war that had begun in the Enlightenment era was the challenge to male dominance and to conventional cultural values of family and sexuality. The sixties created a new wave of feminist movements, often dubbed "second-wave" feminism, that would question patriarchy and male authority. Inspired initially by Betty Friedan's landmark work, *The Feminine Mystique*, influential second-wave authors included Kate Millett, who wrote *Sexual Politics*, a classic work of the new movements; Robin Morgan, a leading activist who wrote the second-wave manifesto *Sisterhood Is Powerful*; and Germaine Greer, who published the *Female Eunuch*.[27] The leading edge of the feminist cultural assault attacked the structure of the family; the denial of women's reproductive rights; and the patriarchal character of the capitalist system that discriminated against women at work and turned them into bullied sex toys, as dramatized in modern sitcoms such as *Mad Men*.

The students' opposition to the Vietnam War was pivotal to the sixties—and it helped to distinguish them as part of a counterculture movement confronting the mainstream and violent bullying culture. Student activists saw the US involvement in Vietnam as militarized bullying of the worst form, justified by American elites as the defense of freedom against communism. The actions of the United States—by claiming that it was fighting to save freedom as it destroyed a poor country—fostered a sense of betrayal in a whole generation.[28] It helped redefine state violence and modern capitalist warfare, especially among youth, as a horrific form of bullying. Against the small nation of North Vietnam, the United States used more bombing tonnage than had been used in all of World War II, in an effort to support an authoritarian regime in the South that was friendly to America and was bullying its own people. Vietnam became a symbol of America as a bully nation, and the sixties' counterculture—in its protest of the war—thus was throwing down the gauntlet to America itself. It rejected the militarized capitalism that had brought on this war—a war that established bullying as a national creed.

The rising role of women and gays in the sixties' counterculture reinforced this challenge to America as a bully nation. Women and gays, along with people of color (who had inaugurated the sixties' movement in their struggle for civil rights), had long been prime targets of bullying and violence inside the country. The new feminist and gay movements gaining strength in the late sixties and seventies viewed male power and violence against women and gays as the core injustice of American society, and some feminists saw gender-based injustice as related to American militarism and Washington's violent bullying of the Vietnamese people. Gloria Steinem, a leading feminist writer and activist, refused to pay taxes in the late 1960s as a protest against the Vietnam War.[29]

African Americans, the originators of the sixties' counterculture—who refused to go to the back of the bus, staged sit-ins at segregated lunch counters, and tried to enroll at segregated universities—had been among those most brutally bullied during and after the slave era. The racist bullying never stopped; it resurfaced in Reconstruction during the Jim Crow era, with lynchings and segregation exemplifying some of America's worst and most violent domestic structural bullying. The black civil rights activists were subjected to brutal violence and even murder as they launched the civil rights movement. Their own repression as leaders of the new movement thus reinforced the sixties as a challenge to institutionalized bullying, dating back to and reflecting centuries of slavery—the ultimate bullying system in America.

Yet even as they confronted the established systems of bullying, the New Left countercultures or movements, as with Enlightenment countercultures, created their own bullying practices. These were pervasive, and they contributed to the New Left's demise.

Consider, for example, the major divisions that arose in regard to violence within the black liberation movement. There were nonviolent antimilitarists such as Martin Luther King, who called the United States "the greatest purveyor of violence in the world today."[30] There were also gun-embracing, violent, and proud bulliers such as the Black Panthers.[31] As the Panthers and similar "black power" groups gained prominence, King and his followers, who had bravely endured beatings and arrests to expose black oppression while demonstrating a real alternative to violent white bullying authority, were now being labeled as sellouts and cowards. The Panthers proclaimed themselves the "vanguard" of the revolution, and many white youth who had previously considered themselves antiwar pacifists accepted them as such. As the vanguard, they could dictate the "correct line" that everyone was to accept.

The fear of being labeled counterrevolutionary squelched debate and bullied leftists into either spouting slogans they felt uncomfortable with or leaving the movement altogether and becoming apolitical; some sought mainstream careers or took a more personal psychological approach to liberation by transforming the use of yoga, meditation, or even drugs into a "touchy-feely" lifestyle. Many sought jobs in the school system or in social services and helped develop the current antibullying agenda.

Bullied into not wanting to appear like uncommitted, privileged, and cowardly white middle-class students, some of those who stayed in the movement might have cheered when they were taunted with the kind of words that both authors of this book heard in that era, such as: "You white middle-class students have shown you can march, but can you kill? I want to see if you can kill." Only a tiny number actually did pick up guns, including some in the Weathermen faction of student activists who conducted bombing campaigns to protest Vietnam in the mid-1970s during the "Days of Rage."[32] They were acclaimed as heroes by some former pacifists who were bullied into accepting the notion that pausing to think, consider consequences, and stick to nonviolence revealed a lack of revolutionary discipline and, more important, a lack of machismo.

Violence is romantic. It creates a sense that you are *doing* something. You are not playing games. You are a committed revolutionary, even if that is self-destructive. Once you turn to violence, there is no turning back. Violence is also a way of separating those who blindly follow from those who will insist upon thinking for themselves. Violence requires discipline. It entails military-like hierarchies, even within tiny factions. It destroys visions of egalitarianism or open debate.

The whole Left and the whole counterculture became deeply divided as more splinter groups and parties, black and white—such as Progressive Labor, the Weathermen, the Spartacus, and the October League—emerged, claiming to be the vanguard. Different parties accused each other of being wimpy or counterrevolutionary.[33] Sectors of the Left and the counterculture of the 1960s and 1970s degenerated into a bullying culture that undermined much of what they originally stood for: nonviolence, opposition to hierarchy, antiauthoritarianism, free expression, and creativity. Some of the most severe bullies rose into the leadership ranks; people who could not accept them either left or were driven out.

Unfortunately, this tendency seems to describe many revolutions launched in the name of liberation, as happened in France, Russia, and China. One of the most sobering books ever written about revolution is George Orwell's *Animal Farm,* in which the pigs lead the other animals into overthrowing the farmer and then become indistinguishable from him.[34] One exception to this degradation of revolutions may be South Africa, but even there, most wealth is still in white hands, partly because of Nelson Mandela's decision not to expel the whites and partly because Mandela's revolutionary group— the African National Congress—was bullied by the United States and other global powers into accepting a capitalist system based on "neoliberal" or austerity policies. Even without external bullying, postrevolutionary South Africa might have embraced dominance and hierarchy. Power produces latent bullying, and it is very tempting to use it. Power can transform the gentle and the sensitive into authoritarian, perhaps even violent, bullies.

Although the movements of the 1960s and 1970s failed to live up to many of their ideals, the coming together of African Americans, women, gays, and affluent white students did test the basic values of the bullying culture. The sixties witnessed a movement driven by those most bullied in America, along with a subculture of elite young people who were rejecting the bullying culture created by their parents. Together, the activists of the sixties era launched a widespread and visionary attack on the culture of the United States and its militarized capitalism, redefining it as a bullying system.

But did it succeed? As with the Enlightenment, the answer is mixed. On the one hand, the sixties created new values and rhetoric that have had enduring effects on America. Women, gays, and African Americans, long subject to systemic and personal bullying, gained new rights and legal protections. Their identity movements growing out of the sixties gave them pride and a sense of strength.

The sixties-based movements—particularly those comprising students, women, gays, and African Americans—helped foster the current antibullying sentiment. For over half a century, the cultural warriors inspired by the 1960s have challenged traditional cultural authority, and they have fought against racist, sexist, or other forms of bullying. The sixties opened up a new conversation on cultural issues that has forced the nation as a whole to question established truths—many based on traditional religious doctrine—about marriage, the family, materialistic consumerism, systemic racism, militarism, and homosexuality. Inevitably, this has helped to bring into focus the bullying that oppressed people have endured. Beyond that and more indirectly, it has also raised broader questions about America as a bully nation.

At the same time, the sixties' counterculture had significant limits and failures. The cultural identity movements of women, gays, and African Americans have not created, as noted earlier, a fresh national consensus about their new values. To the contrary, their movements created the New Right that is fighting back against all the cultural and political changes the sixties tried to enact. The New Right has been especially appealing to white, religious, family-oriented conservatives, particularly in the South and the interior West. In many ways, this is a continuation of the culture wars that have raged since before the Civil War.[35] The one thing these conservatives, who felt denigrated by New Left students and other coastal elites, could cling to was their white caste privilege. The New Right rallied many working-class and rural people against the "elitists" who have allegedly allied themselves with blacks and other racial minorities to undermine their sense of caste identity and worth.[36] The country is now deeply divided on social and cultural issues, resulting in today's culture war. Although the sixties brought a counterculture that has had great influence, the children of that counterculture must now fight their own very tough battles on the social, economic, military, and cultural fronts. It remains unclear which set of values will prevail.

Because the divisions are still so bitter and strong, the legacy of the sixties in changing national institutions and policies has been weak. With the coming of the Reagan revolution, economic inequalities, including job and poverty problems, grew worse than they were in the sixties. Capitalism has become more unequal and punitive, bullying the poor and much of the population with severe austerity policies that are far more harsh than in the sixties. Violence—carried out by the military abroad and by the police and individual shooters at home—has escalated rather than declined. And US militarized capitalism has gained global power and used it to bully more workers and nations around the globe.

The failure of the sixties to soften or reduce bullying also reflects limitations and weaknesses of the counterculture movements. The identity movements around race and gender have largely failed to address issues of class or to challenge the militarized capitalism that helps create the structural bullying of much of the population.[37] Many veterans of the anti-Vietnam movement may oppose the wars in Iraq or Afghanistan, but they have forgotten the fundamental critique of capitalism and militarism. They have implicitly accepted the microparadigm of bullying and failed to embrace the macroparadigm that highlights the structural bullying endemic to our system of militarized capitalism. This dooms any effort to ward off the systemic bullying that we have discussed throughout this book as central to the bullying scourge.

In the current culture war—and the larger politics surrounding it—we need to take seriously the lessons of the earlier countercultural movements. In our concluding chapter, we will offer a few suggestions about how to incorporate the sociological imagination and the macroparadigm to change our bullying culture and reduce the suffering and trauma that bullying inflicts on millions of Americans and people throughout the world.

Are There Solutions?

New Ways to Think about Reducing Bullying

In this book, we have offered a new paradigm for thinking about the causes of bullying. We hope it will lead to a basic shift of thinking, with big implications for scholarship on bullying and for the public's understanding of the problem. But perhaps of greatest importance, our paradigm shift may lead to a new way of thinking about how to alleviate bullying and reduce its pervasive and tragic consequences on institutions, individuals, and society itself.

We have argued that bullying has deep structural and systemic roots and is not simply a problem caused by psychological or psychiatric disorders. This obviously points to the role of the political economy as a target for intervention if we want to reduce societal bullying. If militarized capitalism is the core systemic root of bullying, then modifications in that system are crucial to any meaningful change.

This does not mean that psychological approaches to dealing with individual bullies or victims of bullying should be eliminated. The key to the sociological imagination is the relation between social structure and individual character. Militarized capitalism, operating through transmission institutions such as schools, the military, and the family, plays a pivotal causal role. Thus, interventions in school policies, in the family, and in interpersonal and intrapsychic dynamics are part of any reasonable antibullying approach.

But our analysis suggests that these will be, at best, a bandage rather than a cure—an approach to symptoms rather than the underlying disease. If our new paradigm is correct, the ultimate causes lie in our political economy, and we cannot expect deep and meaningful change until we change our system of militarized capitalism. Of course, we need to treat the military, the school, and the family as parts of the political economy.

Making such a change is a formidable challenge. But because of extreme inequality, environmental crises, spreading wars, and social and other problems in our domestic society, there are many reasons to change our political economy. New movements—whether Occupy Wall Street or the minimum wage movements or environmental movements against climate change or black resistance to police bullying, such as Black Lives Matter—are all rising to take on our militarized capitalism. They will be leaders in the new effort to reduce bullying, sometimes inadvertently, that will make a real difference.

Although we want to suggest a few new "macro" approaches based on our new paradigm, we need to make some initial observations and disclaimers. First, the antibullying movement is already having an impact. Whether or not it has actually reduced bullying behavior, it has changed attitudes toward bullying. Now, bullies can no longer feel confident they will be acclaimed as heroes and leaders. Instead, they risk being shunned or punished in some way. They may even be involuntarily required to undergo therapy, which many will find at least embarrassing. In suggesting new approaches, we do not mean to denigrate the intentions of most opponents of bullying. Rather, we are looking for ways to strengthen the current movement so that it can attract more advocates and develop more effective visions and policies.

Second, we do not believe that bullying can be eliminated. It has been present throughout history, and it exists in nearly every society. This is partly because it is latent in our biological programming, as is evident in the bullying seen in the natural world among animal species. And it is also because bullying is a part of the exercise of power; the elimination of bullying would require the elimination of power, both interpersonally and in economic, political, and military systems. It is far-fetched to imagine this change.

Both the Enlightenment and the sixties led to countercultures that eroded earlier forms of bullying but also created new forms. The Enlightenment weakened medieval forms of church and aristocratic bullying but laid the groundwork for the violence of the French Revolution and, later, the violence of the modern capitalist state and corporate system. As we have seen, the sixties' New Left sometimes fought violence with violence, establishing groups such as the Black Panthers and the Weathermen that romanticized picking up a gun in the name of liberation. This reinforces the idea that even antibullying cultures can produce their own bullying, an idea that is getting new attention today.

Some argue that the current attempt to stop bullying in schools is actually creating a disguised bullying system of its own.[1] It is a way to bully kids and teachers who are not politically correct or don't buy into fashionable ideas about permissiveness, sexism, or racism. Or it can be a means to get your way by accusing those who disagree with you of being bullies.[2] If you are a student, parent, or teacher who believes in old-fashioned discipline, some claim the new antibullying movement will bully you into submission, and they contend that it represents an assault on free speech.[3] The same bullying might be turned on those who reject the new "self-esteem" curriculum or countercultural therapies that claim to change the personalities of bullies.

Nonetheless, it would be unduly pessimistic to argue that we can do nothing about bullying. Serious efforts have been made in recent years in the United States, and successes have been achieved, at least in changing attitudes. Some of the worst forms of bullying and violence in ancient times have been delegitimated and weakened—including slavery and cannibalism. In the last few decades, victims of bullying such as gays, racial minorities, and the disabled have gained more legal and cultural protections.

Our view is that we can achieve better results by restructuring society and the militarism and harsh capitalism that create or reinforce bullying. We want to move toward a new culture and socioeconomic system that discourages bullying rather than rewarding it. The result will not be the elimination of all bullying but rather a reduction in its scale and the level of suffering it inflicts, as well as possibly a reduction in the number of bullies who rise to leadership positions.

This puts us on the path less taken—and the one that follows from the analysis in this book. Bullying must be understood as behavior constructed by hierarchical and violent societal systems, even if it also has biological and psychological roots. Although the current approach has largely been to focus on interpersonal interventions—through psychotherapy or counseling of kids at schools—we want to look at bullying in the world of adults, driven not simply by psychological problems but also by socioeconomic and military institutions that survive and prosper by rewarding bullying.

Comparative national studies of personal bullying—though limited in number and far from conclusive—suggest that there are many developed countries in the world that have less bullying than the United States. Many European countries rank as lower in bullying than the United States, with Sweden and some other Scandinavian countries often rated as particularly low in school and workplace bullying—and in the safety and well-being of children (seen in the conventional paradigm as a measure of protection from bullying).[4] What might explain this? And why might the results actually understate the true differences?

First, Sweden and Denmark, like most European countries, have very small militaries compared to the United States. They embrace a more peaceful way of thinking about the world and managing conflict. Their military systems are defensive and have no capacity for aggression or conquest. Thus, the bullying that stems from militarism does not exist in most countries in Europe today, especially small ones such as Sweden and Denmark.

Second, the studies are measuring rates of personal bullying, but they do not count victims of structural bullying. This excludes millions of victims who suffer from unrecognized forms of structural bullying, such as low-wage workers, foreclosed homeowners, and victims of military or police repression. If we take those who are structurally bullied into account, the numbers of bullied in the United States would soar astronomically and those in Scandinavian countries such as Sweden and Denmark would increase far less, since the latter countries have softer economies and smaller militaries that produce far less institutional bullying.

This points us in an obvious direction. If we want to reduce bullying, we need to embrace economic models more like those in Sweden and Denmark—as well as reduce our militaries to the small, defensive forces found in Scandinavian countries.[5] Making a shift toward the European economic system and approach to international peace is a logical macrostrategy to address the macrobullying generated by US militarized capitalism. At the very least, it will lead to fewer rewards for bullying behavior and make bullies less likely to be perceived as natural leaders.

Sweden and Denmark are capitalist nations, but compared to the United States, they are more egalitarian and compassionate toward workers and the poor; they have more generous social welfare systems and far better job protections, worker training, and benefits.[6] Moreover, they have two macrosystem characteristics that almost certainly reduce both structural and personal bullying. First, inequality is far lower in almost all European countries, especially in Sweden and Denmark. Since inequality of power and wealth is the structural foundation of all bully systems, economic models organized to create more equality will reduce institutional bullying and personal bullying as well.

Second, European nations tend to be more inclusive, viewing all citizens as stakeholders entitled to benefits in their universal welfare states. This means that everyone receives free or inexpensive education, health care, child care, elder care, public transportation, and many other public goods. Universal welfare both reflects and creates more community, and it reduces the distinctions between in-groups and out-groups that define bullying cultures.

Of course, all of this needs to be qualified by the greater cultural homogeneity of European societies and their difficulty in assimilating immigrants from the Middle East, North Africa, and Asia. Even in Scandinavia, immigration has tested the limits of European inclusiveness. Immigrants have been subjected to both institutional and personal bullying, resulting in a rise in violence in these traditionally peaceful and egalitarian societies. This shows, again, the challenge of eroding bullying in societies that are ethnically diverse and that are divided economically between poor immigrants and prosperous white European, native-born peoples.

A third factor, probably related to small militaries, is the European approach to the environment. Scandinavian nations, along with most other European countries, have a much lower per capita carbon footprint than the United States. They are moving far more rapidly than the United States to a renewable energy economy that drastically reduces environmental bludgeoning and bullying. Europeans are seeking to live in harmony with the earth, rather than dominating it for short-term profit.[7]

This turns us back to more general features of European culture. In comparison with Americans, Europeans tend to be more cooperative, less competitive, more generous toward the poor, and less enamored of the reverse Robin Hood austerity politics that enriches the already wealthy in the United States. These egalitarian and antibullying values are linked to a more peaceful and collective approach to world affairs, together with a rejection of the idea of hegemony. Europe is no longer seeking to dominate the world, perhaps sobered by the two world wars that destroyed European empires and their militaristic cultures.[8]

This suggests that perhaps the most important change in the United States would be to let go of the idea of global dominance. American exceptionalism has long promoted this vision, and the twentieth century was the American century—in which the nation was the only true superpower. Many Americans still believe this is the right path for their country, and politicians have campaigned as if it would be suicidal not to embrace it.

But economic and political changes, including the cost of terrible and failed wars in Vietnam, Iraq, and Afghanistan, may, we hope, weaken the American appetite for dominance and military intervention. Americans elected Obama partly for his opposition to Bush's war in Iraq. Obama won a Nobel Peace Prize but quickly reverted to the US elites' commitment to American hegemony or dominance. Nonetheless, millions of Americans are tired of their country's wars and see a higher priority for social and economic reconstruction at home.

Because of this changed attitude, there is an opening through which the antibullying campaign must move. Dominance is the core value of bullying culture. If the United States were to move away from its militaristic view of itself as the world's policeman—which much of the world views as another name for world bully—it would weaken the central macropillar of America as a bully nation. This is arguably the most important political strategy to reduce structural bullying and broader forms of violence in the world.

An effort to embrace more of the egalitarian economics of the European social welfare states would be the natural complement to this antibullying macromovement, as would a shift toward the "share economy" movement and the "new economy" visions advanced by progressive thinkers in the United States. Writers such as Juliet Schor and Gar Alperovitz have laid out new economic visions for a sustainable and democratic economy that would foster a new culture of cooperation and more altruistic and communal values.[9] If we reduce the domination of the superrich at home and seek to invest in public goods for the entire society, we are taking direct aim at the bullying culture. Public investment in infrastructure, especially a new renewable energy system, would create more and better jobs at home that would serve the well-being of the whole planet. Since this would be funded by money taken from reduced military budgets, it would immediately reduce structural bullying. By reducing both militarism and environmental bludgeoning and bullying, while improving the lives of most of our struggling workers currently bullied into insecurity and fear, we would promote the new economy and politics of people at peace with the earth and each other. This is not only good economics and good environmental policy. It is also our best way to live with each other less violently and more humanely, as well as our best prospect for reducing the bullying scourge that is inflicting so much suffering in the United States and the world.

Our God, Our Bully

Israel, Jihad, and the Middle East—
Ancient and Modern

Our shift in ways of thinking about bullying has relevance far beyond the United States. Institutionalized bullying is a major problem in many nations and regions around the world. In this appendix, we look at the Middle East, with an analysis of Israel and some of the Islamic nations and religious groups in conflict with one another and with Israel itself. We hope to show that our concept of institutionalized bullying provides a historical and contemporary window into a new way of viewing much of the world's most important and distressing violence, while also showing how nations or groups that at one period stood out as antibullies can evolve into some of the world's fiercest bullies.

The United States, the focus of this book, is probably the most powerful bullying military empire in the world today, but it has predecessors, among them Rome, Britain, the Mongols, Nazi Germany, the Stalinist Soviet Union, and ancient China. China could offer a challenge again, as could a united Europe. In *The Better Angels of Our Nature*,[1] Steven Pinker suggests that violent bullying has diminished; in fact, he argues, the twentieth was the gentlest and the kindest century in the history of the world. However, that assessment seems dubious when we realize he was talking about a century that brought us to the brink of nuclear annihilation and gave us the two most destructive world wars in all of history, a series of near genocides on several continents, and an environment so polluted that it endangers the survival of the biosphere.

Violent bullying is hardly the exclusive province of vast empires. Tiny Belgium may now pride itself on being one of the world's leading advocates of human rights, but from 1885 to 1908, Belgium's King Leopold II killed, it is estimated, at least 10 million people in the Congo as he enslaved local populations and burned down villages in his efforts to extract ivory and rubber.[2] If we fast-forward a hundred years, we continue to see people facing brutal bullying and a lack of rights in relatively weak poor countries, especially in the Middle East—places labeled by the Western media as terrorist states. As Noam Chomsky affirmed the level of atrocities committed by movements such as the Islamic State of Iraq and Syria, he suggested they are inadvertent by-products of the American invasions of Iraq and Afghanistan:

> ISIS is a monstrosity. There's not much doubt about that. It didn't come from nowhere. It's one of the results of the U.S. hitting a very vulnerable society—Iraq—with a sledgehammer, which elicited sectarian conflicts that had not existed. They became very violent. The U.S. violence made it worse. We're all familiar with the crimes. Out of this came lots of violent, murderous forces. ISIS is one.[3]

When we speak of a terrorist movement, we must remember that *terrorist* itself is a vague, subjective term. If a small group, often without a state, uses violence to resist a powerful nation, it gets described as "terrorist." The mouse becomes a terrorist bully threatening the lion. Chomsky and Edward Herman have suggested the label should be reversed. They say that "the Real Terror Network" is the United States and its clients, such as Israel.[4] The meaning of the word *terrorist,* much like *bully,* may mean quite different things to different people; each side in a conflict may call itself a victim and the other a perpetrator. Were the American invasions of Vietnam, Iraq, and Afghanistan acts of terrorism? How about the bombings of Hiroshima, Nagasaki, and Dresden? Or Israel's incursion into Lebanon or its occupation of the West Bank and Gaza? Powerful nations describe their weak opponents as terrorist to claim they are bullied and acting in self-defense or in defense of a stable global order that provides security for the weak as well as the strong. When he was the head of state, hardly anyone screamed louder against terrorism than the late Israeli prime minister Menachem Begin. When the British controlled Palestine, including what eventually became Israel, London put a price on his head for conducting "terrorism"—the very word they used. He was held responsible for bombing the British army headquarters at the King David Hotel.[5]

Begin's heirs, including Benjamin Netanyahu, still label Arab resistance terrorist as they continue to suppress Palestinian rights and threaten other countries. Partially, but not entirely, as a result of its own recalcitrant policies, Israel does have real enemies. It does have reason to fear that even if it became more tolerant and conciliatory, some Arabs would forever perceive it as an illegitimate representative of Western colonialism—a Jewish incursion dumped by Christians on Muslim territory.

As we look for an example of a small bully nation that, despite its size, wields great influence in the world, we shall focus mainly upon Israel, although it is hardly unique. It is an appropriate choice for several reasons. First, Israel is heavily dependent upon the United States—both the American government, especially the military apparatus, and the self-appointed wealthy leadership of the American Jewish community. Indeed, some people speculate it could not survive without American support. Second, it is heir to a millennia-old history in which one people experienced both ends of the bullying hierarchy. Although their numbers were never large, the Israelites tried to assert bullying power for some of that history. At other times, the Jews were among the world's most vulnerable bullying victims. This suggests the bullying hierarchy is fluid; someone's position on the spectrum can change over time. There is no innate bullying personality or culture; rather, events and resources can make you a bully or a victim, and neither bully nor victim has an automatic claim to moral superiority.

BULLYING BY ISLAMIC NATIONS AND GROUPS:
ISIS, AL QAEDA, AND SAUDI ARABIA

Right now, Israel is powerful enough to bully its neighbors. But it feels vulnerable, and as Chomsky points out, many of its neighbors should not be called nice. They viciously bully their own people and have dreams of—and carry out—bullying of their neighbors, if not the whole world, as France learned in 2015. As of 2015, the American-installed government of Iraq had lost control of much of its territory to ISIS, which is making incursions into Syria and potentially other countries. According to Graeme Wood, anyone who tries to understand ISIS through the logic of modern Western politics will be misled. The group's goal is to impose a medieval caliphate upon the entire world. There, everyone would be subject to sharia, or Koran-based Islamic law, under which any person who questions its authority will face beheading, stoning, crucifixion, or some other form of execution or torture. Since ISIS members believe they operate under divine authority, they are not bound by agreements they may temporarily make with any nation-state; thus, they can never be expected to operate under Western-invented international law. "We can gather that their state rejects peace as a matter of principle; that it hungers for genocide; that its religious views make it constitutionally incapable of certain types of change, even if that change might ensure its survival; and that it considers itself a harbinger of—and headline player in—the imminent end of the world."[6]

Largely as a warning of what is to come and what did come in 2015, ISIS has proudly broadcast beheadings of Western intruders over the international media. Anyone who participates in an election, wears Western clothes, shaves, or drinks alcohol—and perhaps even a person who tries to deal civilly with outsiders or refuses to participate in a stoning—will be deemed an apostate and face severe, if not fatal, consequences. ISIS claims it has the right—no, the duty—to abduct women, even married women, and transform them into concubines.[7] In another video released for international consumption, ISIS shows a married woman being stoned to death by a mob that is led by her father, who proclaims that since she brought dishonor upon the family through adultery, she is no longer his daughter. The woman is bullied into accepting her executioners' definition of reality. She is told, "You must accept God's rule and this is a sin that you have committed." To which she replies, "I say to every woman: preserve your honor . . . and I appeal to every father to pay attention to the surroundings your daughter lives in."[8]

ISIS followers believe any government that refuses to enforce a literal interpretation of sharia, even one that claims to be a caliphate, is illegitimate and must be overthrown. It is understandable why the United States, Israel, and other Western or Muslim countries may feel that ISIS's rampant bullying must be stopped by any means necessary.

ISIS's violent bullying did move beyond the Middle East to endanger the West. In Paris on Friday, November 13, 2015, suicide bombers and gunmen, claiming membership in ISIS, simultaneously attacked a soccer stadium, a concert hall, and several restaurants, killing at least 127 people.[9] Pope Francis, known for his tolerance and universalism, declared that the bombing and shootings were part of a "piecemeal third world war."[10]

Although ISIS calls itself an Islamic state, it is really a large gang (about 30,000 fighters in Iraq and Syria as of 2015) of bullies, violent criminals, and thugs, who embrace an extreme and distorted version of Islam. Relative to large Western powers, they have tiny resources, whether of land, weapons, or people, but they are capable of inflicting serious damage and killing many civilians, both Muslim and non-Muslim. As with the schoolyard bully, ISIS shows that, with a relatively modest amount of power, it is capable not only of bullying the people directly under its control but also intimidating populations through many parts of the world.

The parallels between groups such as ISIS and bullies at school are never discussed in the West, but they are quite striking. Both are wedded to violence—and know how to use it—to establish and maintain their control. Like many bullies in US schools, ISIS members are skillful in using social media to attract followers and attack enemies. And they demonstrate that the bully is capable, with relatively few resources, of spreading great fear and inflicting scarring threats and violence.

The modern West prides itself on freedom of movement, expression, and life style choice, principles that violate a state governed by the ISIS version of Islamic law, under which there is only the truth revealed in the Koran. Diane Foley is the mother of James Foley, a Western journalist who was beheaded by "Jihadi John"; this ISIS leader, whose real name was Mohammed Emwazi, is believed to have been killed in an American bombing raid. Diane Foley offered this tribute to her son: "I hope our country can choose to lead in ways of peace and valuing young Americans who are trying to protect press freedom and our best ideals. That's the part of America I'm proud of. I don't like this bully part."[11]

In an Islam caliphate, there is no need for freedom; it may even be viewed as evil. A few violent acts by a tiny number of people, especially if they are willing to die for Allah, can drive Western states to severely curtail their own citizens' freedom in the name of protecting them. We are all familiar with increased scrutiny at airports in the wake of 9/11. It has become so routine that we hardly think about it. Each violent attack on Western civilians can lead to government policies that further erode freedom. Thus, Islamic fundamentalist groups, such as Al Qaeda or ISIS, although tiny in numbers, can bully the world's richest and most powerful countries into undermining modern Western values. The acts of a few Muslims have intensified Western hostility toward Islam, reducing the freedom of Muslims and leading to a self-fulfilling prophecy—behaviors that affirm that no Muslim can trust a Christian or a Jew. After the Paris attacks, there was talk throughout Europe of increased surveillance of Muslims and a decreased willingness to welcome Syrian refugees fleeing ISIS out of a fear that some of them could be ISIS sympathizers.

ISIS and Western advocates of strong action against it have something in common, which they share with bullies: a xenophobic distrust of anyone outside their culture or control. Many Islamic fundamentalists assume that no matter how much openness or tolerance Westerners—whether Christians or Jews—may profess, they all harbor a secret hatred toward Islam and want to impose their values and culture on the Middle East, as they steal its oil and exploit it economically. Behind any Jew lurks a Zionist, cheering the Palestinian occupation. Similarly, much discourse in the West assumes any Muslim is a potential terrorist anticipating the moment when a global caliphate emerges victorious. As with the schoolyard bullies, ISIS, Al Qaeda, and other Islamic fundamentalists draw deep identity and status distinctions between the inner "saved" group (the "cool" or "in" group in the school) and everyone else. The outsiders, those not in the faith, will be subject to endless threats, humiliation, and verbal or physical violence. This all is in the "natural order of things," reflecting God's will, in the case of ISIS, and the evolutionary differences in strength, cleverness, or toughness in the schoolyard.

When Paris was attacked, France declared war against ISIS, bombing it mercilessly. This will be matched by more attacks from ISIS and more recruitment of young people to ISIS's cause as Muslim civilians die from French and American air strikes. It appears that xenophobic bullying provoked by xenophobic bullying breeds more xenophobic bullying, a variant of bullying eliciting fear and reprisals in schoolyards.

This bullying dynamic plays out in politics as we have shown throughout the book, in ways that reproduce anger, fear, and recruitment to one's own cause, again much as in the schoolyard. Republican presidential candidates seem to believe that American distrust of Muslims will unify their base. Likewise, enmity toward the West—including Christian Europe, the United States, and Israel—is a common cause uniting Muslim fundamentalists who are actually very hostile to each other. Israel itself also has deep internal divisions that could tear the country apart were it not for a sense that all Israelis are under seige by a shared enemy. Saudi Arabia is an absolute monarchy whose royal family enriches itself through controlling much of the world's oil, but the monarchy is under constant peril of being overthrown by its own people. The Israeli lobby tries to minimize American support for the monarchy, but Israel and Saudi Arabia have something in common: they both depend upon military aid from the United States. American militarized capitalism may profess democracy, but for all its power, it is bullied into not being too critical of the Saudi Arabian monarchs for fear that they could cut the oil supply to the West. Saudi Arabia has adopted as its official ideology Wahhabism, an eighteenth-century reading of Islamic law that is little different from the one adopted by ISIS. ISIS has accused the Saudis of not being sufficiently committed to sharia, yet from 2007 to 2010, there allegedly were 345 public beheadings in Saudi Arabia.[12] Sorcery, apostasy, and adultery are included among capital offenses there, and homosexuals are lashed, if not executed. Janine Di Giovanni of *Newsweek* sees little difference between Saudi Arabia and ISIS other than that the former is a recognized state with close ties to the United States. However, because of America's dependency, one gets labeled a legitimate state that the United States may go to war to defend and the other gets labeled as terrorist. As ISIS attacks other Muslim countries, it would like to overthrow the Saudi Arabian monarchy, but it is not clear how different Saudi life would be if ISIS prevailed.

The so-called terrorist organization that destroyed the World Trade Center in New York on September 11, 2001, is, of course, Al Qaeda. Its lifeblood was resentment against American support for Saudi Arabia, and its leader, Osama Bin Laden, envisioned himself as the eventual leader of that country. He too sought a country, if not a world, governed by a literal interpretation of Islamic law. Again, there was little substantive difference between the codes of Al Qaeda, ISIS, and Saudi Arabia, but Al Qaeda accused the Saudis of not being pure enough and ISIS launched the same charge at Al Qaeda.

The United States has difficulty conceiving that ordinary people, on their own, could legitimately be hostile to American intentions and policies: somebody must be misleading them, and there is no such thing as a movement that can emerge spontaneously without hierarchical leadership. The truth is, however, that even though Bin Laden sponsored Al Qaeda, it was a loose confederation, much of which was not under his direct control. In the 1980s, he had received American support because the United States hoped he would help drain the Soviet Union of resources in its invasion of Afghanistan. Similarly, the United States had supported Saddam Hussein because he had gone to war against Iran, which was seen as even more anti-American. Although Bin Laden and Saddam Hussein were actually enemies, the United States assumed no one could possibly attack them without the support of a state, especially one that threatened American interests, and Hussein challenged America's usage of the Persian Gulf as a shipping lane for oil. Somehow, then, Hussein was deemed responsible for 9/11. Feeling its bullying power threatened, the United States wanted to blame a nation-state. It could not admit that a loose confederation without an organized army could ever challenge it. Hence, the United States invaded Iraq, with consequences that are all too well known.[13]

A BULLYING GOD? THE EARLY HISTORY OF THE JEWS

Bullying in the Middle East is nothing new. For millennia, empires rose and fell in the region and nations violently bullied each other (or at least tried to). The ancient Israelites dreamed of a bullying empire, but they never really achieved it. Envisioning themselves, like ISIS, as acting with a divine moral blessing, they worshiped a god who went through several transformations over the centuries but whose earliest images were certainly bullylike. He anointed them as a "chosen people," a status that originally may have made them feel morally free to do whatever they wanted to other nations, particularly the Canaanites, whose land they conquered. Initially, their god promised them virtually the entire known civilized world: "To your offspring, I assign this land, from the river of Egypt to the great river, the Euphrates."[14] This was a god who ordered genocide and then disqualified Israel's first king, Saul, from the throne when he failed to obey a command to kill every man, woman, child, and animal from Amalek.[15] Like the god of ISIS, this divinity required stoning of homosexuals,[16] women who were found not to be virgins at the time of their weddings, and adulterers.[17] Like a schoolyard bully, this god would not tolerate dissent or challenges to his authority or that of his designated leaders. His reactions could be so brutal that the grumblers would soon learn they had better acquiesce and accept their punishment as completely justified.

> The people spoke against God and against Moses, "Why did you make us leave Egypt to die in the wilderness? There is no bread and no water, and we have come to loathe this miserable food." The Lord sent serpents against the people. They bit the people and many of the Israelites died. The people came to Moses and said, "We have sinned by speaking against the LORD and against you."[18]

Capriciously, God tested righteous Job. Robbers took his herds and wealth. His children and most of his servants were killed, and he himself was inflicted with boils. Job did not question God's just intentions, and he begged heaven to explain what he did to deserve his fate. God replied by essentially telling Job he was a little nothing whom God had made and whom God could destroy at whim, someone so inferior that he simply could not understand God's way. To expect God to explain his actions was arrogant:

> Who is this who darkens counsel,
> Speaking without knowledge? . . .

Where were you when I laid the earth's foundations?Have the gates of
   death been disclosed to you?
Have you seen the gates of deep darkness?
If you know these—tell Me.[19]

When Judea was conquered, its people found themselves at the mercy of great empires, and they were forced to abandon any fantasy of glory and domination. Sure enough, their god was transformed from a brutal warlord bully to a protector who provided peace and compassion. Even the early books of the Torah, where God is at his most vindictive, advise the Jews to remember that they had been slaves and strangers and therefore to treat other peoples, especially people over whom they have power, with fairness and generosity: "You shall not oppress a stranger, for you have known the feelings of the stranger, having been strangers yourself in the land of Egypt."[20] The same prophets who warn Israel of total destruction, such as Jeremiah, once they lose their home offer a vision of joy, harmony, and celebration:

The blind and the lame among them . . .
They shall come with weeping
And with compassion will I guide them . . .
Then shall maidens dance gaily.
Young men and old alike,
I will turn their mourning to joy,
I will comfort them and cheer them in their grief.[21]

The prophets offered this hope not just for Israel. There would be a messianic age when all humanity would live in peace and friendship—a world of kindness and sharing, not aggression and hate:

They shall beat their swords into plowshares
And their spears into pruning hooks:
Nation shall not take up
Sword against nation
They shall never again know war.[22]

The Book of Kings, written before Judea was conquered, and the Book of Chronicles, written afterward, both assert that David, the warrior king, was not qualified to build the temple in Jerusalem, the city he conquered and made his capital. However, they offer very different explanations, which suggests a profound change in values before and after the fall of Judea.

Kings suggests he had not yet had the decisive victory "because of the enemies that encompassed him, until the LORD had placed them under the soles of his feet."[23] Chronicles claims the fact that he was a warrior, victorious or not, disqualified him; it declares: "for you have shed much blood on the earth in My (God's) sight."[24]

After a first exile, the Jews were able to return to their homeland, but they lived in the shadow of powerful empires: Persia, Alexander, and Rome. However, a rebellion against Rome ended in a second exile, which persisted for 2,000 years. They wandered among other peoples, where they faced outcast status, expulsions, violence, pogroms, and ultimately the Holocaust. In their pariah position, they clung to the image of their god as one who promises peace, compassion, and comfort, not a bully warlord. They admired scholars, not warriors. In fact, they regarded soldiers as the "scum of the earth." Although they could be aggressive in business or in arguments, they shunned violence. They could manipulate adversaries by going out of their way to appear weak and unthreatening. Humor was a weapon they resorted to far more readily than armaments. Yet even though they often appeared to be compliant bully victims, underneath that veneer rested a defiance that Rabbi Walter Waskow called "God-wrestling."[25] Rabbi Sherwin Wine described this: "The other personality and tradition, the unofficial one was skeptical and angry. It shrugged its shoulders a lot, distrusted all authority, and learned to laugh at the absurdity of things. . . . Its heroes are the angry mockers of authority who conform reluctantly because they have to."[26]

God-wrestling almost certainly helped the Jews survive through 2,000 years of pariah status, and it may account for their having an influence far beyond their demographic numbers. For instance, "although Jews make up only 0.2 percent of the world's population, they win an astonishing 22 percent of Nobel Prizes."[27] In the United States, God-wrestling may explain why Jews are the most liberal and Democratic white ethnic group. In the 2012 election, President Obama won only 39 percent of the white vote[28] but 70 percent of the Jewish vote.[29]

ISRAEL AS A BULLY NATION: FROM VICTIMS TO BULLY

After 2,000 years of wandering as bullied pariahs, largely as the world's compensation for the Holocaust, the Jews got their state back. The way that country, modern Israel, evolved and the culture it adopted suggest that bully and victim are not absolute categories, that you can transform from one to the other, that peace-loving and compassionate victims can be products of circumstances, and that given the opportunity they can become nasty bullies. This may apply to both individuals and nations.

Leaders of the Israeli government consider their nation as the only democracy in the Middle East and believe they are the bearers of civilization in an eternal war against terrorism. Israel pictures itself as a tiny enclave, perpetually besieged by vast hordes of enemies intent on bringing a second holocaust—even though the country can easily overwhelm any likely foe militarily. The Israelis use the 2,000 years of persecution, especially the Holocaust, as a blank check justifying whatever they do. Like a bully, they use that history as a bludgeon, squelching debate. Any gentile critic gets intimidated with the label "anti-Semite," and they try to silence Jewish challengers by calling them "self-haters." Former President Jimmy Carter points out that even in America, politicians dare not defy the Israeli lobby: "It would be almost politically suicidal for members of Congress to espouse a balanced position between Israel and Palestine, to suggest that Israel comply with international law or to speak in defense of justice or human rights for Palestinians."[30]

When Carter proposed this, Abraham Foxman, director of the Antidefamation League, responded, "For a man of his stature and supposed savvy to hold forth that Jews and Zionists have closed off means of discussion is just anti-Semitism."[31]

In a very real sense, the Palestinians are paying the world's price for the 2,000 years of oppression, even though they had little to do with it. This is reminiscent of ancient times when the Canaanites basically paid for what the Egyptians did. Israelis seem to have forgotten the commandment not to persecute the stranger because they have been strangers in someone else's land. The slogan "Never again" has come to mean "Get them before they get you." Instead, it could mean: "We know what it is to wander the earth at the mercy of other nations. Let us take no path which would increase the misery of displaced peoples and make sure no one else goes through a holocaust even vaguely approximating ours."

Carter, along with former Irish president Mary Robinson, has described Israel's treatment of the Palestinians as war crimes. Certainly, bullying is an apt description.

> Israel rejected this opportunity for peace. . . . There is no humane or legal justification for the way the Israeli Defense Forces are conducting this war.

Israeli bombs, missiles, and artillery have pulverized large parts of Gaza, including thousands of homes, schools, and hospitals. More than 250,000 people have been displaced from their homes in Gaza. Hundreds of Palestinian noncombatants have been killed. Much of Gaza has lost access to water and electricity completely. This is a humanitarian catastrophe. ... There is never an excuse for deliberate attacks on civilians in conflict. These are war crimes.[32]

Israeli bullying tactics in the West Bank and Gaza appear to be intended to make sure that the Palestinians never have a viable state that thrives independently of Israeli control—one that can challenge Israeli authority, manage its own resources, develop its own economy, or provide for its own people. After living in the region, Australian journalist Mel Frykberg observed Israeli practices that she called "environmental terrorism,"[33] deliberately intended to impoverish the Palestinians and make life for them in the West Bank unsustainable. Knowing that olive trees are a staple of the Palestinian economy and ever present in the lifestyle, the Israelis have been systematically chopping them down: "According to the Palestinian Authority (PA) and the Applied Research Institute Jerusalem (ARIJ), approximately 800,000 olive trees have been uprooted since Israel occupied the West Bank and Gaza in 1967."[34]

After the Palestinians are bullied into leaving, the Israelis can claim the land is abandoned and seize it, as the Palestinians find themselves unable to legally protect their property.

The Israelis' treatment of the Arabs is motivated by more than fear or an economic desire to control land and resources. It is also an attempt to show the world that they are no longer the wimps—the schlemiels—who could be pushed around for 2,000 years only to march into the gas chambers. There is a sense that if old Jews were too weak or peace-loving to fight back, they deserved their bullied fate. New Jews are now tough. No one had better mess with them.[35] Israeli tourist posters show soldiers with machine guns praying at the Western Wall, the surviving relic of the old Jerusalem temple. (We decided we had better not call it by its old name, the Wailing Wall, because that implies weakness and mourning; Israelis view their control of the Western Wall as a sign of triumph.) The god they now worship is more like the warrior bully of the early books of the Hebrew Bible than the god of compassion and universality of the later books. They shun the culture that evolved in eastern Europe in the last few centuries before the Holocaust. They have replaced the language of that culture, Yiddish, with Hebrew, the language of the ancient warrior bully god. Here is an excerpt from a conversation between Yiddish novelist Isaac Singer and Israeli prime minister Menachem Begin in 1978, the year they both won the Nobel Prize:

> "With Yiddish," Begin shouted, "we could not have created any navy; with Yiddish, we could have no army; with Yiddish, we could not defend ourselves with powerful jet planes; with Yiddish, we would be nothing. We would be like animals."
>
> Isaac sat with hands folded in his lap and shrugged his shoulders. "Nu," he said sweetly to the hushed crowd, "since I am a vegetarian, for me to be like an animal is not such a terrible thing."[36]

Although they were obsessed with Jewish survival, it was the goal of Begin and his successors to transform the Jews into "a people like everyone else"; they would forget their universalistic, pacifistlike, humanist, "God-wrestling" traditions and instead be tied to a land where they could assert militaristic bullying power. The death of an individual Jew would be as deplorable as anyone else's, but the survival of Jews as a people matters only if they are a distinctive culture with unique gifts. Ironically, their status as pariah bully victims helped them to develop such a culture. Access to bullying power has made them new enemies, not brought them security or safety, and becoming "a people like any other" may destroy their distinctive culture as effectively as any enemy ever could.

Notes

CHAPTER 1: RETHINKING BULLYING

1. Katherine Newman, Cybelle Fox, Wendy Roth, Jal Mehta, and David Harding, *Rampage: The Social Roots of School Shootings* (New York: Basic Books, 2005).

2. Jessie Klein, *The Bully Society: School Shootings and the Crisis of Bullying in America's Schools* (New York: NYU Press, 2013).

3. A quick look at the entry on "Bullying" on *Wikipedia* immediately makes clear the psychological focus in the reigning scholarship and public discourse. The entry also cites many of the leading scholarly works in this area. See "Bullying," *Wikipedia,* posted at http://en.wikipedia.org/wiki/Bullying#Definitions. For standard approaches, see Eve M. Brank, Lori A. Hoetger, and Katherine P. Hazen, "Bullying," *Annual Review of Law and Social Science* 8 (December 2012): 213–230, doi:10.1146 /annurev-lawsocsci-102811-173820, retrieved October 28, 2013; Elizabeth Bennett, *Peer Abuse Know More! Bullying from a Psychological Perspective,* Infinity, January 1, 2006, ISBN 978-0-7414-3265-0, retrieved October 29, 2013.

4. C. Wright Mills, *The Sociological Imagination* (Oxford: Oxford University Press, 1958).

5. Klein, *Bully Society.*

6. Robert Zemeckis, *Back to the Future,* NBC Universal, Hollywood, CA, 1985.

7. Jeff Kinney, *The Diary of a Wimpy Kid* (New York: Amulet, 2007).

8. Carrie Goldman, *Bullied: What Every Parent, Teacher and Kid Needs to Know about Ending the Cycle of Fear* (New York: Harper, 2013).

9. For examples, see Alisha R. Cardemil, Esteban V. Cardemil, and Ellen H. O'Donnell, "Self-Esteem in Pure Bullies and Bully/Victims: A Longitudinal Analysis," *Journal of Interpersonal Violence* 25, no. 8 (August 2010): 1489–1502, doi:10.1177 /0886260509354579.PMID20040706, rtrieved October 29, 2013; George M. Batsche and Howard M. Knoff, "Bullies and Their Victims: Understanding a Pervasive Problem in the Schools," *School Psychology Review* 23, no. 2 (1994): 165–175; Edward M. Levinson, "Assessment of Bullying: A Review of Methods and Instruments," *Journal of Counselling & Development* 82, no. 4 (2004): 496–503, doi:10.1002/j.1556-6678.2004 .tb00338.x, retrieved October 29, 2013.

10. See David Karp, *Speaking of Sadness* (New York: Oxford University Press, 1996). See also Peter Breggin, *Toxic Psychiatry: Why Therapy, Empathy and Love Must Replace the Drugs, Electroshock and Biochemical Theories of the "New Psychiatry"* (New York:

St. Martin's Press, 1994); Gary Greenberg, *The Book of Woe* (New York: Blue Rider Press, 2013); Robert Whitaker, *The Anatomy of an Epidemic: Magic Bullets, Psychiatric Drugs and the Astonishing Rise of Mental Illness in the US* (New York: Broadway Books, 2011); Daniel Carlet, *Unhinged: The Trouble with Psychiatry* (New York: Free Press, 2010); and Stewart Kirk and Tomi Gomory, *Mad Science: Psychiatric Coercion, Diagnosis and Drugs* (New York: Transaction, 2013).

11. Eric Lax, *Woody Allen: A Biography* (Cambridge, MA: Da Capo Press, 2000), p. 162.

12. Karp, *Speaking of Sadness*. See also David Karp, *Is It Me or My Meds?* (Cambridge, MA: Harvard University Press, 2006).

13. C. Wright Mills and Hans Gerth, *Character and Social Structure* (Boston: Mariner, 1964).

14. Mills, *Sociological Imagination*.

15. Mills and Gerth, *Character and Social Structure*.

16. C. Wright Mills, *The Power Elite* (Oxford: Oxford University Press, 1957).

17. Edward Herman and Noam Chomsky, *Manufacturing Consent: The Political Economy of the Mass Media* (New York: Pantheon, 2002). See also our prior work, Charles Derber and Yale Magrass, *Morality Wars* (Boulder, CO: Paradigm, 2010).

18. Mills, *Sociological Imagination*. See also Charles Derber and Yale Magrass, *Capitalism: Should You Buy It?* (Boulder, CO: Paradigm, 2014), esp. chaps. 1 and 2.

19. Mills, *Power Elite*. See also G. William Domhoff, *Who Rules America? The Triumph of the Corporate Rich*, 7th ed. (New York: McGraw-Hill, 2013).

20. Domhoff, *Who Rules America?* See also Derber and Magrass, *Capitalism: Should You Buy It?*

21. We discuss militarized capitalism in two earlier books. The military side is addressed in Derber and Magrass, *Morality Wars*, esp. chaps. 1–3. The economic and political sides are described in *Capitalism: Should You Buy It?*

22. See Charles Murray, *American Exceptionalism: An Experiment in History* (Washington, DC: AEI Press, 2013).

23. Thomas Piketty, *Capital in the Twenty-First Century* (Cambridge, MA: Harvard University Press, 2014).

24. See ibid. See also Charles Derber, *The Disinherited Majority: Capital Questions—Piketty and Beyond* (Boulder, CO: Paradigm, 2015); Chuck Collins, *99 to 1: How Wealth Inequality Is Wrecking Our World and What We Can Do about It* (San Francisco: Berrett-Koehler Press, 2012); and Joseph E. Stiglitz, *The Price of Inequality: How Today's Divided Society Endangers Our Future* (New York: Norton, 2013).

25. Charles Derber, *Hidden Power* (San Francisco: Berrett-Koehler Press, 2005).

26. Stopbullying.gov, "Bullying Definition: What Is Bullying," posted at http://www.stopbullying.gov/what-is-bullying/definition/.

27. "Bullying," *Wikipedia* (emphases in the original).

28. For the psychological paradigm, this is made explicit in a 2010 report by the American Psychological Association; see Clayton R. Cook, Kirk R. Williams, Nancy G. Guerra, Tia E. Kim, and Shelly Sadek, "Predictors of Bullying and Victimization in

Childhood and Adolescence: A Meta-analytic Investigation," *School Psychology Quarterly* 25, no. 2 (2010): 65–83, doi:10.1037/a0020149, retrieved October 28, 2013.

29. For this focus in the psychological paradigm, see Kipling D. Williams, Joseph P. Forgas, and William Von Hippel, eds., *The Social Outcast: Ostracism, Social Exclusion, Rejection, and Bullying* (Australia: Psychology Press, 2013).

30. Jessie Klein gives the most attention to societal factors, including a chapter on the capitalist economy, but her work concentrates overwhelmingly on gender as the critical social hierarchy. See Klein, *Bullying Society*.

31. J. Juvonen, S. Graham, and M. Schuster, "Bullying among Young Adolescents: The Strong, the Weak, and the Troubled," *Pediatrics* 112, no. 6 (December 2003): 1231–1237.

32. Theodore Roosevelt quoted in John T. Bethel, "A Splendid Little War," *Harvard Magazine*, November 1998.

33. Charles Derber, *Corporation Nation: How Corporations Have Taken Over Our Lives and What We Can Do about It* (New York: St. Martin's Press, 2000).

34. Wendy Craig, Yossi Harel-Fisch, Haya Fogel-Grinvald, Suzanne Dostaler, Jorn Hetland, Bruce Simons-Morton, Michal Molcho, Margarida Gaspar de Mato, Mary Overpeck, Pernille Due, and William Pickett, HBSC Violence & Injuries Prevention Focus Group and HBSC Bullying Writing Group, "A Cross-national Profile of Bullying and Victimization among Adolescents in 40 Countries," *International Journal of Public Health* 54, supp. 2 (September 2009): 216–224, doi:10.1007/s00038-009-5413-9, posted at http://www.ncbi.nlm.nih.gov/pmc/articles/PMC2747624/.

35. Andrew Bacevich, *The New American Militarism* (New York: Oxford University Press, 2013), and Noam Chomsky, *Hegemony or Survival: America's Quest for Global Dominance* (New York: Holt, 2004).

36. See Noam Chomsky and Robert McChesney, *Profit over People: Neoliberalism and Global Order* (New York: Seven Stories Press, 2011). See also Charles Derber, *People before Profit* (New York: Picador, 2003), and Derber and Magrass, *Morality Wars*, esp. chap. 3 on the US exercise of global imperial power.

37. Mills, *Sociological Imagination*, and Mills, *Power Elite*.

38. See chapter 4. See also Piketty, *Capital in the Twenty-First Century*, and Derber, *Disinherited Majority*.

39. Charles Derber, *Marx's Ghost* (Boulder, CO: Paradigm, 2012).

40. Todd Gitlin, *Occupy Nation: The Roots, the Spirit and the Promise of Occupy Wall Street* (New York: It Books, 2012).

41. Martin Scorsese, *The Wolf of Wall Street*, Paramount, Hollywood, CA, 2013.

42. Oliver Stone, *Wall Street*, 20th Century Fox, Hollywood, CA, 1987.

43. See Derber and Magrass, *Capitalism: Should You Buy It?* esp. chap. 6. See also Derber, *Disinherited Majority*, esp. chaps. 5–8.

44. Derber and Magrass, *Morality Wars*.

45. Ibid., esp. chaps. 1–3.

46. Noam Chomsky, *Deterring Democracy* (New York: Hill and Wang, 1992).

47. Michelle Alexander, *Mass Incarceration in the Age of Color-Blindness* (New

York: New Press, 2012). See also Charles Derber, *The Wilding of America,* 6th ed. (New York: Worth, 2015).

48. Ayn Rand, *Atlas Shrugged* (New York: Signet, 1957).

49. Derber, *Disinherited Majority.*

50. Derber and Magrass, *Morality Wars,* esp. chaps. 1–3.

51. Naomi Klein, *This Changes Everything: Capitalism vs. the Climate* (New York: Simon & Schuster, 2014). See also Charles Derber, *Greed to Green* (Boulder, CO: Paradigm, 2008).

52. See chapter 5. See also Klein, *This Changes Everything.*

53. Howard Zinn, *People's History of the United States* (New York: Harper, 2005).

CHAPTER 2: CAPITAL BULLYING

1. Dave Jamieson, "Pro-union Burger King Worker Disciplined for Poor Pickle Placement," *Huffington Post,* October 1, 2014, posted at http://www.huffingtonpost .com/2014/10/01/burger-king-workers-were-_n_5914526.html.

2. Ibid.

3. Ibid.

4. Ibid.

5. Karl Marx and Frederick Engels, *The Communist Manifesto* (New York: Empire Books, 2011). See also Derber, *Marx's Ghost.*

6. Piketty, *Capital in the Twenty-First Century.*

7. Ibid.

8. Ibid., p. 27.

9. Ibid.

10. Gregory Claeys, "The 'Survival of the Fittest' and the Origins of Social Darwinism," *Journal of the History of Ideas* 61, no. 2 (April 2000): 223–240.

11. Francis J. Bremer, *Puritanism: A Very Short Introduction* (New York: Oxford University Press, 2009). For the classic view of the relation of Protestantism to worldly success, see Max Weber, *The Protestant Ethic and the Spirit of Capitalism,* 2nd ed. (New York: Routledge Classics, 2001).

12. Richard Sennett and Jonathan Cobb, *The Hidden Injuries of Class* (New York: Norton, 1993).

13. For a discussion of Romney's view of makers and takers, drawn from Ayn Rand's notions of productives and moochers, see Derber and Magrass, *Capitalism: Should You Buy It?*

14. See ibid., where we develop these points at some length.

15. Ayn Rand, *Atlas Shrugged* (New York: Plume, 1999). See also Rand and Nathaniel Branden, *The Virtue of Selfishness* (New York: Signet, 1964).

16. Paul Krause, *The Battle for Homestead, 1880–1892: Politics, Culture and Steel* (Pittsburgh, PA: University of Pittsburgh Press, 1992).

17. "Dedicate Three Pump House Memorials," *Battle of Homestead News,* n.d., posted at http://www.battleofhomesteadfoundation.org/archives/2005_Jan.pdf.

18. David Brody, *Steelworkers in America: The Nonunion Era* (Champaign-Urbana: University of Illinois Press, 1998), pp. 57–58.

19. Phillip Foner, *History of the Labor Movement in the US,* vol. 2 (New York: International Publishers, 1975).

20. Julfikar Ali Manik and Jim Yardley, "Building Collapse in Bangladesh Leaves Scores Dead," *New York Times,* April 24, 2013, p. 1, posted at http://www.nytimes.com /2013/04/25/world/asia/bangladesh-building-collapse.html?pagewanted=all&_r=0 .more. See also "Savar Building Collapse," *Wikipedia,* posted at http://en.wikipedia .org/wiki/2013_Savar_building_collapse, and Derber, *Wilding of America,* p. 51.

21. Manik and Yardley, "Building Collapse in Bangladesh."

22. For a discussion of exit power in globalization, see Charles Derber, *People before Profit* (New York: Picador, 2003), chaps. 2 and 3.

23. The concept of exit power was first developed by Albert Hirschman in his enormously influential work *Exit, Voice and Loyalty: Responses to Decline in Firms, Organizations and States* (Cambridge, MA: Harvard University Press, 1970).

24. Derber, *Wilding of America,* p. 55.

25. Charles Kernaghan, "High Tech Misery in China," in the Institute for Global Labor and Human Rights newsletter of February 9, 2014.

26. Colman McCarthy, "Adjunct Professors Fight for Crumbs," *Washington Post,* August 22, 2014, posted at http://www.washingtonpost.com/opinions/adjunct-profes sors-fight-for-crumbs-on-campus/2014/08/22/ca92eb38-28b1-11e4-8593-da634b 334390_story.html.

27. Ibid.

28. Ibid.

29. Ibid.

30. Robin Roenker, "The Rise of the Temporary Worker," *Lane Report,* May 7, 2014, posted at http://www.lanereport.com/31575/2014/05/the-rise-of-the-temporary -worker/.

31. "40% of America's Workforce Will Be Freelancers by 2020," *Quartz,* March 20, 2013, posted at http://qz.com/65279/40-of-americas-workforce-will-be-freelancers-by -2020/.

32. Charles Derber, "Working Paper on Contingent Work," mimeo, 1988. For Derber's full published discussion of contingent work, see his *Corporation Nation,* chap. 5.

33. Derber, "Working Paper on Contingent Work."

34. Ibid.

35. Jonathan Hughes, *The Vital Few* (Boston: Houghton Mifflin, 1966), p. 238. See also Thomas C. Leonard, "Origins of the Myth of Social Darwinism: The Ambiguous Legacy of Richard Hofstadter's Social Darwinism in American Thought," *Journal of Economic Behavior and Organization* 71 (2009): 37–51.

36. "The Cleveland Massacre," *American Experience,* PBS, Boston, 2013.

37. David Steitfield, "Amazon and Hachette Resolve Dispute," *New York Times,* November 13, 2014, posted at http://www.nytimes.com/2014/11/14/technology/amazon -hachette-ebook-dispute.html?_r=0.

38. "Apple Sues Samsung for $2bn as Tech Rivals Head Back to Court," *Guardian,* March 30, 2014, posted at www.theguardian.com/technology/2014/mar/31/apple-sues-samsung-for-2bn, and "Smartphone Patent Wars," *Wikipedia,* http://en.wikipedia.org/wiki/Smartphone_patent_wars.

39. Laura Stampler, "These Are the Ten Biggest Brand Bullies in the US," *Business Insider,* March 26, 2013, posted at http://www.businessinsider.com/heres-why-lance-armstrong-is-one-of-the-biggest-trademark-bullies-in-america-2012-3?op=1.

40. Personal story told by the CEO of the company to Derber, Boston, August 2014.

41. See Paul Baran and Paul Sweezy, *Monopoly Capital: An Essay on the American Economic and Social Order* (New York: Monthly Review Press, 1966).

42. Chris Pane, *Who Killed the Electric Car?* Sony Pictures, Los Angeles, 2006.

43. Naomi Klein, *No Logo: Taking on the Brand Bullies* (New York: Picador, 2009).

44. Karl Marx, *Capital,* vol. 1, *A Critique of Political Economy* (New York: Penguin Classics, 1992).

45. Derber, *Greed to Green.*

46. Klein, *Bully Society.*

47. Thorstein Veblen, *Theory of the Leisure Class,* 3rd ed. (New York: Dover Reprints, 1994).

48. Stuart Ewen, *Captains of Consciousness: Advertising and the Social Roots of the Consumer Culture* (New York: Basic Books, 2001).

49. Juliet Schor, *Born to Buy: The Commercialized Child and the New Consumer Culture,* reprint ed. (New York: Scribner, 2005).

50. Derber, *Wilding of America,* chap. 5.

51. Jim Klein and Martha Olson, *Taken for a Ride,* PBS, Boston, 1966.

52. Louis Brandeis quoted in Stephan Gowans, "The United States vs. Democracy," Swans, blog, May 6, 2002, posted at http://www.swans.com/library/art8/gowans31.html.

53. Marx and Engels, *Communist Manifesto.*

54. Derber and Magrass, *Capitalism: Should You Buy It?* See also Derber, *Corporation Nation,* esp. chap. 8.

55. Kenneth P. Vogel, *Big Money: 2.5 Billion Dollars, One Suspicious Vehicle, and a Pimp—On the Trail of the Ultra-rich Hijacking American Politics* (New York: Public Affairs, 2014), and John Nichols and Robert McChesney, *Dollocracy: How the Money and Media Election Complex Is Destroying America* (New York: Nation Books, 2013).

56. Domhoff, *Who Rules America?*

57. John Anderson, *Follow the Money: How George W. Bush and the Texas Republicans Hog-Tied America* (New York: Scribner, 2007).

58. Matthew Josephson, *The Robber Barons* (New York: Mariner Books, 1962). See also Derber, *Corporation Nation,* chap. 1.

59. Jay Newton-Small, "Don't Cry for K Street: Federal Lobbying Is Down, but Profits Are Up," *Time,* August 8, 2013, posted at http://swampland.time.com/2013/08/08/dont-cry-for-k-street-federal-lobbying-is-down-but-profits-are-up/.

60. Rachel Cooper, "What Is a Lobbyist?" About.com, 2014 (no further date), posted at http://dc.about.com/od/jobs/a/Lobbying.htm.

61. Derber, *People before Profit*, chaps. 2 and 3.

62. Ibid.

63. Oscar Guardiola-Rivera, *Story of a Death Foretold: The Coup against Salvador Allende* (London: Bloomsbury, 2013).

CHAPTER 3: ENVIRONMENTAL BULLYING

1. For a discussion of the indigenous cultures' growing impact on our views about the environment and on environmental movements, see the work of the Pachamama Alliance, a global coalition of environmental activists rooted in the Indigenous People's Movement. For a general discussion of their perspective and publications, see the Pachamama Alliance homepage, http://www.pachamama.org/about. See also Klein, *This Changes Everything*, op. cit., and Derrick Jensen, *Endgame*, vol. 1, *The Problem of Civilization* (New York: Seven Stories Press, 2006).

2. David Chamovitz, *What a Plant Knows: A Field Guide to the Senses*, repr. ed. (New York: Scientific American/Farrar, Straus and Giroux, 2013). See also Gareth Cook, "Do Plants Think?" *Scientific American*, June 5, 2012, posted at http://www.scientific american.com/article/do-plants-think-daniel-chamovitz/.

3. Jenkins, *Endgame*; see also Chamovitz, "What a Plant Knows."

4. Jenkins, *Endgame*.

5. Peter Singer, *Animal Liberation: The Definitive Classic of the Animal Movement* (New York: Harper Perennial Modern Classics, 2009).

6. Ibid.

7. John Bellamy Foster, *The Ecological Rift: Capitalism's War on the Earth* (New York: Monthly Review Press, 2011).

8. Klein, *This Changes Everything*; Bill McKibben, *Earth: Making a Life on a Tough New Planet* (New York: St. Martin's Press, 2011); and Derber, *Greed to Green*.

9. Stefan G. Chrissanthos, *Warfare in the Ancient World* (Westport, CT: Praeger, 2008), p. 80.

10. M. Wheelis, "Biological Warfare at the 1346 Siege of Caffa," *Emerging Infectious Diseases* 8, no. 9 (2002), posted at http://wwwnc.cdc.gov/eid/article/8/9/01-0536 _article.

11. Paul Martin, *Twilight of the Mammoths* (Berkeley: University of California Press, 2007).

12. James Fink, *The Automobile Age* (Cambridge, MA: MIT Press, 1990), p. 136, chap. 5.

13. Herman Daly and Jonathan Cobb, *For the Common Good* (Boston: Beacon Press, 1994).

14. John Bellamy Foster, *The Vulnerable Planet: A Short Economic History of the Environment* (New York: Monthly Review Press, 1999), and Klein, *This Changes Everything*. See also Derber, *Greed to Green*.

15. Klein, *This Changes Everything*. See also Derber, *Greed to Green*.

16. Quote cited in Phillip Jones Griffith, *Agent Orange: Collateral Damage in Vietnam* (London: Trolley Books, 2004). See also "Agent Orange Record: A Continuing Legacy of the Vietnam War," posted at http://www.agentorangerecord.com/impact _on_vietnam/environment/defoliation.

17. Animal League Defense Fund, "Animal Fighting Case Study: Michael Vick," Animal Defense League website on the history of the Michael Vick case, January 2011, posted at http://www.aldf.org/resources/laws-cases/animal-fighting-case-study -michael-vick/.

18. Ibid.

19. Ibid.

20. Jim Gorant, *The Lost Dogs: Michael Vick's Dogs and Their Tale of Rescue and Redemption* (New York: Gotham, 2011). See Gorant as cited in Animal League Defense Fund, "Animal Fighting Case Study."

21. Animal League Defense Fund, "Animal Fighting Case Study: Michael Vick."

22. Ibid.

23. Matthew Bershadker, "Why We Can't Forget Michael Vick's Dog-Fighting Past," New York Post.com, March 26, 2014, posted at http://nypost.com/2014/03/26 /why-we-cant-forget-michael-vicks-dog-fighting-past/.

24. PETA, "Animal Abuse and Human Abuse: Partners in Crime," People for the Ethical Treatment of Animals, posted at http://www.peta.org/issues/companion -animal-issues/companion-animals-factsheets/animal-abuse-human-abuse -partners-crime/.

25. Ibid.

26. Ibid.

27. John Bellamy Foster, *Marx's Ecology: Materialism and Nature* (New York: Monthly Review Press, 2000).

28. Quote from Pew Commission on Industrial Farm Animal Production, cited in "Ending Factory Farming," Farming Forward, posted at http://www.farmforward .com/farming-forward/factory-farming.

29. PETA, "Factory Farming: Cruelty to Animals," n.d., posted at http://www.peta .org/issues/animals-used-for-food/factory-farming/.

30. Ibid.

31. Rachel Carson, *Silent Spring* (Boston: Houghton Mifflin, 1962).

32. Graham Land, "Monocrop Farming: Green Revolution or Environmental Blunder of Historic Proportions?" Greenfudge.org, September 24, 2009, posted at http:// www.greenfudge.org/2009/09/24/monocrop-farming-green-revolution-or-environ mental-blunder-of-historic-proportions/.

33. Foster, *Marx's Ecology*.

34. Frederick Engels cited in Derber, *Marx's Ghost*, p. 96.

35. Derber, *Greed to Green*, chaps. 9–10.

36. Daly and Cobb, *For the Common Good*; Derber, *Greed to Green*.

37. Klein, *This Changes Everything*.

38. Ibid.; Foster, *Ecological Rift*; and Derber, *Greed to Green*.

39. Dan Lamothe, "Climate Change Threatens National Security, Pentagon Says," *Washington Post*, October 13, 2014, posted at http://www.washingtonpost.com/news /checkpoint/wp/2014/10/13/climate-change-threatens-national-security-pentagon-says/.

40. Worldwatch Institute report quoted in PETA, "Fight Global Warming by Going Vegetarian," PETA report, n.d., posted at http://www.peta.org/issues/animals -used-for-food/global-warming/.

41. These themes about capitalism are developed by John Bellamy Foster in several important books. See especially his *Ecological Rift* and *Marx's Ecology*.

42. Klein, *This Changes Everything*, and Jensen, *Endgame*.

43. Derber is grateful to Derrick Jensen, who shared some of these insights with him and has written about this theme in a number of his books, cited elsewhere in this chapter.

44. William H. Young, "Capitalism and Western Civilization: Social Darwinism," National Association of Scholars, April 19, 2012, posted at http://www.nas.org/articles /capitalism_and_western_civilization_social_darwinism.

45. Derber and Magrass, *Capitalism: Should You Buy It?* chap. 10.

46. Foster, *Ecological Rift*, and Foster, *Marx's Ecology*.

47. Juliet Schor, *True Wealth* (New York: Penguin, 2011).

48. Derber and Magrass, *Capitalism: Should You Buy It?* esp. chap. 10.

49. See Francis Moore Lappe, *EcoMind: Changing the Way We Think, to Create the World We Want* (New York: Nation Books, 2013), esp. chaps. 1 and 2, and Derber, *Disinherited Majority*. See chapter 11.

50. John Kenneth Galbraith, *The Affluent Society*, 40th anniversary ed. (New York: Mariner, 1998).

51. Klein, *This Changes Everything*.

52. Juliet Schor is our most important writer on consumerism today. See Schor, *Born to Buy*. See also Schor, *True Wealth*.

53. Schor, *True Wealth*, and Derber, *Greed to Green*, chap. 10.

54. Derber and Magrass, *Capitalism: Should You Buy It?* chap. 10.

55. Juliet Schor, "Reading Capital in the Athropocene," in Derber, *Disinherited Majority*, pp. 108–112.

56. Derber, *Wilding of America*.

57. Ibid.

58. Dan Lamothe, "Climate Change Threatens National Security, Pentagon Says," and Emily Atkin, "Pentagon: Global Warming Poses 'Immediate Risk' to National Security," ClimateProgress, October 14, 2014, posted at http://www.thinkprogress.org /climate/2014/10/14/3579338/pentagon-global-warming-national-security/.

59. Klein, *This Changes Everything*, p. 444.

60. Ibid.

61. Ibid.

62. Anneke Campbell and Thomas Linzey, *Be the Change: How to Get What You Want in Your Community*, 2nd ed. (New York: Gibbs-Smith, 2009).

1. Noam Chomsky, *Failed States: The Abuse of Power and the Assault on Democracy* (New York: Metropolitan Books, 2007), and Andrew Bacevich, *Washington Rules: America's Path to Permanent War* (New York: Metropolitan Books, 2011).

2. This distinction between personality and structural imperatives is spelled out in Charles Derber, *Sociopathic Society: A People's Sociology of the United States* (Boulder, CO: Paradigm, 2013).

3. Bacevich, *New American Militarism*, and Derber and Magrass, *Morality Wars*.

4. Center for American Progress, "A User's Guide to the Fiscal Year 2015 Defense Budget," April 24, 2014, posted at https://www.americanprogress.org/issues/security /report/2014/04/24/88516/a-users-guide-to-the-fiscal-year-2015-defense-budget.

5. See Donald Kagan, Gary Schmitt, and Thomas Donnelley, *Rebuilding America's Defenses: Strategy, Forces and Resources for a New Century* (Washington, DC: Project for the New American Century, 2000), posted at https://web.archive.org/web /20130501130739/http://www.newamericancentury.org/RebuildingAmericasDefenses .pdf. See also the homepage for the Project of the New American Century at https:// web.archive.org/web/20130112203305/http://www.newamericancentury.org/.

6. Kagan, Schmitt, and Donnelley, *Rebuilding America's Defenses*, p. ii.

7. Ibid., p. iv.

8. Ibid.

9. Ibid.

10. William Kristol et al., "Open Letter to the President," *Weekly Standard*, September 20, 2001, posted at http://www.weeklystandard.com/Content/Public/Articles /000/000/000/040pvmoi.asp?page=2.

11. Kagan, Schmitt, and Donnelley, *Rebuilding America's Defenses*, pp. v–vi.

12. William Kristol, "Liberate Iraq," *Weekly Standard*, May 14, 2001, posted at newamericancentury.org, accessed May 28, 2007.

13. Barack Obama, "Statement by the President on ISIL," September 23, 2014, posted by the White House at http://www.whitehouse.gov/the-press-office/2014/09 /10/statement-president-isil-1.

14. Henry Kissinger, excerpted from "Brainy Quotes," quote posted at http://www .brainyquote.com/quotes/quotes/h/henryakis101648.html.

15. Derber and Magrass, *Morality Wars*, chaps. 1–3.

16. Noam Chomsky, "United States, Global Bully," *Le Monde Diplomatique*, December 2001, posted at http://www.matrixmasters.com/wtc/chomsky/bully/bully .html.

17. Chomsky, *Deterring Democracy*. See also Noam Chomsky, *Power Systems: Conversations on Global Democratic Uprisings and the New Challenges to US Empire* (New York: Metropolitan Books, 2013).

18. Noam Chomsky, *The Essential Chomsky*, ed. Anthony Arnove (New York: New Press, 2008).

19. Stephen Kinzer, *Overthrow: America's Century of Regime Change from Hawaii to Iraq* (New York: Times Books, 2007).

20. Ibid.

21. Review of Kinzer's book posted on Amazon at http://www.amazon.com /Overthrow-Americas-Century-Regime-Change/product-reviews/0805082409.

22. Bruce Ackerman, "Obama's Betrayal of the Constitution," *New York Times,* September 12, 2014, posted at http://www.nytimes.com/2014/09/12/opinion/obamas -betrayal-of-the-constitution.html?_r=0.

23. Gar Alperovitz, *Atomic Diplomacy* (London: Pluto, 1994).

24. NBC Learn K-12, "President Truman on His Decision to Drop the Atomic Bomb," August 6, 2005, posted at http://www.archives.nbclearn.com/portal/site/k-12/flat view?cuecard=4962.

25. Jeff Faux, "Why Republicans Oppose the Iran Agreement: Follow the Money," *Huffington Post,* July 30, 2015, posted at http://www.huffingtonpost.com/jeff-faux/why -republicans-oppose-th_b_7905218.html.

26. Joseph Gerson and John Feffer, "Empire and Nuclear Weapons," Foreign Policy in Focus, November 30, 2007, posted at http://www.fpif.org/empire_and_nuclear _weapons/.

27. "First Taiwan Strait Crisis: Quemoy Matsu," posted at http://www.global security.org/military/ops/quemoy_matsu.htm.

28. Thomas D. Friedenbach, *Eisenhower's Nuclear Policy toward China, September 1954–April 1955* (n.p.: Whitman College, 2011).

29. See the discussion of the Cuban missile crisis in William Schwartz and Charles Derber, *The Nuclear Seduction* (Berkeley: University of California Press, 1990).

30. Francis Gavin, *Nuclear Statecraft: History and Strategy in America's Atomic Age* (Ithaca, NY: Cornell University Press, 2012), p. 108.

31. Ibid., p. 116. See also Alex Wellerstein, "Nixon and the Bomb: 'I just want you to think big, Henry!'" *Restricted Data: The Nuclear Secrecy Blog,* October 25, 2013, accessed April 10, 2015, http://blog.nuclearsecrecy.com/2013/10/25/nixon-and -the-bomb/.

32. Cited in Gerson and Feffer, "Empire and Nuclear Weapons."

33. Joseph Gerson and John Feffer, "The Romance of Ruthlessness," Foreign Policy in Focus, November 30, 2007, posted at http://fpif.org/empire_and_nuclear _weapons/.

34. Barack Obama, "Statement by the President on ISIL."

35. See Jonathan Turley, "Obama: I Do Not Need Congressional Approval to Go to War with ISIS," September 10, 2014, posted on his blog at jonathanturley .org/2014/09/10/obama-i-do-not-need-congressional-approval-to-go-to-war-with -isis/.

36. Scott Shane, "Drone Strikes Said to Set a Dangerous Precedent," *New York Times,* April 14, 2115, p. A5.

37. Turley, "Obama: I Do Not Need Congressional Approval."

38. On the day the Senate torture report was released, the *New York Times* ran a banner headline that read SENATE PANEL FAULTS CIA OVER BRUTALITY AND DECEIT IN TERRORISM INTERROGATIONS, filling the paper that day with stories such as Mark Mazetti, "Failure of Oversight Is Outlined—Agency Defends Program," *New York*

Times, December 10, 2014, pp. A1 and A12, and Scott Shane, "Portraying a Broken Agency," *New York Times,* December 10, 2014, pp. A1 and A16.

39. Quote cited in Mazzetti, "Failure of Oversight."

40. Dwight D. Eisenhower, *Mandate for Change* (New York: Doubleday, 1994), p. 372.

41. In this section, we are drawing heavily on the authoritative history of the Vietnam War by historian Gabriel Kolko. See his *Anatomy of a War* (New York: New Press, 1994).

42. Curtis E. Lemay quoted in "What They Said," *New York Times,* May 1, 1975, posted at http://partners.nytimes.com/library/world/asia/050175vietnam-quotes .html.

43. This and much of the description here relies on a report by a US soldier: see Joe Allen, "Vietnam: The War the U.S. Lost," *International Socialist Review (ISR),* no. 40 (March-April 2005).

44. M. Bilton and K. Sim, *Four Hours of My Lai: The Hugh Thompson Story* (Los Angeles: Acadian House, 1992), pp. 204–205.

45. James Duffy cited in "Winter Soldier Investigation," Testimony given in Detroit, Michigan, on January 31, 1971, and February 1–2, 1971. Testimony of the 1st Air Cavalry Division, part 2. The full text of the investigation is available at http://lists .village.virginia.edu/sixties/HTML_docs/Resources/Primary/Winter_Soldier/WS _entry.html.

46. Lyndon B. Johnson, "Speech to the Associated Press Luncheon, April 20, 1964," posted at http://millercenter.org/president/lbjohnson/speeches/speech-5659.

47. Kolko, *Anatomy of a War.*

48. John F. Kennedy cited in Stanley Karnow, *Vietnam: A History* (New York: Penguin, 1986), p. 248.

49. John Kerry quote cited at http://www.searchquotes.com/quotes/about /Vietnam/.

50. McNaughton quote cited in Kolko, *Anatomy of a War,* p. 113.

CHAPTER 5: THE LAND OF THE SLAVE AND THE HOME OF THE BULLY

1. "The Royal Proclamation—October 7, 1763," The Avalon Project, Lillian Goldman Law Library, Yale Law School, New Haven, CT.

2. See http://www.archives.gov/exhibits/charters/declaration_transcript.html.

3. John L. Sullivan, "The Great Nation of Futurity," *United States Democratic Review,* 1839.

4. *Encyclopedia Britannica,* 2014, s.v. "Mexican-American War."

5. "Native American Words—Tsa-la-gi-ti-a-ye-li," Spirit_cherokee.webs.com, retrieved April 20, 2013.

6. Robert Leckie, *The Wars of America* (Roswell, GA: Castle Books, 1998), p. 537.

7. "The Middle Passage," *The Terrible Transformation,* PBS.org, 2000.

8. Olaudah Equiano, *The Interesting Narrative of the Life of Olaudah Equiano or Gustavus Vassa the African* (London: n.p., 1789).

9. Solomon Northrup, *Twelve Years a Slave* (Auburn, NY: n.p., 1853).

10. Jim Kirwan, *Slavery Transformed America,* video, pt. 3, November 25, 2009.

11. David Pilgrim, *What Was Jim Crow,* exhibit, Museum of Racist Memorabilia, Ferris State University, Big Rapids, MI, September 2000.

12. D. W. Griffith, *Birth of a Nation,* DVD, Alpha Video, Narbeth, PA, 2005.

13. Charles Chestnutt Digital Archive, Berea College, Berea, KY, 2007.

14. Rakesh Kochhar, Richard Fry, and Paul Taylor, "Wealth Gaps Rise to Record Highs between Whites, Blacks, Hispanics," *Pew Social Trends,* July 2011.

15. Jack Healy, "Ferguson, Still Tense, Grows Calmer," *New York Times,* November 26, 2014.

16. Al Baker, J. David Goodman, and Benjamin Mueller, "Beyond the Chokehold: The Path to Eric Garner's Death," *New York Times,* June 13, 2015.

17. Ray Sanchez, "What We Know about the Controversy in Sandra Bland's Death," CNN, July 21, 2015, posted at http://www.cnn.com/2015/07/21/us/texas-sandra-bland-jail-death-explain/.

18. Matt Pearce and Dexter Thomas, "Deputy Who Threw South Carolina Student in Class Is under Federal Investigation," *Los Angeles Times,* October 27, 2015.

19. Death Penalty Information Center, 2015, www.deathpenaltyinfor.org/race--death.

20. Michelle Alexander, *The New Jim Crow* (New York: New Press, 2012).

21. Aaron Morrison, "Black Unemployment Rate 2015: In Better Economy, African-Americans See Minimal Gains," *International Business Times,* March 8, 2015.

22. Kwane Ture and Charles Hamilton, *Black Power: The Politics of Liberation* (New York: Vintage, 1992).

23. Joseph Farah, "The Militarization of the Domestic Police," *WorldNetDaily,* November 6, 1997.

24. Diane Cecilia Weber, "Warrior Cops: The Ominous Growth of Paramilitarism in American Police Departments," *Cato Institute Working Papers* (regular series evaluating government policies and offering proposals for reform), no. 50, August 26, 1999.

25. Krissah Thompson, "Arrest of Harvard's Henry Louis Gates Jr. Was Avoidable, Report Says," *Washington Post,* June 30, 2010.

26. Reena Flores, "Donald Trump: 'Anchor babies' aren't American citizens," *CBS News,* August 19, 2015.

27. Karen Finney, "Punish Bachmann," *The Hill,* July 23, 2012.

28. Lucy Madison, "Romney on Immigration: 'I'm for "self-deportation,"'" *CBS News,* January 24, 2012.

29. Daniel Angster and Salvatore Colleluoiri, "IA Radio Host Jan Mickelson: Enslave Undocumented Immigrants Unless They Leave," *Media Matters for America* (website), August 19, 2015.

30. Ana Gonzalez-Barrera and Jens Krogsta, "U.S. Deportations of Immigrants Reach Record High in 2013," Pew Research Center, October 2, 2014.

1. Barack Obama, acceptance speech delivered at the Democratic National Convention, Los Angeles, September 6, 2012.

2. "Before Rebranding, the US Dept. of Defense Was Called the 'Department of War,'" *Forgotten History*; 2008, posted at http://www.forgottenhistoryblog.com/before-rebranding-the-us-dept-of-defense-was-called-the-department-of-war/.

3. Theodore Roosevelt, speech delivered at Harvard University, Cambridge, MA, February 25, 1907.

4. Boy Scouts of America, *Boy Scout Handbook* (Irving, TX: Boy Scouts of America, 1982), p. 529.

5. Wayne LaPierre, press conference, Washington, DC, December 21, 2012.

6. Alfred Lord Tennyson, "Charge of the Light Brigade," 1853.

7. Graeme Wood, "Why We Fear and Admire the Military Sniper," *Boston Globe*, January 16, 2015.

8. Stephen Losey, "Obama's Mark on the Military," *Military Times*, December 21, 2014.

9. Hamilton Nolan, "Don't Ask, Don't Tell, Faggot: Inside the Marines Boot Camp," *Gawker*, May 21 2013, posted at http://gawker.com/dont-ask-dont-tell-faggot-inside-marine-corps-boot-509032688.

10. Ibid.

11. "Military Veterans: What Are Your Best Stories from Basic Training/Bootcamp," *Reddit*, San Francisco, November 10, 2014.

12. Stanley Kubrick, *Full Metal Jacket*, Warner Bros., Hollywood, CA, 1987.

13. Ibid.

14. "Military Veterans."

15. Wes Van Horn, "7 Soldiers Share Their Craziest Basic Training Stories," *Playboy*, December 9, 2014.

16. "Military Veterans."

17. Mathew Daly, "Senate Approves Bill Aimed at Reducing Suicide Epidemic among Veterans," *Huffington Post*, February 3, 2015, posted at http://www.huffingtonpost.com/news/veteran-suicide.

18. Abby Phillip, "Trial of Eddie Routh, Killer of Chris Kyle, Will Be Darkest Chapter of 'American Sniper,'" *Washington Post*, January 22, 2015.

19. Emily Schmall, "Report Faults Army's Ability to Predict Violence," Associated Press, January 24, 2015.

20. Manny Fernandez, "Death Penalty for Rampage at Fort Hood," *New York Times*, August 28, 2013.

21. "From Decorated Veteran to Mass Murderer," CNN, posted at www.cnn.com/CNN/Programs/people/shows/mcveigh/profile.html.

22. Christopher Goffard, Joel Rubin, and Kurt Streeter, "Manhunt for Christopher Dorner," *Los Angeles Times*, December 8, 2013.

23. Jake Tapper and Chelsea Carter, "An American Hero: The Uncommon Valor of Clint Romesha," CNN, February 8, 2013.

24. Michael Moore, *Bowling for Columbine*, Dog Eat Dog Films, New York, 2002.

25. Russ Thurman, "Industry Enters Golden Era, Firearms Sales Set Records," *Shooting Industry*, July 2012.

26. Thom Hartmann, "The Second Amendment Was Ratified to Preserve Slavery," *Truth-Out*, January 15, 2013, posted at http://www.truth-out.org/news/item/13890-the-second-amendment-was-ratified-to-preserve-slavery.

27. Paul Theroux, *Deep South* (Boston: Houghton Mifflin, 2015), p. 106.

28. "Global Study on Homicide," United Nations Office on Drugs and Crime, posted at https://www.unodc.org/gsh/2012.

29. Schmall, "Report Faults Army's Ability."

30. Julie Watson, "Meditating Marines: Military Tries Mindfulness to Lower Stress," NBC News, January 20, 2013.

31. Andrew Perzo, "Gen. Patton Struck Two Soldiers in August 1943," *American Press* (Lake Charles, LA), August 10, 2014.

32. Ibid.

33. James Risen, "American Psychological Association Bolstered C.I.A. Torture Program, Report Says," *New York Times*, April 30, 2015.

34. Buck Henry and Joseph Heller, *Catch 22*, Paramount, Hollywood, CA, 1970.

35. Jerry Lembcke, *PTSD* (Lanham, MD: Lexington, 2013), p. 10.

36. Ibid., p. 80.

37. Ibid., p. 36.

38. Mark Koba, "U.S. Military Spending Dwarfs Rest of World," NBC News, February 24, 2014.

39. Henry Blodget, "The Average CEO Earns More in an Hour Than the Average Employee Earns in a Month," *Business Insider*, April 10, 2013, posted at http://www.businessinsider.com/the-average-ceo-earns-more-in-an-hour-the-the-average-employee-earns-in-a-month-2013-4.

40. Malcolm Brown and Shirley Seaton, *The Christmas Truce* (London: Pan, 1999).

41. Alfred Bryan, "I Didn't Raise My Boy to Be a Soldier," Edison Collection, Library of Congress, 1915.

42. Eugene Debs, speech delivered at Canton, OH, June 16, 1918.

43. David Kennedy, *The American Pageant* (Boston: Houghton Mifflin, 2006), p. 716.

44. Nicholson Baker, "Why I Am a Pacifist: The Dangerous Myth of the Good War," *Harper's*, May 2011, pp. 41–50.

45. Tom Brokaw, *The Greatest Generation* (New York: Random House, 2001).

46. Russell W. Glenn, "Man against Fire," *Vietnam Magazine*, April 2002.

47. Wood, "Why We Fear."

48. Ibid.

49. Staff Sergeant Barry Sadler and Robin Moore, "Ballad of the Green Berets," RCA Victor, New York, 1966.

50. Andy Mager, "We Ain't Marching Anymore," *Non-violent Activism*, War Resister League, New York, March-April 2000.

51. Jessica Mitford, *The Trial of Dr. Spock* (St. Louis, MO: McDonald, 1969).

52. Morton Halperin, Jerry Berman, Robert Borosage, and Christine Marwick, *The Lawless State: The Crimes of the U.S. Intelligence Agencies* (New York: Penguin, 1976).

53. Ronald Reagan (1980) quoted in Patrick Hagopian, *The Vietnam War in American Memory* (Amherst: University of Massachusetts Press, 2011), p. 38.

54. C. N. Trueman, "Stab in the Back Legend," HistoryLearningSite.co.uk, 2014.

55. Denver Nicks, "Private Manning and the Making of Wikileaks," *This Land,* Tulsa, OK, September 23, 2010, posted at http://thislandpress.com/2011/02/08/private-manning-and-the-making-of-wikileaks-2/.

56. Glenn Greenwald, Ewen MacAskill, and Laura Poitras, "Edward Snowden: The Whistleblower behind the NSA Surveillance Revelations," *Guardian,* June 11, 2013.

57. Lisa Lef, "Mother's Vigil Recalls Quiet, Dedicated Son," Associated Press, August 13, 2005.

58. John Kerry, speech delivered at the Democratic National Convention, Boston, July 29, 2004.

59. Clint Eastwood, *American Sniper,* Village Roadside Pictures, South Yarra, Victoria, Australia, 2015.

60. Monica Davey and Manny Fernandez, "Security in Ferguson Is Tightened after Night of Unrest," *New York Times,* November 25, 2014.

61. Bart Jansen, "Curfew over, Baltimore Looks for Recovery," *USA Today,* May 4, 2015.

62. William Boykin quoted in Greg Corombos, "U.S. General: America Craves More 'Heroes' Like Chris Kyle," WND Radio, February 3, 2015.

63. Jerry Lembcke, *The Spitting Image* (New York: NYU Press, 1998).

64. Andrew Adamson and Vicky Jenson, *Shrek,* DreamWorks, Universal City, CA, 2001.

65. "'March against Death' Commences in Washington, D.C.," *This Day in History,* History Channel, November 13, 1969, posted at http://www.history.com/this-day-in-history/march-against-death-commences-in-washington-d-c.

66. Judith Orr, "Fort Hood: Iraq and Afghanistan—The Resurgence of Anti-war Cafes," *Socialist Review,* October 2009, p. 341.

67. Jessie Kindig, "Draft Resistance in the Vietnam War," Antiwar and Radical History Project, Seattle, WA, 2008.

68. Martin Luther King, "Beyond Vietnam," Clergy and Laymen Concerned about Vietnam, Riverside Church, New York, April 4, 1967.

Chapter 7: Schooling for Bullies

1. Thomas Hughes, *Tom Brown's School Days* (Oxford: Oxford University Press, 2008).

2. Ibid., chap. 8.

3. Bertolt Brecht, *The Threepenny Opera* (New York: Grove Press, 1994).

4. Andrew Carnegie, *Triumphant Democracy* (New York: Charles Scribner's Sons, 1886), p. 101.

5. Henry Giroux, "Schooling and the Myth of Objectivity: Stalking the Politics of the Hidden Curriculum," *McGill Journal of Education* (1981): 282–304.

6. Alfie Kohn, "The Costs of Overemphasizing Achievement," *School Administrator*, November 1999, posted at http://www.alfiekohn.org/article/costs-overemphasizing -achievement/.

7. Jody Fester, "Military Recruit Provisions under the No Child Left Behind Act," *Congressional Research Service Report to Congress*, January 8, 2008, posted at www .dtic.mil/dtic/tr/fulltext/u2/a494158.pdf.

8. "Chain of Command & Battalion Staff," Furr High School NJROTC, posted at everything.explained.today/Junior_Reserve_Officers'_Trining_Corps, retrieved June 11, 2009.

9. New York Civil Liberties Union, letter from attorneys Donna Lieberman and Jeffrey Fogel to principal David Greco, October 12, 2005, posted at www.nyclu.org /files/greco-followup.pdf.

10. Title 10 U.S. Code § 2031—Junior Reserve Officers' Training Corps.

11. Frederick Wiseman, *High School*, Osti Productions, Philadelphia, 1968.

12. Lee Jenkins, "Reversing the Downslide of Student Enthusiasm," *School Administrator* 69, no. 5 (May 2012): 16–17.

13. Roald Dahl, *Matilda* (London: Puffin, 2007).

14. Arne Duncan, www.twitter.com/arneduncan, US Department of Education, 2012.

15. Nancy M. Sanders and Karen Kearney, eds., "Performance Expectations and Indicators for Education Leaders," Counsel of Chief Education Officers, Washington, DC, 2008, posted at https://www.wested.org/resources/performance-expectations -and-indicators-for-education-leaders/; also Harold Knoff, "Evaluating Classroom Climate, Safety and Classroom Management Using Brief Class-Room Walk Through," Arkansas Department of Education, 2011.

16. Diane Ravitch, *Reign of Error* (New York: Vintage, 2014).

17. Lynne Cheney, *Telling the Truth* (New York: Touchstone, 1996).

18. Jonathan Zimmerman, "Why Is American Teaching So Bad?" *New York Review of Books*, December 4, 2014.

19. Rachel Morello, "Teacher Turnover Is Higher than Ever," *State Impact Indiana*, July 17, 2014, posted at http://indianapublicmedia.org/stateimpact/2014/07/17/study -teacher-turnover-higher/.

20. Zimmerman, "Why Is American Teaching So Bad?"

21. Michelle Rhee, "Poverty Must Be Tackled but Never Used as an Excuse," *Huffington Post*, September 5, 2012, posted at http://www.huffingtonpost.com/michelle -rhee/poverty-must-be-tackled-b_b_1857423.html.

22. Ravitch, *Reign of Error*.

23. Diane Ravitch, "A Letter to My Friends and Readers," 2014, posted at diane ravitch.com/what-you-can-do.

24. Samuel Bowles and Herbert Gintis, *Schooling in Capitalist America* (New York: Harper, 1977), pp. 42 and 43.

25. Klein, *Bullying Society*, p. 30.

26. D. A. Kinney, "From Nerds to Normal," *Sociology of Education* 66 (1993): 21–40; P. A. Adler, S. J. Kless, and P. Adler, "Socialization to Gender Roles," *Sociology of Education* 65 (1992): 169–187.

27. Klein, *Bullying Society,* p. 86.

28. Ibid., p. 156.

29. Paul Willis, *Learning to Labor* (New York: Columbia University Press, 1977), p. 34.

30. Ibid., p. 87.

31. Ibid., p. 80.

32. Ibid., p. 95.

33. Ibid., p. 39.

34. Klein, *Bullying Society,* p. 3.

35. Sennett and Cobb, *Hidden Injuries of Class.*

36. Ibid., pp. 158 and 159.

37. Klein, *Bullying Society,* p. 99.

38. Baran and Sweezy, *Monopoly Capital,* chap. 5.

39. Goldman, *Bullied,* p. 33.

40. Ibid., p. 38.

41. Ibid., p. 27.

42. Ibid., p. 37.

43. Klein, *Bullying Society,* p. 99.

44. Helen Kennedy, "Phoebe Price, South Hadley High School's 'New Girl' Driven to Suicide by Teenage Cyber Bullies," *New York Daily News,* March 29, 2010.

45. "The Murder of Reena Virk," CBS News, April 12, 2005.

46. Klein, *Bullying Society,* pp. 37 and 38.

47. Ibid., p. 67.

48. *Metro Boston,* untitled article, November 12, 2014.

49. Rosalind Wiseman, *Queen Bees and Wannabees* (New York: Three River Press, 2003).

50. Tina Fey, *Mean Girls,* Paramount Pictures, Los Angeles, 2004.

51. Richard DeGrandpre, *Ritalin Nation* (New York: Norton, 2000).

52. Trevor Romain, *Bullies Are a Pain in the Brain* (Minneapolis: Free Spirit, 1997).

53. Ibid., p. 2.

54. Ibid., p. 3.

55. Ibid., p. 68.

56. Ibid., pp. 16 and 18.

57. Ibid., p. 32.

58. Ibid., p. 57.

Chapter 8: The Heartless World

1. Christopher Lasch, *Havens in a Heartless World* (New York: Norton, 1995).

2. Leontine Young, *The Fractured Family* (New York: McGraw-Hill, 1973).

3. Jeff Levinson, *Mill Girls of Lowell* (Malden, MA: History Compass, 2007).

4. Noel Langley, Florence Ryerson, and Edgar Allen Woolf, *The Wizard of Oz*, MGM, Hollywood, CA, 1939.

5. Genesis, *English Standard Bible* (Wheaton, IL: Crossway, 2011).

6. Brittany Garcia, "Romulus and Remus," *Ancient History Encyclopedia* (West Sussex, UK: n.p., 2013).

7. William Shakespeare, *Hamlet* (New York: Simon & Schuster, 2012).

8. David Starkey, *Six Wives: The Queens of Henry VIII* (New York: Harper, 2004).

9. "Married Women's Property Laws,"*American Women,* Library of Congress, American Memory, posted at https://memory.loc.gov/ammem/awhhtml/awlaw3/property_law.html, retrieved February 3, 2013.

10. Douglas Chung, "Confucianism: A Portrait," in *A Sourcebook for Earth's Community of Religions,* ed. Joel Beversluis (Grand Rapids, MI: CoNexus Press, 1995).

11. Arthur P. Wolf and Chieh-shan Huang, *Marriage and Adoption in China, 1845–1945* (Palo Alto, CA: Stanford University Press, 1980), p. 87.

12. Deuteronomy 21:18–21, *English Standard Bible* (Wheaton, IL: Crossway, 2010).

13. Ibid., 22:13–29.

14. Karl Polanyi, *The Great Transformation* (Boston: Beacon, 2001).

15. Joseph Stein, *Fiddler on the Roof,* United Artists, Hollywood, CA, 1971.

16. Karl Marx and Frederick Engels, *The Communist Manifesto* (Rockland, MD: Wildside Press, 2008), p. 11.

17. Jamie Gumbrecht, "In Sweden, a Generation of Kids Who've Never Been Spanked," CNN, November 9, 2011.

18. Richard Santorum, Republican Debate, Orlando, FL, September 22, 2011.

19. Tim La Haye, *Battle for the Mind* (Tappan, NJ: Revell, 1980).

20. Tim La Haye, *Battle for the Family* (Tappan, NJ: Revell, 1984).

21. La Haye, *Battle for the Mind,* p. 60.

22. Tony Perkins, "FRC Gets to the Bottom of Spanking," *Washington Watch Daily,* Washington, DC, December 26, 2007.

23. James Dobson, *The Strong-Willed Child* (Carol Stream, IL: Tyndale Momentum, 1992), p. 37.

24. Ibid., pp. 53–54.

25. Ibid., p. 235.

26. Richard Santorum, http://www.brainyquote.com/quotes/quotes/r/ricksantor425210.html.

27. "10 Questions with Rick Santorum," *New York Times,* March 1, 2012.

28. Connor Friedersdorf, "Rick Santorum's Case for Big Government," *Atlantic,* June 9, 2011, posted at http://www.theatlantic.com/politics/archive/2011/06/rick-santorums-case-for-big-government/240174/.

29. Richard Santorum, speech delivered at First Redeemer Church, Forsyth County, GA, February 19, 2012.

30. "Mike Huckabee Calls Natalie Portman's Pregnancy 'Troubling,'" *Wall Street Journal,* March 4, 2011.

31. Howard Kurtz, "Huckabee Rips Critics of 'Libido' Comments," Fox News Politics, January 24, 2014.

32. William Fruet, *Wedding in White,* Video Service, Toronto, Canada, 1972.

33. See www.longtermcare.gov/costs-how-to-pay/costs-of-care/2010.

34. Carmen DeNavas-Walt and Bernadette Proctor, "Income and Poverty in the United States: 2014," US Census Bureau, US Department of Commerce, Washington, DC, September 2015.

35. Glenn D. Braunstein, "Caring for Aging Parents Is a Labor of Love—with a Cost," *Huffington Post,* April 15, 2013, posted at http://www.huffingtonpost.com/glenn-d -braunstein-md/caregivers-aging-parents_b_3071979.html.

36. Karl Marx, "Estranged Labor," in *Economic & Philosophical Manuscripts of 1844* (Radford, VA: Wilder Publications, 2011).

37. Norman Lear, *All in the Family,* CBS, Hollywood, CA, 1971–1979.

38. Norman Lear, "Two's a Crowd" episode, *All in the Family,* 1978.

39. "Don't Trust Anyone over 30, Unless It's Jack Weinberg," *Berkeley (CA) Daily Planet,* April 6, 2000.

40. George Bernard Shaw, *Major Barbara* (New York: Penguin, 2001), Act 1.

41. Gertude Berg and Dan Greenburg, *How to Be a Jewish Mother* (New York: Pocket Book, 1965).

42. Nia Vardalos, *My Big Fat Greek Wedding,* HBO Films, Toronto, Canada, 2002.

43. Tom Astle and Matt Ember, *Failure to Launch,* Paramount, Hollywood, CA, 2006.

44. Alan Bjerga, "U.S. Child Born in 2010 May Cost $226,920 to Raise," *Bloomberg News,* June 9, 2011.

45. Yvonne Abraham, "Less Is More. Really," *Boston Globe,* December 25, 2014.

46. Alanna Vagianos, "30 Shocking Domestic Violence Statistics That Remind Us It's an Epidemic," *Huffington Post,* October 23, 2014, posted at http://www.huffington post.com/2014/10/23/domestic-violence-statistics_n_5959776.html.

47. Melissa Jeltsen, "Arkansas Governor Signs Domestic Violence Bill Dubbed 'Laura's Law,'" *Huffington Post,* April 2, 2015.

48. "Domestic Violence: Statistics & Facts," Safe Horizon, New York, posted at www.safehorizon.org/page/domestic-violence-statistics--facts-52.html.

49. Eileen Meehan and Jackie Byars, "Telefeminism: How Lifetime Got Its Groove: 1984–1997," in *The Television Studies Reader,* vol. 1, no. 1 (London: Psychology Press, 2004), pp. 33–51.

50. Ken Englade, *Murder in Boston* (New York: St. Martin's Press, 1990), pp. 2–5.

51. Terrence McCoy, "Oscar Pistorius Sentenced to Five Years in Killing of Girlfriend," *Washington Post,* October 21, 2014.

52. Benjamin Morris, "The Rate of Domestic Violence Arrests among NLF Players," *FiveThirtyEight Datalab,* July 31, 2014.

53. "Jodi Arias Will Get a Video Call for Christmas, Juan Martinez Fights Back," *Examiner,* Denver, CO, December 24, 2014.

54. Vardalos, *My Big Fat Greek Wedding.*

55. Arlie Hochschild, *The Second Shift* (New York: Viking, 2012).

56. Norman Lear, "Edith Breaks Out," *All in the Family,* 1975.

57. Stein, *Fiddler on the Roof.*

58. Ibid.

59. Vardalos, *My Big Fat Greek Wedding.*

60. Jackie Gleason, "The Babysitter," *The Honeymooners,* CBS, New York, 1956.

61. Raymond Romano, "Marie's Meatballs," *Everyone Loves Raymond,* Warner Bros., Burbank, CA, 1996.

62. Raymond Romano, "The Dog," *Everyone Loves Raymond,* Warner Bros., Burbank, CA, 1997.

63. Raymond Romano, "Lucky Suit," *Everyone Loves Raymond,* Warner Bros., Burbank, CA, 2002.

64. Dorothy Cebula, "The Kid's Inheritance," Medford Leas, NJ, May 11, 2014, posted at www.medfordleasblog.org/the-kids-inheritance.

65. *London Daily Mail,* April 9, 2012, posted at http://www.dailymail.co.uk/news /article-2127515/Be-nice-children-Theyll-chose-nursing-home-And-tips-grown -know.html.

CHAPTER 9: THE ANTIBULLYING MOVEMENT

1. "Anti-bullying," *Wikipedia,* posted at http://www.en.wikipedia.org/wiki/Anti -bullying_legislation.

2. "The Bullying Stops Here," National Bullying Prevention Awareness Month, October 2011, posted at http://www.thebullyingstopshere.org/events/.

3. See "Anti-bullying," *Wikipedia.*

4. James Brooke, "Gay Man Dies from Attack, Fanning Outrage and Debate," *New York Times,* October 13, 1998, posted at http://www.nytimes.com/1998/10/13/us /gay-man-dies-from-attack-fanning-outrage-and-debate.html. A series of *New York Times* reports about Matthew Shepard have been collected and posted online by the *Times*; see "Matthew Shepard News—The New York Times," posted at http://www .nytimes.com/topic/person/matthew-shepard.

5. Matthew Shepard Foundation, "The Foundation's Story," May 13, 2015, posted at http://www.matthewshepard.org/our-story.

6. We discuss this in Derber and Magrass, *Capitalism: Should You Buy It?* See also Derber, *Marx's Ghost.*

7. This argument was prefigured by sociologist Daniel Bell in the 1960s, setting off a spate of work on the new "knowledge economy" and the change from assembly-line industrial work to a high-technology capitalism. See Bell, *The Coming of Post-industrial Society: A Venture in Social Forecasting* (New York: Basic Books, 1976).

8. Richard Florida, *The Rise of the Creative Class—Revisited,* rev. and expanded ed. (New York: Basic Books, 2014).

9. See George Packer, "Change the World: Silicon Valley Transfers Its Slogans— and Its Money—to the World of Politics," *New Yorker,* May 27, 2013, posted at http:// www.newyorker.com/magazine/2013/05/27/change-the-world.

10. Ibid. See also John Markoff, "Searching for Silicon Valley—A Place and a

State of Mind," *New York Times,* April 16, 2009, posted at http://www.nytimes.com/2009/04/17/travel/escapes/17Amer.html?pagewanted=1&_r=0.

11. Lucas Shaw, "Sundance: 'Whiplash' Sweeps Top Dramatic Awards," WRAP Covering Hollywood, January 25, 2014, posted at http://www.thewrap.com/sundance-whiplash-sweeps-top-awards/.

12. Alice Park, "The Tiger Mom Effect Is Real, Says Large Study," *Time,* May 5, 2014, posted at http://time.com/88125/the-tiger-mom-effect-is-real-says-large-study/.

13. See the discussion of this topic in chapter 8.

14. For a good analysis of the culture wars as they impact the United States and American politics today, see Thomas Frank, *What's the Matter with Kansas? How Conservatives Won the Heart of America* (New York: Holt Paperbacks, 2005).

15. Ibid.

16. Ibid.

17. Jonathan I. Israel, *Radical Enlightenment: Philosophy and the Making of Modernity, 1650–1750* (New York: Oxford University Press, 2002), p. 3.

18. Jonathan I. Israel, *A Revolution of the Mind: Radical Enlightenment and the Intellectual Origins of Modern Democracy* (Princeton, NJ: Princeton University Press, 2011), pp. 49–50.

19. Spinoza cited in ibid., p. 159.

20. Mark Kishlansky, Patrick Geary, and Patricia O'Brien, *A Brief History of Western Civilization: The Unfinished Legacy,* vol. 2, *Since 1555,* 5th ed. (New York: Longman, 2007). See also Richard Hooker, "The Philosophes" (1996), http://www.richard-hooker.com/sites/worldcultures/ENLIGHT/PHIL.HT/.style.

21. Israel, *Revolution of the Mind.*

22. Dorinda Outram, *Panorama of the Enlightenment* (Los Angeles: Getty Publications, 2006), pp. 29ff.

23. Hooker, "Philosophes." See also Israel, *Revolution of the Mind.*

24. Charles Derber, William Schwartz, and Yale Magrass, *Power in the Highest Degree: The Coming of a New Mandarin Order* (New York: Oxford University Press, 1991).

25. Todd Gitlin, *The Sixties: Days of Hope, Days of Rage* (New York: Bantam, 1993).

26. Ibid. See also Richard Flacks, *Making History: The American Left and the American Mind* (New York: Columbia University Press, 1988).

27. Betty Friedman, *The Feminine Mystique,* reprint ed. (New York: Norton, 2001); Kate Millett, *Sexual Politics,* reprint ed. (Champaign-Urbana: University of Illinois Press, 2000); Robin Morgan, *Sisterhood Is Powerful* (New York: Vintage, 1970); Germaine Greer, *The Female Eunuch,* reprint ed. (New York: Harper Perennial Classics, 2008).

28. Gitlin, *Sixties.*

29. On Gloria Steinem's war protest, see "Writers and Editors War Tax Protest," *New York Post,* January 30, 1968. Robin Morgan, a leading feminist and antiwar activist with Steinem, wrote many books, including *Sisterhood Is Powerful.*

30. King made this antiwar statement in his speech at Riverside Church in New York City on April 4, 1967. For a commentary, see David A. Love, "America Is the Greatest

Purveyor of Violence in the World Today," *Huffington Post,* May 25, 2011, posted at http://www.huffingtonpost.com/david-a-love/america-is-the-greatest-p_b_820729 .html.

31. For a discussion of the Black Panther Party, see Joshua Bloom and Waldo E. Martin, Jr., *Black against Empire: The History and Politics of the Black Panther Party* (Berkeley: University of California Press, 2012). See also Hugh Pearson, *The Shadow of the Panther: Huey Newton and the Price of Black Power in America* (Boston: Da Capo Press, 1994).

32. Bernardine Dohrn, Bill Ayers, and Jeff Jones, *Sing a Battle Song: The Revolutionary Poetry, Statements, and Communiqués of the Weather Underground, 1970–1974* (New York: Seven Stories Press, 2006). See also Dan Berger, *Outlaws of America: The Weather Underground and the Politics of Solidarity* (Oakland, CA: AK Press, 2006).

33. Mark Rudd, "The Death of SDS," Markrudd.com, posted at http://www.mark rudd.com/?sds-and-weather/the-death-of-sds.html.

34. George Orwell, *Animal Farm,* 50th anniversary ed. (New York: Signet Classics, 1996).

35. Michael Kazin, *The Populist Persuasion* (Ithaca, NY: Cornell University Press, 1998). See also Todd Gitlin, *Twilight of Common Dreams* (New York: Holt, 1996).

36. Frank, *What's the Matter with Kansas?* See also Derber, *Hidden Power.*

37. Gitlin, *Twilight of Common Dreams.*

EPILOGUE: ARE THERE SOLUTIONS?

1. Izzy Kalman, "Anti-bullying Laws Are a Violation of the Golden Rule, " reprinted by Kalman from *Psychology Today* and posted at Resilience to Bullying, March 25, 2010, http://www.psychologytoday.com/blog/psychological-solution-bullying/201003 /anti-bully-laws-are-violation-the-golden-rule.

2. Ibid.

3. John Vettese, "Are New School Anti-bullying Laws Fair, or Unreasonable?" Annenberg Classroom, n.d., posted at http://www.annenbergclassroom.org/speakouts.aspx ?name=are-new-school-anti-bullying-laws-fair&AspxAutoDetectCookieSupport=1.

4. Office of Research, UNICEF, "Child Well-Being in Rich Countries: A Comparative Overview," posted at RC11 Research Findings—UNICEF, http://www.google.com /url?sa=t&rct=j&q=&esrc=s&source=web&cd=1&ved=0CB4QFjAA&url=http%3A %2F%2Fwww.unicef.org%2Fmedia%2Ffiles%2FRC11_Key_Findings_Final_EN .docx&ei=9vKFVLOjK4GcgwT4qYS4BA&usg=AFQjCNEVKX_Jm44ykEk1bYheKY vWw-UqQg&bvm=bv.80642063,d.eXY.

5. For a discussion of the Scandinavian model, see Robert Kuttner, *The Economic Illusion* (Philadelphia: University of Pennsylvania Press, 1987). See also Jeremy Rifkin, *The European Dream* (New York: Tarcher, 2005).

6. Kuttner, *Economic Illusion.*

7. Derber, *Greed to Green.*

8. Rifkin, *European Dream.*

9. Schor, *True Wealth*. See also Gar Alperovitz, *What Then Must We Do? Straight Talk about the Next American Revolution* (White River Junction, VT: Chelsea Green, 2013).

Appendix: Our God, Our Bully

1. Steven Pinker, *The Better Angels of Our Nature* (New York: Penguin, 2011).

2. Martin Ewans, *European Atrocity, African Catastrophe: Leopold II, the Congo Free State and Its Aftermath* (New York: Routledge Curzon, 2002).

3. Noam Chomsky, *Democracy Now,* March 2, 2015, posted at http://www.democ racynow.org/2015/3/2/noam_chomsky_opposing_iran_nuclear_deal.

4. Edward Herman, *The Real Terror Network* (Boston: South End, 1999).

5. J. Bowyer Bell, *Terror Out of Zion* (New York: St. Martin's Press, 1996), p. 172.

6. Graeme Wood, "What ISIS Really Wants," *Atlantic,* March 2015.

7. Letta Tayler, "Those Who Should Speak Out Have Not Done So," *Prospect Magazine* (London), November 13, 2014.

8. Kayla Ruble, "Islamic State Releases Video Allegedly Showing Woman Being Stoned to Death by Her Father," *Vice News,* October 21, 2014.

9. "Deadly Attacks across Paris," CBS News, November 13, 2015, posted at http://www.cbsnews.com/pictures/deadly-attacks-paris-france.

10. Kim Bellware, "Pope Says Paris Terror Attacks Part of 'Piecemeal Third World War,'" *Huffington Post*, November 15, 2015.

11. Ryan Grenoble, "Family, Friends of 'Jihadi John' Victims React to News of His Likely Death," *Huffington Post,* November 13, 2015, posted at http://www.huffington post.com/entry/jihadi-john-killed-family-reacts_564611eee4b045bf3deecc35.

12. Janine di Giovanni, "When It Comes to Beheadings, ISIS Has Nothing over Saudi Arabia," *Newsweek,* October 14, 2014.

13. Bill Moyers, "A Brief History of Al Qaeda," *PBS,* July 20, 2007.

14. Genesis 15:18, *Tankakh: The Jewish Bible* (Philadelphia: Jewish Publications Society, 1984), p. 22.

15. Samuel I 15, in ibid., pp. 440 and 441.

16. Leviticus 20:13, in ibid., p. 187.

17. Deuteronomy 22, in ibid., pp. 308 and 309.

18. Numbers 21:5–7, in ibid., p. 243.

19. Job 38:2–18, in ibid., pp. 1394 and 1395.

20. Exodus 23:9, in ibid., p. 120.

21. Jeremiah 31, in ibid., p. 837.

22. Isaiah 2:4, in ibid., p. 619.

23. 1 Kings 5:17, in ibid., p. 524.

24. Chronicles I 22:7–8, in ibid., p. 1562.

25. Arthur Waskow, *God-Wrestling* (New York: Schocken, 1978).

26. Rabbi Sherwin Wine, "Jewish Identity," *Humanist Judaism* (Autumn 1985): 7 and 8.

27. Julie Bien, "5 Reasons Jews Win So Many Nobel Prizes," *Jewish Journal*, October 9, 2013, posted at http://www.jewishjournal.com/thebulletinbored/item/5_reasons_jews_win_so_many_nobel_prizes.

28. Chris Cillizza and Jon Cohen, "President Obama and the White Vote? No Problem," *Washington Post*, November 8, 2012.

29. Jeremy Ben-Aminov, "America's Jewish Vote," *New York Times*, November 12, 2012.

30. Jimmy Carter quoted in *Los Angeles Times*, December 6, 2006.

31. Abraham Foxman, *Jewish Week*, New York, December 15, 2006.

32. Jimmy Carter and Mary Robinson, "How to Fix It," *Foreign Policy*, August 4, 2014, posted at http://www.foreignpolicy.com/2014/08/04/how-to-fix-it/.

33. Mel Frykberg, "Environmental Terrorism Cripples Palestinian Farmers," *Truthout*, April 14, 2015, posted at http://www.truth-out.org/news/item/30188-environmental-terrorism-cripples-palestinian-farmers.

34. Ibid.

35. Paul Breines, *Tough Jews* (New York: Basic Books, 1992).

36. Miriam Weinstein, *Yiddish* (New York: Ballantine Books, 2001), p. 127.

Index

"Employment-at-will," 45, 46
Emwazi, Mohammed "Jihadi John," 219
Engels, Friedrich, 70, 71
Enlightenment, 200–201, 202, 209
    as antibullying movement, 200
    counterculture and, 198, 199, 200, 203
Environment
    capitalism and, 76
    as externality, 63, 73, 78
    preserving, 68
Environmental bullying and bludgeoning, 21, 59, 60, 61, 62, 75, 76, 213
    capitalist, 71, 79
    climate change and, 63, 65, 73–82
    corporate, 65, 68–73
    destructive forms of, 64–65
    industrial agriculture and, 70
    justice and, 81
    militaristic capitalism and, 65
    mind-set of, 64
    renewable energy and, 212
Environmental damage, 69, 70, 71, 72, 73
    climate change and, 79, 80
    commodity growth and, 77
    competition and, 74
Environmentalists, 29, 60, 75, 82, 209
Equality, 199, 200
    democracy and, 10, 11
    familiarity and, 177
    myth of, 150
Evangelists, 80, 171
Everyone Loves Raymond, 22, 186–187
Exceptionalism, 10, 11, 212
Exit power, 39–42, 57, 58

Facebook, legal action and, 48
Factory farms, 69, 82
Failure to Launch (movie), 180
Family
    bond/escaping, 180
    bullying by, 161, 181–188

capitalism and, 160–161, 161–162, 166, 168, 172, 176, 183
    cultural values of, 202
    culture wars and, 168–172
    economic institutions and, 162
    as independent entity, 171
    love and, 181, 188
    patriarchy and, 183
    patterns, 23
    power and, 178
    precapitalist, 162–165
    schools and, 169
    traditional, 166, 167, 168, 181
    transition, 165–168
    weakening of, 172–173, 173–175
Family Research Council (FRC), 169, 170
Farabundo Marti National Liberation Front (FMLN), 90
Fascism, 27, 200
Fast Food Forward Network, 30–31
Fast Food Organizing Network, 31
Federal Bureau of Investigation (FBI), 133, 187
Federal Emergency Management Agency (FEMA), 80
Feffer, John, 92, 95
Female Eunuch (Greer), 202
Feminine Mystique, The (Friedan), 202
Femininity, standards of, 152, 153
Feminist movement, 162, 202, 203
Feudalism, 160, 161, 166, 201
Fey, Tina, 155, 156
Fiddler on the Roof, 166, 184
Finding Your Roots (PBS), 110
Foley, Diane, 219
Foley, James, 219
Ford, Henry, 191–192
Foreign policy, 19, 84, 86, 91, 98, 101
Foster, John Bellamy, 70, 73
Fox, Michael J., 4
Foxman, Abraham, 225
Fox News, 171

Revenge, 31, 150, 188
Rhee, Michelle: on teachers/bullying,
144
Rice, Ray, 182
Richland County, bullying in, 109
Robber barons, bullying by, 56
Roberts, Doris, 186
Robinson, Mary, 225
Rockefeller, John D., Sr.: bullying by,
47–48, 56, 58
Rolls Royce, 51
Romain, Trevor, 158–159
Roman Empire, Jews and, 224
Romano, Raymond, 186–187
Romesha, Clinton, 120
Romney, Mitt, 35, 111
Roosevelt, Theodore, 14, 84, 115
Rousseau, Jean-Jacques, 199

Samsung, legal action and, 48
Sandinistas, 90
Santorum, Richard "Rick," 169, 170, 171
Saudi Arabia
    bullying by, 217–221
    ISIS and, 220–221
Schools
    adapting to, 157
    families and, 169
    as great equalizers, 150
    industrial capitalism and, 137
    institutional bullying and, 139
    militaristic capitalism and, 137,
        138–141, 159
    public/private, 137, 138, 139
    segregated, 146
Schor, Juliet, 52, 213
Sears Roebuck, 52
Second Amendment, 121
Security, 86, 178
    border, 112
    job, 43, 46
    national, 194
    psychological, 160
Segregation, 108–109, 146, 201

Self-defense, 16–17, 28, 86, 114
Self-esteem, 121–122, 148, 159, 210
Sennett, Richard, 150
September 11th, 219, 221
Service Employees International Union
    (SEIU), 31
Service sector, culture of, 193
Sexism, 201, 210
Sexuality, cultural values of, 202
Sexual orientation, 13, 191
Sexual Politics (Millett), 202
Shaken-infant syndrome, 61
Shakespeare, William, 163
"Share economy" movement, 213
Sharia, 217, 221
Shaw, George Bernard, 179
Sheehan, Cindy, 131
Shepard, Matthew, 189–190, 191
Shock Factor: American Snipers in the
    War on Terror (Coughlin), quote
    from, 129
Shrek (movie), 135
"Silent Night," singing, 127
Silent Spring (Carson), 70
Silicon Valley, antibully surge and, 193
Singer, Isaac, 227
Singer, Peter, 61
Sisterhood Is Powerful (Morgan), 202
Slaughtering, violence of, 69–70
Slavery, 29, 68, 103, 105–107, 111, 210
    bullying and, 107, 203
    restoring, 108
Slaves, 106, 114, 121
    bullying and, 138
    citizenship and, 108
    selling of, 107
Smithfield Farms, 3, 59
SNCC. See Student Nonviolent
    Coordinating Committee
Snowden, Edward, 131
Social change, movements for, 29
Social Darwinism, 28, 34–35, 36, 77
    competition and, 192
    general philosophy of, 76

Torture, 65–66, 118, 217
  bullying and, 98
Toys "R" Us, branding by, 51
Trade laws, 54
Tradition, erosion of, 165–168
Transportation, public, 53, 211
Truman, Harry, 92, 93, 95
Trump, Donald, 3, 111, 112, 189
Twelve Years a Slave (Northrup), quote
    from, 106–107
Tyson, 3, 59, 69

Unemployment, 45, 110, 149
Unions, 30–31, 38, 41
  busting, 45, 54
United Automobile Workers (UAW), 41
United Fruit, 90
"United States, Global Bully"
    (Chomsky), 89
University of Massachusetts–
    Dartmouth, 173, 179
US Air Force, 99
US Army Corps of Engineers, 80
US Army Rangers, 110
US Bureau of Labor Statistics, 44
US Constitution, 82
US Department of Agriculture, 181
US Department of Defense, 114, 122
US Department of Homeland Security,
    27
US Department of Veterans Affairs, 122
US Department of War, 114
US Marine Corps, 116–117, 123
US Navy SEALs, 110, 116
US Supreme Court, 54

Values, 8, 103, 113, 188, 193
  alien, 173
  alternative, 175
  antibullying, 195, 212
  bullying, 67, 130, 132, 160, 161, 169,
    174, 181, 194
  capitalist, 63, 73, 74, 76, 138, 150–151,
    176, 192

core, 10, 114, 213
cultural, 14, 20, 129, 152, 202
egalitarian, 212
Enlightenment, 201, 202
family, 170, 171, 179, 197, 198
military, 114, 116, 120
moral, 121
school, 88
traditional, 172, 197
transmitting, 161
Vardalos, Nia, 180, 187
Veblen, Thorstein: conspicuous
    consumption and, 51
Vick, Michael: bullying by, 65–66
Victims, 2, 4, 61, 156–157, 211
  authority figures and, 159
  bullying, 158–159, 208
  empowering, 183
Vietnam syndrome, 131, 132
Vietnam Veterans against the War, 131–132
Vietnam War, 129, 130, 140–141, 201, 203
  bullying and, 98–102, 134, 157
  as game of chicken, 101
  protesting, 135, 202, 204
Violence, 7, 8, 14, 86, 89, 113, 149, 203,
    219, 224
  acceptance of, 195
  animal species and, 60
  boys/girls and, 150
  bullying and, 122, 126, 129, 181, 182,
    183, 215–216
  community watch, 111
  cure for, 126
  discipline and, 204
  domestic, 182
  gun, 121
  judgment of, 148
  military, 123, 206
  physical, 16, 150, 168, 220
  school, 57
  self-defense and, 16–17
  slaughtering and, 69–70
  verbal, 220
Virginia Tech, 2